MW00578934

Aftershock

Meghan Beck
2010
Uni- of- Guelph

AFTERSHOCK

ANTI-ZIONISM AND ANTISEMITISM

BY DAVID MATAS

THE DUNDURN GROUP
TORONTO

Copyright © David Matas, 2005

All rights reserved. No part of this publication may be reproduced, stored in a retrieval system, or transmitted in any form or by any means, electronic, mechanical, photocopying, recording, or otherwise (except for brief passages for purposes of review) without the prior permission of Dundurn Press. Permission to photocopy should be requested from Access Copyright.

Copy-Editor: Andrea Pruss
Design: Andrew Roberts
Printer: Webcom

Library and Archives Canada Cataloguing in Publication

Matas, David
    Aftershock : Anti-Zionism and Antisemitism / David Matas.

Includes bibliographical references and index.
ISBN-10: 1-55002-553-8
ISBN-13: 978-1-55002-553-8

    1. Antisemitism. 2. Zionism. I. Title.

DS145.M38 2005   305.892'4   C2005-901766-X

1   2   3   4   5   09   08   07   06   05

We acknowledge the support of the Canada Council for the Arts and the Ontario Arts Council for our publishing program. We also acknowledge the financial support of the Government of Canada through the Book Publishing Industry Development Program and The Association for the Export of Canadian Books, and the Government of Ontario through the Ontario Book Publishers Tax Credit program, and the Ontario Media Development Corporation.

Care has been taken to trace the ownership of copyright material used in this book. The author and the publisher welcome any information enabling them to rectify any references or credit in subsequent editions.

J. Kirk Howard, President

Printed and bound in Canada.
Printed on recycled paper.

www.dundurn.com

Dundurn Press
8 Market Street, Suite 200
Toronto, Ontario, Canada
M5E 1M6

Gazelle Book Services Limited
White Cross Mills
Hightown, Lancaster, England
LA1 4X5

Dundurn Press
2250 Military Road
Tonawanda NY
U.S.A. 14150

"Naively, I was convinced that antisemitism died in Auschwitz."

— Elie Wiesel, New York, June 21, 2004, United Nations.

TABLE OF CONTENTS

ACKNOWLEDGMENTS

THOUGH there are many individuals I want to thank, I first of all have to acknowledge B'nai Brith Canada as an organization. From the time I first became active in their advocacy work in 1979, the organization has provided unstinting institutional support. I participated in many of the events that led to the conclusions this book sets out as a B'nai Brith Canada representative.

Because so many for so long within B'nai Brith have offered their support, it is invidious to name just some of them. I will inevitably omit the names of others who should be mentioned. I nonetheless cannot help but name Rochelle and Sid Wilner, Frank Dimant, Stephen Scheinberg, Marvin Kurz, Ruth Klein, Anita Bromberg, Karen Mock, Karen Lazar, Amos Sochaczevski, Toni Silberman, Amy Goldstein, Dan Mariaschin, Klaus Netter, Harold Davis, Ted Greenfield, Hershie and Marilyn Frankel, Brian and Harriet Morris, Aurel Braun, Jules Kronis, Lou Ronson, Conrad Winn, Lyle Smordin, Moishe Smith, Rubin Friedman, Gordon Wiseman, Joseph Ben-Ami, Alan Yusim, and Leigh Halprin.

As well, I acknowledge the unfailing efforts of Stan Urman, executive director of the Center for Peace in the Middle East, East Orange, New Jersey, to promote justice for Jews from Arab countries. The chapter in this book on that subject was drawn from a report I co-authored with him.

Rebecca Holtzman, Arthur Gillman, and Floralove Katz provided me with a steady stream of insights, communications, and support. Irwin Cotler, now Attorney General and Minister of Justice for Canada, and Anne Bayefsky of the Hudson Institute in New York have contributed both wisdom and eloquence on the subject matter of this book. I have learned from listening to them and reading them.

Trevor Anderson guided me through the law of restrictive covenants. David Weisstub helped me with Jewish Holocaust theology.

Felice Gaer and Sybil Kessler of the Jacob Blaustein Institute have spurred and organized international initiatives to attempt to grapple with anti-Zionist–based antisemitism. The chapter on the differences between Jewish and general human rights organizations in combatting antisemitism draws from a paper I wrote for a Jacob Blaustein Institute workshop in Vienna in 2003.

Finally, I have to thank Dundurn Press, my publishers. This is the second book they have published of mine. (They published *No More: The Battle against Human Rights Violations* in 1994.) I am, of course, grateful to any publisher that would venture to publish even one of my books. But for a publisher who has already published one book of mine to publish a second bespeaks a confidence in me that I cherish.

INTRODUCTION

YOUSEF SANDOUGA firebombed the Edmonton Beth Shalom Synagogue in the early morning of November 1, 2000. He brought to the synagogue two Molotov cocktails, each bottle filled with gasoline into which he had inserted a wick. He set one alight and threw it at a window. The firebomb broke the window but did not enter the building. It started a fire on the outside wall. Sandouga set himself on fire attempting light the second Molotov cocktail. He rolled on the ground to extinguish the flames on his clothing and fled. While rolling on the ground, he dropped his cellphone.

The synagogue's caretaker, who lived in a residence next door, saw Sandouga flee. She found the cellphone. Her son and the firefighters they called put out the fire. The damage was limited to scorched bricks, burned vegetation, and two broken windows. The firefighters found gasoline spread along the wall of the synagogue where the Molotov cocktail had been thrown. A conflagration had been narrowly averted.

Through the cellphone, the police were able to track down Sandouga. He had been treated for burns at the Royal Alex Hospital shortly after the attack.

Sandouga was prosecuted for arson and pleaded guilty. In an agreed statement of facts, he stated that he attacked the synagogue "out of frustration with events in the Middle East." The trial judge sentenced Sandouga to one year in jail. The Court of Appeal, on a prosecution appeal of sentence, increased the punishment to two and a half years in prison.[1]

A fire accelerant was thrown through the window of the United Talmud Torahs elementary school library in Montreal in the early morning of April 5, 2004. The ten-thousand-volume library was destroyed. Books were burned, charred, covered in soot, melted, or damaged from the water used to extinguish the fire. Only twenty-five books, sitting separately in a box, survived. All six of the library windows were broken. Snow that morning fell through the windows onto the piles of blackened books. The library served 230 students. Estimated damage was $300,000.

A note, two pages long, was left duct-taped to the door of the school. The director-general of the school, Sidney Benudiz, got to the school before the police did, saw the note, and transcribed it before the police took it away. What Benudiz wrote down, in translation from its original French, was this:

> Here is the consequence of your crimes and your occupation. Here
> is the response to your crimes and your occupation. Here are the

results of your assassinations. Here is where you are being led by the terrorist Ariel Sharon. Today our target was an empty building. Our goal was to simply sound the alarm without causing death. But this was only the beginning. If your crimes continue in the Middle East, our attacks will continue. We are not targeting Quebec. We are targeting you, Israelis and Zionists. The next time we will hit you more strongly. Watch yourself. The Brigades of Sheik Ahmed Yassin.

Sleiman Elmerhebi pleaded guilty to the firebombing and was sentenced in January 2005 to forty months in prison. His mother, Rouba Elmerhebi Fahd, was charged as an accessory.

What is going on here? What could possibly be the connection between a synagogue in Edmonton, an elementary school library in Montreal, and the Middle East?

The Court of Appeal in the Edmonton case wrote that the attack "was motivated by revenge against the Jewish community for events that had taken place in Palestine." The revenge motivation of the attack on the Montreal elementary school library is apparent from the note. But what would lead anyone to think that attacking a religious institution in Edmonton or a children's library in Montreal could be revenge for events that happened thousands of miles away, across the Atlantic and the Mediterranean, in another country, another continent?

This book is an attempt to answer that question. There has been a dramatic increase in attacks against the Jewish community, both its people and its institutions, worldwide in recent years. These attacks are, for the most part, no longer the work of the neo-Nazi lunatic fringe. Rather, like the attack on the Edmonton synagogue or the Montreal children's library, they have a Middle Eastern connection.

The ideology of antisemitism has shifted. It still maintains its old myths of Jewish world conspiracy, Jewish control of the media, and Jewish demonization. But it has added a new and potent element: Jews as a criminal population because of their perceived support for a mythical criminality of the Jewish state. The note on the school library, presumably addressed to its users — Montreal Jewish children and their parents — refers to "your crimes." This book is an attempt to explain the reality and the threat of this new antisemitism.

I have already written a quartet of books attempting to draw out the lessons of the Holocaust. In *Justice Delayed: Nazi War Criminals in Canada*,[2] I wrote of the need to bring war criminals and criminals against humanity to justice. In *Closing the Doors: The Failure of Refugee Protection*,[3] I urged the protection of refugees. In *No More: The Battle against Human Rights Violations*,[4] I argued for the need for individuals, through non-governmental organizations, to oppose human rights violations worldwide. In *Bloody Words: Hate and Free Speech*,⁵ I contended that hate speech must be prohibited.

And that, I thought, was that. The lessons I had drawn from the Holocaust were legacies of its victims, of value more to others than to the Jewish community, who had suffered through the Holocaust an irreparable loss.

Through these writings, I had become sensitized to the workings of bigotry and the warnings of genocide. Because of this sensitization, I was stunned and horrified to see the rise of attacks against the Jewish people. Antisemitism had again become respectable. Jews again faced the threat of destruction.

But how did that happen? How did we get from the Holocaust to the threat of a new devastation of the Jewish people within the lifetime of survivors of the Holocaust?

The title of this book, though only one word, suggests the answer. There is a direct link between the Holocaust and the threats the Jewish people face today. The Holocaust was an earthquake of the human soul. It laid bare a yawning gap of depravity. Today's antisemitism is an aftershock of that earthquake, a reminder of that tragedy and a warning of the risks that lie ahead.

Because this book attempts to refute allegations that the Jewish people are a criminal people because of their actual or presumed support for a criminal Jewish state, it necessarily involves legal argument. Several chapters contain international law discussions. The idea is to inform the general public so that a person who is not an international lawyer can see how flimsy these accusations are.

Chapter one sets the stage by looking at the Durban World Conference Against Racism. That conference highlighted the close connection between anti-Zionism and antisemitism.

Chapter two examines the manner in which anti-Israel discourse has turned into anti-Jewish discourse. Attempts to demonize the State of Israel have turned into antisemitism.

Chapter three examines specific allegations of human rights violations made against Israel. Israel is accused of the worst crimes known to humanity, not because of what has happened, but because of what anti-Zionists want to happen: the end of Israel as a Jewish state.

Chapter four discusses the specific accusation of occupation. It addresses the theory that the occupation by Israel of the West Bank and Gaza is the root cause of the global attacks against Jews.

Chapter five considers a specific war crimes charge against Israel. The charge is that the settlements on the West Bank and Gaza are a war crime, the crime of transfer of civilian populations to occupied territory.

Chapter six examines yet another accusation against Israel, that its security barrier violates international law. The advisory opinion of the International Court of Justice (informally called the World Court) on the barrier is analyzed.

Chapter seven deals with the claim that there is a Palestinian right of return to Israel. The chapter argues that there is no such right.

Chapter eight shows the patterns of prejudice flowing from anti-Zionism. Anti-Zionism may be distinctive in its ideology, but it is classic in its consequences. It fits the mould of all forms of bigotry.

Chapter nine details the corruption of international human rights institutions caused by anti-Zionism. Anti-Zionism, like any prejudice, does not harm just its victims. It harms everyone.

Chapter ten sets out the consequences of the new antisemitism. This new form of antisemitism has many of the old results. Jews suffer today from the new antisemitism in many of the same ways they suffered from the old.

Chapter eleven contrasts the treatment of Palestinian refugees and Jewish refugees from Arab countries. The contrast highlights the hypocrisy implicit in anti-Zionism.

Chapter twelve sets out the centrality of the Holocaust both to Israel and to human rights standards and institutions. The chapter argues that the Holocaust is unique.

Chapter thirteen discusses why the Jews must have a state and why that state must be in Israel for the rights of Jews everywhere to be respected. The connection between the right to self-determination of peoples and the right of Israel to exist is made.

Chapter fourteen discusses how to work with anti-racist and religious communities to combat the antisemitism that is anti-Zionism. Antisemitism is both racism and religious intolerance.

Chapter fifteen examines the different ways in which Jewish community organizations and general human rights organizations combat antisemitism.

Chapter sixteen looks at strategies for combatting anti-Zionism. Strategies are considered for Canada, for Arab and Muslim countries, and for the United Nations.

The conclusion argues for the need for Jewish ethics to address anti-Zionism. It ends by asserting that the struggle against anti-Zionism is the struggle for human rights.

One theme of my earlier Dundurn book is that human rights violations have ideological causes. This book, in a sense, is a case study of that theme, exploring anti-Zionism as an ideological cause of antisemitic actions.

W HAT is civil society when it stops being civil? That question was posed by the non-governmental organization (NGO) Forum Against Racism at Durban in August 2001. The forum preceded by three days and overlapped by two the inter-governmental World Conference Against Racism.

The NGO forum and the intergovernmental conference were held at neighbouring venues. The forum was held in tents set up outside and within the oval of the Durban Kingsmead Cricket Grounds. The conference was held across the street at the Durban International Convention Centre.

Non-governmental forums have been paralleling intergovernmental forums for decades. They are a lobbying opportunity, a chance to present an unofficial perspective, a reality check, presenting to the media and the world more than just the official line.

However, despite their extensive history, each new forum is a new experience. The non-governmental world is, by its nature, not institutionalized. Any group of individuals anywhere and for any purpose can form a non-governmental organization. Along with the few well-established, well-known organizations, there are thousands of organizations that represent just a few individuals and a very specific cause. Each new NGO forum is a new anarchy.

The non-governmental world is impoverished. Financing is threadbare. Insofar as money can solve organizational problems, it is a solution not ready at hand.

There have been attempts to produce some order out of the chaos. The Office of the United Nations High Commissioner for Human Rights has an NGO liaison office that tries to provide some support to NGOs. However, not many people make a business of attending international NGO forums. Each gathering throws up a whole new crowd, focused on its own issues and unaware of how to organize an NGO forum or function within one. The befuddled lead the bewildered.

In the past, despite the mayhem, participants in the forums have managed to muddle through. Goodwill has managed to overcome the obstacles of disorgani-zation and miscommunication.

The Durban NGO forum presented a whole new experience, a landmark for the NGO world, an event of significance beyond the confines of the fight against racism. The Durban NGO forum was plagued by a group of NGOs who had a political agenda, not a human rights agenda, and who were willing to stop at nothing to realize that agenda. Goodwill was not at hand to put order into the disarray. Rather, the inexperience of the organizers and the absence of both clear rules and institutional structures meant that those with a political agenda were able to turn the NGO forum away from human rights.

The planned end product of the World Conference Against Racism was a declaration and program of action to combat racism. The NGO forum organizers decided to attempt to produce their own declaration and program of action in order to influence the development of the intergovernmental document. Even if there had been clear rules and an experienced organization, such an attempt would have been fraught with difficulties. The non-governmental community does not speak with one voice, and sometimes speaks with conflicting voices. Consensus is rare.

To compound their difficulties, the organizers of the forum decided to include in their declaration and program of action the voices of the victims, speaking about their victimization. The trouble with that notion is that in times of war, both sides typically see themselves as the victims and their enemies as the perpetrators. A plan to produce a consensus declaration that gave a voice to the victims would require victims on both sides to agree. Otherwise, the document would be internally contradictory or, to avoid the contradiction, one set of victims' voices would be stilled.

When, on top of all that, the rules were not clear and the organization was a shambles, an attempt to produce an NGO declaration and program of action became an invitation to disaster. In such a situation it was all too easy for it to become the voice not of the many, but of a few — the wildest and most determined extremists.

The non-governmental world is no holier than the governmental world. Powerlessness does not sanctify. What distinguishes governments from non-governmental organizations, aside from money and power, is the range of interests. Governments are multi-faceted, inevitably trying to juggle a number of different interests or causes simultaneously. Non-governmental organizations have the luxury of specialization. They can and do devote themselves to only one cause or a small number of causes.

However, there is nothing inherently worthy about the causes of non-governmental organizations. Non-governmental organizations are as likely to preach human rights violations as human rights, and they are as likely to resort to violence and incitement to violence as governments are. Non-governmental organizations are, after all, like governments, just people, and often the same people on their way into or out of government.

Non-governmental human rights organizations have the luxury of an exclusive focus on human rights that governments cannot afford. Non-governmental political organizations are more easily obsessed by the monomania of their political causes. Governments are brought face to face with reality when they attempt to put their ideas into practice. Non-governmental ideologists can live in a fantasy world.

There has been a tendency for non-governmental human rights organizations to focus on abuses by governments. The explanation for this is, in part, historical. The non-governmental human rights movement arose during the Cold War when governments in the East were totalitarian and client governments of the West were authoritarian. Governments were strong, and opposition groups were weak. Now, big brother has been replaced by little brother. Instead of communist regimes in the East and national security regimes in the West, we have state collapse and fragmentation, free-for-alls where warlords, terrorists, and the mafia reign — too little government rather than too much.

The non-governmental human rights world has been slow to adapt to this changing reality. Human rights NGOs are so used to mobilizing civil society to call governments to account and seeing other non-governmental organizations as potential allies that they find it hard to grapple with threats to human rights from the non-governmental world.

Human rights NGOs have learned to be suspicious of governments that mouth the human rights vocabulary and do little else. Governmental human rights hypocrisy is easily identified and condemned. These same human rights NGOs have been far less likely to scrutinize the incantation of human rights platitudes by political non-governmental organizations.

The naïveté and misdirection of human rights NGOs have created an opportunity for political NGOs. Political activists who have little regard for human rights use human rights discourse to discredit and delegitimize their opponents. They turn to human rights NGOs to endorse their cause and to condemn their opponents as human rights violators. Human rights NGOs, as often as not, have been blind to this political manipulation and have bought into the agenda of those political movements that use the proper human rights vocabulary.

Political NGOs are sometimes non-governmental in name only. Human rights NGOs are reluctant to take money from governments for fear that it might compromise their independence. Political NGOs are not as reluctant and are often financed by sympathetic governments. GONGOs, government-organized NGOs, have been a traditional feature of communist regimes, but they proliferate wherever repression is found.

The turmoil of NGO forums, the naïveté of human rights NGOs, and the fixations of politicized NGOs all came together in Durban to produce a witches' brew. The atmosphere was poisoned, and so was the result. The source of the mess, unsurprisingly, was politics in the Middle East.

In the war between Palestinians and Israelis, both sides see themselves as victims. Israelis see the Palestinians and their supporters as perpetrators, unwilling to accept the existence of the State of Israel and terrorizing its population. Palestinians see Israel and the Jews as denying them their homeland and committing crimes against them to suppress their claim to that homeland.

The organized Jewish community did not even consider asking the World Conference Against Racism or the NGO forum to endorse the view that the Palestinian Authority is intent on terrorism and violence and opposed to the peaceful settlement of the Middle East conflict. Anti-Zionist organizations, however, showed a good deal more nerve.

For the anti-Zionists, both the NGO Forum Against Racism and the World Conference Against Racism became a continuation of the war against Israel by other means. Anti-Zionists sought to have language included in both the NGO forum's and the intergovernmental conference's Declaration and Program of Action that accused Israel of the worst crimes known to humanity: genocide, war crimes, crimes against humanity, colonialism, ethnic cleansing, and apartheid.

Anti-Zionist advocates attempted to appropriate the voice and victimization of the Jewish people by denying them the use of the words *antisemitism* and *Holocaust*. The Palestinian Caucus called for the reintroduction of the United Nations resolution equating Zionism with racism, the only UN resolution in the last fifty years that has been formally repealed. The Palestinian Caucus asserted a non-existent Palestinian right of return and called for a repeal of the Israeli Law of Return.

Given anti-Zionist ambitions, the question for both the NGO Forum Against Racism and the World Conference Against Racism became whether they would be able to defend themselves from turning into a forum and conference endorsing racism and incitement to hatred. Would the fanaticism of the enemies of Israel carry the day?

The basic element of the NGO forum was the caucus. It was caucuses that voted in the plenary, not individuals or organizations. It was caucuses that submitted the texts that formed the component parts of the NGO Forum Against Racism Declaration and Program of Action. It was caucuses that ran the thematic commissions during the forum where discussions of text were held. But despite the centrality of caucuses to the forum, there were never any clear, written rules about who could form a caucus, how a caucus could be formed, or by when a caucus had to be formed. In practice, any group of individuals could signify to the organizers that they wished to form a caucus based on a region or victim group or theme, and status was bestowed. At the last minute a deadline was imposed of two days before the closing plenary. At that point there were forty-one caucuses. Some were formed, it seemed, just for the purpose of piling up votes. The anti-Zionist cause, in particular, ended up having four caucuses: Palestinian, Arab and the Middle East, Environmental Racism, and Colonialism and Foreign Occupation.

When it came to the plenary, several groups realized that they were disenfranchised, not being part of any caucus. They asked to be allowed to form caucuses then and there. Those at the head table agreed, insisting only that there be at least ten in the hall who wanted to join the caucus. Within a few minutes, several new caucuses were formed, including Sikhs, Pakistan, Refugees, and South Asia, and additional voting cards were given out. As the queue for new voting cards grew, the plenary had second thoughts. They decided to have a vote on the new procedure and repudiated it. The decision was, no new caucuses. So the new voting cards handed out had to be handed back in.

The thematic commissions were equally problematic. In theory, the thematic commissions at the forum were the place to discuss components of the text of the forum's Declaration and Program of Action. Each thematic commission was run by a caucus. The Commission on Antisemitism, for instance, for which I was the rapporteur, was run by the Jewish Caucus.

There were only twenty-five thematic commissions, considerably fewer than the number of caucuses. Those who were not part of any caucus and those whose caucuses were not running a thematic commission were left to choose amongst the thematic commissions.

Voting in commissions was as perplexing as voting in plenary. There were rules circulated for commissions saying that there would be majority rule if there were no consensus. But a majority of whom? The rules did not say. Was it a majority of the relevant caucus, or a majority of whoever happened to be around at the time? The first alternative was exclusionary, but the second was far worse: it would allow those antagonistic to the aims of the caucus and the voices of its victims to overwhelm the caucus and take away from the victims the chance to speak of their victimization.

The litany of bungles and confusions seemed never-ending. Before Durban, the NGO Forum Against Racism Declaration and Program of Action had gone through several drafts that seemed to please almost nobody. At Durban, the press kits contained an early draft that had been rejected by the International Steering Committee. The delegates' kits had no draft. Instead, delegates were instructed to find a draft on the Internet, though few had access to computers.

Rather than circulate a prior draft to the thematic commissions for comment, the organizers tried to do something specific and up to date. Each thematic commission was given new language specific to its theme for comment. The language was drawn from prior drafts and other submissions the organizers and the drafting committee had received. Only text relevant to the theme was given to each commission to prevent commissions from wandering off into other areas, commenting on language submitted by other caucuses.

The trouble with this approach was that it meant that each caucus could prepare comments on only a small part of the text, that relevant to the theme of the commission that the caucus ran. The rest of the text was not before the commission for comment.

As well, the organizers failed to take into account the inevitable delays in producing new texts. The texts that each commission had to consider were delivered sometimes a few minutes before, sometimes even after the commissions had begun their deliberations. Needless to say, there were not sufficient copies for those present. Most people present at commissions were discussing texts that were not in front of them.

The Commission on Antisemitism had its own special problem — an invasion of hostile elements. As the forum organizers suggested, the commission was divided into two parts. The first part was a sequence of short presentations defining antisemitism and presenting victims' stories. The second was discussion of the commission's contribution to the overall Declaration and Program of Action.

Towards the end of the first part, a number of participants who were supporters of the Palestinians and hostile to the existence of Israel and the work of the commission jumped up and started haranguing the commission non-stop. At the same time, about one hundred people (almost doubling the attendance), many of them wearing kafiyas (a checkered scarf symbolizing support for the Palestinian cause), stormed the commission.

Continuation of the commission became impossible. The last speaker, Peleg Reshef, chair of the World Union of Jewish Students, shouted out his presentation, and the commission recessed. After the recess, the commission split into six working groups to allow discussion and to draft different components of the antisemitism part of the Declaration and Program of Action.

The split, after a fashion, worked. The troublemakers were able to make life difficult for a few of the working groups, but not for all of them. Many of invaders left when they realized that their audience, the commission plenary, was fragmented.

The Jewish Caucus met every night at the Durban Jewish Club, down the road from the Kingsmead Cricket Ground. Yehuda Kay, national director of the South African Jewish Board of Deputies, was the caucus meetings facilitator. At the caucus meeting the night following the commission, each working group reported to me. From those reports and the prior texts, along with the help of other members of the Jewish Caucus, I stitched together a report to the Drafting Committee for the NGO forum's Declaration and Program of Action. One clause stated:

> We are concerned with the prevalence of anti-Zionism and attempts
> to delegitimize the State of Israel through wildly inaccurate charges
> of genocide, war crimes, crimes against humanity, ethnic cleansing
> and apartheid, as a virulent contemporary form of antisemitism
> leading to firebombing of synagogues, armed assaults against Jews,
> incitements to killing, and the murder of innocent Jews, for their
> support for the existence of the State of Israel, the assertion of
> the right to self-determination of the Jewish people and the
> attempts, through the State of Israel, to preserve their cultural
> and religious identity.

Antoine Madelin of the International Federation for Human Rights was the member of the NGO Drafting Committee appointed as liaison with the Commission on Antisemitism. One of the federation's affiliates is LAW, a Palestinian-led group. LAW was also represented on the steering committee of the NGO forum.

When I handed in our text, Antoine was not pleased. He tried to persuade me to remove the quoted clause, arguing that it was justifiable to criticize the policies of Israel and that the Palestinian language was directed at policies only. I explained to him that this was not the way the Jewish Caucus saw it and stood firm.

The troublemakers at the Commission on Antisemitism, not satisfied with the vitriolic anti-Israel language they had already produced in the Palestinian Caucus, tried to eliminate the report of the Commission on Antisemitism from the NGO forum's Declaration and Program of Action, complaining that the commission was invalid because we did not continue in the plenary that they made impossible to conduct. Seven of them filed a formal complaint with the overall Steering Committee on the basis that the Commission on Antisemitism had no plenary discussion, only working group discussions, that there was no consensus, and that no vote was taken on the report of the commission, as the rules required.

My answer to that, when asked by the International Steering Committee, was that there was a consensus amongst members of the victim group, the Jewish Caucus, and that no caucus should have to count the votes of those who would oppress the group the caucus represented. The Steering Committee, it seemed, accepted that answer, because the report of the Commission on Antisemitism, including the parts accusing Israel of all the worst crimes and asserting that these accusations were antisemitism and incitement to hatred, remained in the draft presented to the overall plenary. Neither Antoine nor the Steering Committee felt that they had the authority to remove language agreed to by a caucus. The Drafting Committee did edit out some of the contradictory language, relegating it to one paragraph rather than the several in which the Jewish Caucus had inserted it. But the substance remained.

The plenary was something else. It was held on Saturday, the Jewish Sabbath. Keeping the Sabbath holy is one of the Ten Commandments in the Torah. While some people in the Jewish community, including me, are not all that religious, many are observant. The institutional Jewish community respects all Jewish religious holidays. The Jewish Caucus could not participate in the Saturday plenary. Individuals could attend as observers only, not to represent the Jewish Caucus. That is what I did.

The rules for the plenary provided that any caucus could propose an amendment to text emanating from another caucus. A decision on the proposed amendment would be made by a majority of caucuses: one caucus, one vote.

The Jewish Caucus had proposed an amendment deleting all the anti-Zionist paragraphs in the text and prepared a statement to speak to it. But we were not going to attend. Someone who was not Jewish volunteered to give the statement for us so that our voice could be heard.

Throughout the process, the Drafting Committee, the Steering Committee, and SANGOCO (the South African NGO coalition that was the host on the ground for the NGO forum) all, in various ways, showed sympathy for the anti-Zionist cause and insensitivity to the Jewish Caucus. They were not impartial and made no real effort to appear impartial.

As it turned out, the plenary was postponed to Saturday after sundown, when the Jewish Caucus could and did attend. However, that postponement did not happen out of respect for human rights principles or for religious accommodation of the Jewish Caucus. Rather, it was an effect of the continuing disorganization of the forum.

On Saturday morning, when everyone was supposed to review, discuss, and vote on the text that the Drafting Committee had put together from the contributions of the various theme commissions, there was no text to discuss, in any language. For no apparent reason, there were copies distributed in French of an earlier draft of the Declaration and Program of Action, which we were told to disregard. The text we needed to look at was still being photocopied. It would not be available until later in the day. So the plenary was postponed until after what was still called, despite its inappropriate name, the closing ceremonies.

The delay of the plenary to Saturday evening to accommodate the need for copies shows that it could have been postponed to accommodate the Jewish Caucus. The fact that it was not shows how little regard the organizers gave to fairness. The only concession the organizers made to the Jewish Caucus was to exempt them from the rule that only caucuses of more than ten participants present at the plenary scheduled for Saturday daytime could propose amendments to the text and vote.

At the plenary, individuals were not allowed to speak, only caucus representatives. Each caucus was allowed to speak only once during the whole plenary, for only five minutes, to explain any amendments it proposed. The chair appointed security to guard the floor mikes and deny access to anyone the chair did not recognize.

A document titled "Agenda and Procedures for adoption of the Declaration and Program of Action" stated, "Guiding Principle: We reaffirm the following principle, that the victims of racism and related intolerance have the right to describe their own realities of racism and related intolerance as they experience it. The NGO community supports them in this document in describing these realities of racism and related intolerance for themselves."

In spite of that guiding principle, the World Council of Churches, speaking for the Ecumenical Caucus, proposed the deletion from the text on antisemitism the paragraph protesting anti-Zionism. Their reason was that this clause contradicted the pro-Palestinian clauses elsewhere in the document. The chair called a vote on this proposed deletion, without giving the Jewish Caucus or, indeed, anyone, an opportunity to speak.

Several caucuses abstained, but only four — the Jewish, European, Roma, and Eastern and Central European caucuses — voted against. After this vote, the Jewish Caucus and the Eastern and Central European Caucus walked out. The Asian Descendants Caucus subsequently told the Jewish Caucus that they were so confused by what was going on that they voted in favour even though they intended to voted against.

We heard reports that later that evening the European Caucus and the Roma Caucus also walked out. The Roma Caucus, before they walked out, took the microphone to explain that they were leaving because they could not approve the hate language contained in the NGO documents. We also heard that the Arab Caucus proposed the addition of paragraphs, which the plenary accepted, that expanded the definition of antisemitism to include Arabs as victims. At about four in the morning, with about seventy-five people left and fifteen caucus representatives, the plenary approved the Declaration and Program of Action. At the end of the day, the paragraph from the Commission on Antisemitism protesting anti-Zionism was the only paragraph that the plenary deleted from the draft document.

The Eastern and Central European Caucus, the Cultural Diversity Caucus, the South Asia Caucus, and the Peace Caucus each circulated statements rejecting the NGO Declaration and Program of Action and the process that generated it. The Eastern and Central European Caucus statement included a petition that scores of NGOs signed:

> … the process of compilation and adoption of the NGO Forum Declaration and Program of Action was neither transparent nor democratic and permeated with procedural violations. The draft documents were not submitted to the delegates in a timely manner and the rules of procedure were unclear and repeatedly changed; the discussion was heavily restricted. Finally the delegates were not given an opportunity to vote on the draft documents in their entirety. This enables us to affirm that the documents cannot be considered adopted by the NGO Forum and are not consensus documents.
>
> We believe that as a result of this flawed process, the contents of the documents include unacceptable concepts and language …
>
> We must emphasize that the language of the chapter "Palestine" as well as the deliberate distortions made to the chapter "Antisemitism" is extremely intolerant, disrespectful and contrary to the very spirit of the World Conference …

The European Roma Rights Centre, which signed this statement, issued its own statement as well.

> The European Roma Rights Centre (ERRC) is saddened to conclude that it cannot endorse the 72-page NGO Declaration and Programme of Action submitted yesterday to the organisers of the World Conference against Racism in Durban on behalf of the NGO Forum. "These documents contain inappropriate language fuelling precisely the kind of hatred and racism the Durban gathering was meant to challenge," said Dimitrina Petrova, Executive Director of ERRC. "We cannot but deplore the fact that an event of such importance for Roma and other victims of discrimination was apparently hijacked by biased activists, forcing through their own agenda. The aggressive exclusion of Jewish participants by fellow NGO colleague and the accompanying, blatantly intolerant anti-Semitic spirit plaguing the entire process, prompted us to firmly distance ourselves from this Forum's unfortunate outcome."

The Cultural Diversity Caucus statement declared:

- the Conference has, under cover of the democratic system of the United Nations, developed governmental documents with racist content:
- the Middle East is not a racial conflict, but only a political-cultural conflict, which is not relevant to the Conference;
- it is not true that Israel is committing genocide, ethnic cleansing, much less apartheid ...
- the Conference has not blocked racist language from intergovernmental and non-governmental documents and has not respected human rights ...

For the above reasons, we request: ...

- To reject the intergovernmental and non-governmental documents from this Conference ...

The South Asia and Peace caucuses declared, in a statement signed by several other NGOs:

> 1) The declaration has not been drafted in a transparent manner. The drafts were presented at odd hours without giving proper notice to the plenary.

2) The process of drafting was not democratic. Out of a large number of NGO's/Caucuses, only a few were represented in the Drafting Committee while some NGO's were over represented. the drafting committee was not democratically constituted,

3) The process of drafting was highly politicized with certain NGO's taking definite political stances on specific issues …

Even the Drafting Committee rejected the process. Six members of the committee, but not Antoine, issued a statement:

> The proposal by the Ecumenical Caucus to delete a paragraph from the submissions made by the Anti-Semitism Thematic Commission and the subsequent walk out by members of the Anti-Semitism Thematic Commission in the midst of a general uproar was certainly not conducive, in our minds, to the intent and objectives of the Plenary.
>
> As members of the Drafting Committee we indicated to the International Steering Committee our unhappiness with the way the plenary had been conducted …

United Nations High Commissioner for Human Rights Mary Robinson played an ambiguous role. Prior to the Durban meeting there was a sequence of preparatory regional meetings, including one in Tehran for Asia. According to Congressman Tom Lantos, head of the American delegation to Durban,[6] she took no action to attempt to overcome the ban on attendance of Israeli government representatives but merely tried to appease. In the other regional preparatory meetings, she opened with appeals to governments to recognize and confront their own present-day problems of discrimination. In Tehran, however, there was no such appeal.

In a statement to the press after the conclusion of the Tehran conference, which ended with a one-sided anti-Israel concluding document, she congratulated the Tehran delegates on their degree of consensus and urged them to carry on in the fight against racism. She characterized the meeting as a productive dialogue between civilizations. When asked about the inflammatory rhetoric directed at Israel, she stated, "The situation in the Palestinian occupied territories was brought up at the meeting and it is reflected in the final declaration."

At a preparatory meeting in Geneva in August just prior to the Durban Conference, Robinson refused to reject the notion in the draft Durban conference text that the wrong done to the Jews in the Holocaust was equivalent to the pain suffered by the Palestinians in the Middle East. Instead, as Lantos reports, she discussed "the historical wounds" of antisemitism and of the Holocaust on the one hand, and "the accumulated wounds" of displacement and military occupation on the other. Instead of insisting that it was inappropriate to single out Israel in the context of a World Conference Against Racism, she condoned it by referring to the "need to resolve protracted conflict and occupation, claims of inequality, violence and terrorism, and a deteriorating situation on the ground." Tom Lantos wrote, "It was clear to me that Mrs. Robinson's intervention during the Geneva talks represented the *coup de grace* on efforts to save the [Durban] conference from disaster."

When she got to Durban, Robinson switched gears. She rejected the language of the NGO forum's concluding document, refusing to recommend its adoption by the intergovernmental World Conference. She said publicly, "It's sad for me that for the first time I can't recommend to delegates that they pay close attention to the NGO Declaration." She was "disheartened and dismayed" by the inappropriate language accusing Israel of genocide. She called the document "unacceptable and hurtful." She added, "I am aware of and condemn those whose words and actions in Durban were themselves intolerant, even racist." When presented with the antisemitic literature being distributed at the Kingsmead Cricket Grounds Robinson said, "When it comes to this, I am a Jew."[7]

But as the Durban inter-governmental conference ended, Robinson stuck her head back in the sand. In her closing address, she said, "We have succeeded." She congratulated the delegates for reaching consensus, blithely ignoring that both Israel and the United States had walked out.

McGill University gave Mary Robinson an honourary doctorate on June 4, 2004. It should not have been given. Honourary doctors are meant to be examples to students. Their careers are held up to emulation. But Mary Robinson behaved dishonourably. While she could not control anti-Zionist governments, she could control what she said and did. Her record shows that she was not prepared to stand up to attempts to turn the conference into an anti-Zionist platform. The office of United Nations High Commissioner for Human Rights is a human rights leadership pulpit. She abused this pulpit to give comfort to the anti-Zionist cause.

The offensive wording in the NGO forum's Declaration and Program of Action gave only an inkling of the pervasive antisemitism at the forum, which became an arena of antisemitism, a stadium of hatred.

On entry to the forum grounds, every participant was accosted by virulent antisemitic slogans, pamphlets, slurs, and chants. There was a steady stream of incidents of people from the Jewish Caucus being threatened, verbally abused, and harassed for no other reason than that they were Jewish and had stood up for the rights of the Jewish people. Anyone who was Jewish felt unwelcome and unwanted.

An officially sanctioned booth of the Arab Lawyers Union handed out antisemitic hate propaganda that violated international human rights and South

African legal standards — cartoons portraying Jews with hooked noses, blood dripping from fangs, with pots of money surrounding the victims. *The Protocols of the Elders of Zion*, a czarist forgery, along with other traditional antisemitic literature, was on sale at the forum. The Afro-Brazilian National Congress handed out a flyer with the headline "Down with the Nazi-Israel Apartheid." Similar flyers and posters were plastered all over the official information tent, as well as tents allocated for regional meetings.

T-shirts were freely distributed with both the official NGO forum logo and symbols inciting hatred and violence towards the Jewish state, including the phrase "End Israeli Apartheid." Marches and chants of an antisemitic nature went on throughout the forum, with participants shouting, "Zionism is racism" or "Israel Nakba." (*Nakba* is Arabic for "catastrophe.")

Many comments were directed at Jewish participants. "You do not belong to the human race." "Chosen people? You are cursed people." "Why haven't the Jews taken responsibility for killing Jesus?" "They've sucked our blood all these years." At a rally on Friday, August 31, there was a poster reading "Hitler should have finished the job." At another rally during the forum, a person shouted, "Kill the Jews." These sorts of comments were incessant, endemic.

The invasion of the Commission on Antisemitism on Tuesday, August 28, by hostile elements was a harbinger of things to come. On Thursday, August 30, the Jewish Caucus held a press conference in the forum's media tent, chaired by Rabbi Abraham Cooper of the Simon Wiesenthal Institute of Los Angeles. A group hostile to the concerns of the caucus invaded the press conference and shouted it down too. The din created by agitators chanting "Zionism is racism" prevented journalists from asking us questions. One of the anti-Zionist rabble-rousers shouted at me while I was at the press conference, "You are killing our children."

This was the second time in my life I had been accused of murder. The first time I was eight. A playmate accused me of killing Jesus Christ. Unaware of both antisemitism and Christian theology at the time, I replied, lamely, that I had killed no one. However, the charge seemed so bizarre, that an eight-year-old could be guilty of killing someone who died almost two thousand years ago, it stuck with me. I appreciate now, though I did not then, the seriousness of the charge, the danger it posed for me and for the whole Jewish community.

Collective guilt leads to collective punishment. That is presumably what the anti-Zionist accuser had in mind. He accused me of killing Palestinian children because he wanted to punish me, as a member of the Jewish community, by denying to me the right to membership in a people that enjoys the right to self-determination.

The rally at the forum on August 31 was supposed to be against racism, but it turned into a rally against the Jewish people. The demonstrators took their march, not to the city hall or national government buildings or consular offices, but to the Durban Jewish Club, blocking its access and threatening its occupants.

The Jewish Caucus, though it normally met in the evening, had scheduled its Friday meeting for that afternoon, so as not to conflict with the oncoming Sabbath, which started at sundown Friday evening. Security officials closed off the Jewish Club to protect against an invasion from the demonstrators.

At the last minute, the caucus meeting was rescheduled to the lobby coffee shop of the Hilton Hotel. As many members as possible were advised of the change through cellphones. So the Jewish Caucus was relegated to a hotel lobby to meet and plan about the forum plenary that, because of the Sabbath, they could not attend.

The forum ended as badly as it began. It began, at least for me, with the Commission on Antisemitism being invaded by hostile elements. It ended with the Jewish Caucus plenary walkout. The Jewish Caucus, after voting alone, walked out to applause and shouts of "Get out of Palestine" and "Free Palestine."

During the forum, anti-Zionist agitators interrupted not just the Jewish Caucus press conference, but private media interviews as well. They broke into interviews of Jewish Caucus representatives, answering the questions the reporter asked the Jewish Caucus representative and not giving the representative a chance to respond.

One anti-Zionist apologist broke into an interview that a Reuters reporter was conducting with me and Anne Bayefsky. The reporter asked the anti-Zionist apologist to move on, but he refused. We had to walk away from him to carry on the interview. We then had to leave the Kingsmead Cricket Grounds because security staff advised us our safety was at risk.

The organizers of the forum did nothing to prevent the dissemination of hatred and incitement to hatred. Indeed, some of the organizers actively particicipated in it. There were police on the grounds who occasionally interposed themselves between anti-Zionist demonstrators and Jewish delegates when things seemed to be getting out of hand. However, that was the only effort made by anyone to control the situation.

A gang of terrorists operating under the name Popular Front for the Liberation of Palestine hijacked a number of planes in 1970 in order to garner publicity for their cause. The result was the installation of metal detectors and security checks at airports around the world. The hijacking of the NGO Forum Against Racism by a new generation of anti-Zionists is going to require a global response just as momentous. For future NGO forums, organizers are going to have to install hate detectors. They must not allow the fanaticism of a few to deny the fundamental human rights of the many.

Though the blame for the deterioration of the NGO forum lies primarily with the NGOs themselves, the UN must share some responsibility, because the UN gave money to NGOs to organize and attend the forum — including NGOs whose commitment to sowing hatred against the Jewish people was obvious from the start. Money was given to the host NGO, SANGOCO, for organization, without adequate supervision or insistence that minimal standards be respected.

The NGO Forum Against Racism showed the need for a democratic voting structure, an independent mechanism for the adjudication of disputes, the articulation and enforcement of standards of respect and civility, and an adequate security structure. In short, the non-governmental forum demonstrated the need for government.

The Durban NGO forum told us what civil society becomes when it ceases to be civil. It is an unruly mob, a kangaroo court, a bunch of bullies and cowards, a collection of tricksters and suckers.

Neither the World Conference Against Racism nor the NGO Forum Against Racism ended up being, in the main, about the fight against racism. Instead, most of the debate and deliberations at both meetings were devoted to Middle East politics. Indeed, given the persistence of Arab attempts to delegitimize the state of Israel by criticizing it of the worst crimes imaginable and by minimizing or generalizing the human rights violations that gave Israel birth, both the NGO forum and the World Conference became venues for racism.

Nonetheless, at the end of the day, the intergovernmental conference, though it produced an unsatisfactory document, was not as wacky as the NGO forum. However, it did end up with text expressing concern for the plight of the Palestinians under foreign occupation.

Additional text supported a right of return of refugees to their homes. The text was under the rubric "Middle East" and appeared to be a coded reference to Israel.

The World Conference document can be condemned, by virtue of these texts, for wandering off into a political area that had nothing to do with racism and for taking part in the dispute over whether Palestinians who have never set foot in Israel and never had any legal status granted by the state have a right to enter Israel en masse. The inclusion of pro-Palestinian text in what was supposed to an anti-racism document suggested that the fight against racism meant siding with the Palestinians against Israel.

However, the World Conference document was not the incitement to hatred against Jews that the NGO forum document was. In the struggle for respect for human rights, historically it is governments that are called to account, and NGOs doing the accounting. It is governments that violate human rights and NGOs that promote respect for those rights.

In Durban, the tables were turned. The NGO document diminished and tarnished rights far more than the intergovernmental document did. After Durban, non-governmental organizations cannot say with a straight face that they always articulate ideals for governments to follow. In Durban, NGOs lost their innocence. They articulated and incited human rights violations that governments had the good sense not to mimic.

Both the intergovernmental conference and the NGO forum, by providing a venue and a platform for incitement to hatred against Jews, set back, rather than advanced, the fight against racism. Neither should have been convened. State delegates and non-governmental representatives who came to Durban to fight racism were caught up in a rearguard struggle to prevent the endorsement of racism.

Both the conference and the forum were a colossal waste of time and money. No one who is serious about opposing racism would cite the Declaration and Program of Action of either the conference or the forum in support of their cause.

Canada was on the verge of walking out on the World Conference throughout. The Americans and the Israelis did walk out on Monday, September 3. The Jewish Caucus, including the organization I represented, B'nai Brith Canada, decided the next day to join the walkout. B'nai Brith International President Richard D. Heideman, in a statement made on behalf of the Jewish Caucus, said, "The United Nations was founded to promote human rights and international security. This conference, though, has undermined these principles." The government of Canada stayed, according to United Nations Ambassador Paul Heinbecker, "only because we wanted to have our voice decry the attempts at the conference to delegitimize the state of Israel, and to dishonour the history of the Jewish people."

The Aboriginal Caucus also walked out, on Friday, September 7, and asked all those sympathetic to the rights of indigenous people to join them. The focus of their concern was the endorsement of those provisions of the World Conference Declaration that denied that the term "indigenous peoples" has any international law rights implications.[8] Their statement said, "It is inconceivable and unacceptable that something of this nature would occur at a place where the rights of peoples were to be discussed and protected."

Civil society careened out of control, with a group of passengers trying to drive it off the road. The smash-up that occurred was, nonetheless, avoidable.

What led, in the end, to the wreckage of the forum was the feebleness of the support the Jewish anti-racist organizations received from other anti-racist groups. While the Cultural Diversity, Asian Descendants, Roma, Eastern and Central European, South Asia, Peace, and European caucuses each in their own way expressed their voices in solidarity, most did not.

The Canadian government delegation met with and briefed Canadian NGOs every day during the World Conference. At the briefing of Tuesday, September 4, my statement that B'nai Brith Canada had pulled out of the conference and had asked Canada to do the same was met with widespread incomprehension. Most Canadian NGOs were so wrapped up in their issues that an attack on their colleagues took second place.

Nobel Peace Prize laureate Elie Wiesel called the Durban meetings "an enterprise of disgrace … a moral catastrophe." He wrote, "The content was wholly unadulterated hatred and cruelty, whose expressions ought to outrage any decent and cultured human being."

The anti-racism community from around the world came to Durban to fight racism. Yet, when they found racism staring them in the face, most of them looked the other way.

The NGO community decided that confronting their colleagues at the Kingsmead Cricket Ground was just not cricket. So they walked away from the game.

Wiesel reminded us, "Hatred is like a cancer. It spreads from cell to cell, from organ to organ, from person to person, from group to group." In Durban, the global anti-racist community set back the fight against racism by failing to combat the racism in front of their noses.

Only three days after the conference ended, terrorists hijacked four planes in the United States, crashed into the Pentagon and the World Trade Center, and killed three thousand people. On hearing the news, thousands of Palestinians poured into the streets of the West Bank and Gaza to celebrate, chanting "God is Great" and distributing candy to passersby.

While those at Durban could not have anticipated the terrorist attacks on the United States, no one who was at the Kingsmead Cricket Grounds would have been surprised by the Palestinian reaction of joy. Some parts of the world have developed a culture of hatred against Israel and American support for Israel as fierce as the Nazi hatred of Jews before the Second World War.

Wiesel said, "What is painful is not that the Palestinians and the Arabs voiced their hatred, but the fact that so few delegates had the courage to combat them." The overall response of the human rights community, in the face of real and immediate racism was "that is a legitimate victim's perspective," or "let's talk about something else."

This was the third World Conference Against Racism, after those of 1978 and 1983, that was consumed by anti-Zionism. If the global community wants to convene a fourth conference, it will either have to wait for anti-Zionism to end or lay in its defences to prevent anti-Zionism from overwhelming its deliberations.

CHAPTER TWO
From Anti-Zionism to Antisemitism

S ̲ɪ̲x̲ᴛ̲ʏ̲ years after the Holocaust, within the lifetime of many of its survivors, suicide bombers in Israel are killing Jews because they are Jewish. The Jewish community globally is under verbal and physical attack for its support of Israel. Synagogues and Jewish community centres around the world are being torched and firebombed. Antisemitic graffiti is everywhere.

How could this be happening? How could a community that has suffered so grievously so recently be subject again to the crazed hatred of fanatics consumed with a passion for killing Jews?

To answer that question, we have to look at the response of the global community to the Holocaust. The current antisemitism is a perversion of the legacy of the Holocaust.

The community of nations responded to the Holocaust with the assertion of human rights and the creation of the state of Israel. Both of these remedies have been perverted. Those opposed to the existence of the State of Israel have turned these twin shields into swords to be used in attacking the Jewish community worldwide.

The root cause of the revival of antisemitism is, in a word, anti-Zionism.[9] To talk of anti-Zionism as a root cause of human rights violations against the Jewish community worldwide may seem to miss the mark. It might be more accurate to say anti-Zionism is a human rights violation. And indeed, there is a key element of human rights that anti-Zionism violates just by being what it is — the right to self-determination. Zionism is the expression of the right to self-determination of the Jewish people. Anti-Zionism, by definition, denies and rejects this right by denying the right to a state for the Jewish people. Anti-Zionism is a form of racism. It is the specific denial to the Jewish people of a basic right to which all the peoples of the world are entitled.

After the Second World War, the horrors of the Holocaust discredited traditional antisemitism. Yet antisemitism did not die. For many member states of the United Nations it turned into anti-Zionism. Israel became the Jew amongst nations, condemned for sins it did not commit, targeted for destruction, almost friendless and alone.[10]

There is a tiny minority of Orthodox Jews who believe that the return of the Jewish people to the Land of Israel should await the coming of the Messiah. There are a few secularists who oppose the existence of any and all nation states, who propose for all peoples, in the words of Isaac Deutscher, "wider frameworks for their existence."[11] Though these people, in their own ways, oppose the existence of the State of Israel, they are not true anti-Zionists.

The nation state and the right to self-determination of peoples are post-Biblical concepts. True anti-Zionists are bigots, accepting and endorsing the right to self-determination of all peoples except the Jewish people. They attempt to obfuscate their own bigotry by hiding behind the messianism of a minority of Orthodox Jews or the heterodoxy and iconoclasm of those opposed to all nation states.

The reason I refer to anti-Zionism as a root cause of human rights violations rather than a human rights violation of its own is that anti-Zionism leads to violations of human rights above and beyond those conveyed by its literal meaning. Anti-Zionism advocates denial of the right to self-determination of the Jewish people. Every advocate of anti-Zionism preaches this denial.

Not all advocates of anti-Zionism preach the killing and maiming of innocent Jews, though, of course, some do. One cannot say that every single one of the promoters of anti-Zionism sees these killings as part of an ideal he or she is working to achieve. However, even the anti-Zionism of those who refrain from overt incitement leads to murders. Anti-Zionism generates abuses that must horrify every rights-respecting person, regardless of his or her views on the existence of the State of Israel. And it is these abuses, stemming from anti-Zionism, that are a powerful argument against anti-Zionism.

The evolution into human rights violations and the killing of innocent Jews has made the faults of this ideology manifest. The killing of innocent Jews is the logic of anti-Zionism made unrelenting.

Attacking the existence of Israel has meant attacking the reasons given for the existence of Israel both within and outside the Jewish community. Thus it is impossible to understand the rhetoric against Israel without understanding why Israel is there. Israel exists because of the Holocaust, because of antisemitism and as a place of refuge for Jews fleeing persecution, for the cultural survival of the Jewish people and their right to self-determination, because of the ties of the Jewish people to the land of Israel, and because of international acceptance and recognition. The logic of anti-Zionism requires attacking each and every one of these reasons for the existence of Israel.

Israel came into existence not just after the Holocaust, but because of the Holocaust. Although the Holocaust was concentrated in continental Europe, it was a crime in which the whole world shared by killing Jews or by denying refuge to Jews or by granting a haven to their murderers. The singularity of the Holocaust is elaborated in a later chapter of this book.

The Holocaust required a global response, not just a European response. The Holocaust made evident to the global community that the Jewish people needed their own state and that, in the case of the Jewish people, the right to self-determination meant the right to statehood.

It would have been inhumane to expect the Jewish people, after the Holocaust, to live in the countries of their persecutors. And their persecution was an enterprise in which the whole world shared. This argument is more fully set out in a later chapter of this book.

The rebuttal to that reason for the existence of the State of Israel amongst anti-Israel advocates is either Holocaust denial or Holocaust trivialization. The examples of Holocaust denial in the Arab and Muslim world are endless.

For example, Yacoub Zaki of the Muslim Institute of London stated on a Muslim radio station, Radio 786, in Cape Town, South Africa, in May 1998: "I accept that 1 million-plus Jews died during the Second World War, but I dispute the fact that they were murdered, that they were killed by gassing. These people died, like other people in the camps, from infectious diseases, particularly typhus."[12]

A sermon from the mosque of Sheikh Ijlin in Gaza preached by Sheikh Ibrahim Madhi and broadcast on Palestinian Authority television in January 2002 stated: "One of the cursed actions of the Jews is what is called the Holocaust, that is to say, the massacre of the Jews by Nazism. But revisionist historians have proved that this crime rumoured against some Jews was manipulated by Jewish leaders and became a political tactic. So you can see who are the Jews against whom we struggle."[13]

Mahmoud Abbas or Abu Mazen, chief PLO negotiator for the Oslo peace accords and a former prime minister of the Palestinian Authority under Yasser Arafat, wrote a book in 1983 titled *The Other Side: The Secret Relationship between Nazism and the Zionist Movement*. The book suggested that the number of Jews killed in the Holocaust was "peddled" by the Jews, but that in fact "the Jewish victims may number six million or be far fewer, even fewer than one million." Abbas justified the book as part of the war with Israel.[14]

One example of Holocaust trivialization was the Durban NGO Forum Against Racism and the overlapping intergovernmental World Conference Against Racism. Each meeting began with draft texts. Both meetings were preceded by a number of regional and global meetings that prepared those draft texts. At those regional and global meetings, where a proposed text was disagreed on, the proposal was put in square brackets. Texts where there was agreement were not bracketed.

The draft intergovernmental Durban declaration had the phrase "holocausts/Holocaust" in square brackets, meaning that the use of the word *Holocaust* in the singular with a capital "H" was in dispute. The purpose of this square bracketing was to deny the reality of the Holocaust, to suggest that other violations of human rights, including those alleged against Israel by anti-Israel advocates, were themselves holocausts. Anne Bayefsky said that this square bracketing questioned "the reality of Jews as the victims of the most heinous crimes committed against a people in history."[15]

At the end of the day, the plural and the small "h" disappeared from the intergovernmental conference's concluding declaration. However, the fact that the Holocaust was an issue indicates one dimension of Israel negation.

The Holocaust was global, not just European. It had a Middle Eastern dimension, because of the failure of the states of the Middle East to offer protection to Jewish refugees before, during, and after the Holocaust. Jewish refugees were protected and resettled in the Middle East without hindrance only after the creation of the State of Israel.

Until the creation of the State of Israel, the United Kingdom was nominally responsible for shutting Jews out of Palestine. However, Britain, in saying "no" to Jews attempting to find refuge in Palestine and in running an anti-Jewish blockade, was carrying out the intransigent will of the local Arab leadership.[16]

The crimes committed against the Jews were crimes against humanity, not just crimes against Jews or Europeans. The notion that the Holocaust was a European crime that should be remedied in Europe is a denial of the universality of human rights, a rejection of the common humanity we all share. It is an assertion that the harm was inflicted on "others," not on everybody. Humanity cannot be compartmentalized into geographical components. The obligation to remedy these wrongs falls on the whole global community.

The most notorious Nazi war criminal alive today, Alois Brunner, is reportedly living in the Meridien Hotel in Damascus, Syria, under the name Dr. Georg Fischer.[17] Brunner was in charge of the operations that sent Jews in Austria, Germany, Greece (in Salonika), and France (in Drancy) to concentration camps and death. He was personally responsible for sending over one hundred thousand Jews to these camps. Germany asked Syria for Brunner's extradition as long ago as 1987. In 1991 the European Parliament voted to condemn Syria for continuing to harbour him. The immunity that Syria gives Brunner to this day is blatant and continuing proof that the Holocaust remains a Middle Eastern crime as well.

A connected reason for the existence of Israel is the reality of antisemitism, not just during the Holocaust, but today. The fact is that Israel exists as a bulwark against global antisemitism.

One anti-Zionist rebuttal to that has been pretending that antisemitism does not exist. For years it was impossible to have the United Nations condemn antisemitism. The United Nations Commission on Human Rights each year passed resolutions condemning racism, but refused to mention antisemitism in those resolutions. Condemnation of antisemitism has only in the last few years appeared in these resolutions. The Vienna World Conference on Human Rights of 1993 omitted reference to antisemitism in its concluding document, despite the efforts of some states to put it there.

I attended the United Nations Commission on Human Rights in 1997 as a non-governmental representative. That year the resolution on racial intolerance was mired in a debate about whether antisemitism would or would not be mentioned. The African delegations, led by Egypt, put out a version of the resolution on racism without any reference to antisemitism. A Turkish draft condemned antisemitism. Then ensued a prolonged debate over whether to include antisemitism in the resolution, exclude it from the resolution, or keep in the preamble and drop it from the operative paragraphs. The resulting compromise was a mention of antisemitism in the preamble, but not in any of the fifty-one operative paragraphs.[18]

To a person unaware of Middle Eastern politics, the notion that a condemnation of antisemitism would be the subject of intensive debate would seem incredible. Why would Egypt lead a charge to have the UN avoid the mention of antisemitism? The only explanation is an unwillingness to acknowledge a wrong that justifies the existence of Israel.

A second response to the justification for Israel as a haven from antisemitism has been denial or appropriation of the victimization of the Jewish people, of antisemitism itself. The word *antisemitism* was coined in the nineteenth century by William Marr of Germany to describe opposition to Jews and Judaism, and has consistently been used ever since as meaning hatred of Jews or discrimination against Jews.[19] Like the Holocaust that was its result, the very existence of antisemitism has prompted those against Israeli to contort and distort its meaning.

At the Durban NGO forum, anti-Israel advocates arranged to have inserted into the final Declaration and Program of Action the words "anti-Arab racism is another form of antisemitism" and "Arabs as a Semitic people have also suffered from alternative forms of antisemitism."[20] This attempt had nothing to do with racism against Arabs and everything to do with undercutting a rationale for the existence of the State of Israel.

Another, crude, response to the existence of Israel as a haven from antisemitism is that antisemitism is right. Opposition to the existence of Israel has given the old myths of antisemitism new life.

Anti-Zionism is a both a new and an old antisemitism. Some forms of anti-Zionism would make no sense if Israel did not exist. Other forms of anti-Zionism are as old as antisemitism itself, repeating the traditional antisemitic myths, with an attempt to give them an anti-Israeli twist. Anti-Zionism has adopted this old antisemitism and made it its own.

For instance, Omayma al-Jalahma, a professor at King Faisal University and a columnist for the Saudi newspaper *al-Riyadh*, wrote in a March 2002 column that Jews use the blood of Christian or Muslim children in pastries for Purim. An English translation on the Internet sparked protest and his firing from the newspaper.

A website called Radio Islam, hosted in Sweden, offers *The Protocols of the Elders of Zion*. *The Protocols* are a forgery manufactured in czarist Russia attempting to show Jews conspiring to dominate the world.[21]

A Saudi government newspaper, *Al-Watan*, in January 2002 ran an article accusing Jews of a conspiracy to run the world. The headline was "The Jewish organizations are implementing their strategic hellish plan to take over the world."[22]

The official newspaper of the Palestinian Authority, *Al-Hayat Al Jadeeda*, picked up on *The Protocols'* theme. The paper asserted the existence of "a greater Zionist plan which is organized according to specific stages that were determined when *The Protocols of the Elders of Zion* were composed."[23]

Adolf Hitler's *Mein Kampf*, in Arabic translation, has become a bestseller in the Palestinian territories. It is being sold elsewhere around the world where there are large Arab populations.[24]

These are a few examples of a widespread, persistent trend. Anti-Israel venom has given new life and won new adherents to old antisemitic myths. Two chapters of this book elaborate on this theme, showing the patterns of prejudice and the harvest of hate.

Israel exists as a haven for Jews fleeing persecution. The Holocaust dictates not only that there should be a Jewish state, but also what kind of state it should be. The failure by countries around the globe to grant refuge to Jews fleeing the Holocaust and its aftermath tells us that a Jewish state has to be a refuge for Jews from all over the world.

The anti-Zionist rebuttal to the argument for Israel as a place of refuge is that the Israeli Law of Return is racist, that Zionism is racism. While condemning the Law of Return as racist, the anti-Israel community, in a piece of double-talk, asserts a right of return for some 6.5 million descendants of Palestinians who at one time lived in the territory of Israel. A later chapter of this book on accusations of Israeli human rights violations sets out in detail why the Law of Return is not racist.

The survival of Israel is also necessary for the cultural survival of the Jewish people around the world. The chapter of this book on Israel and the right to self-determination elaborates why that is so.

This connection between the Jewish people and the land of Israel has led to the strange anti-Zionist position that today's Jews are not descendants of the ancient Jews but rather of a group of Crimean converts called Khazars. Dr. Mustafa Mahmud writes, "Israel is today populated by people who are not descendants of the Children of Israel, but rather a mixture of slaves, Aryans and the remnants of the Khazars, and they are not Semites. In other words, people without an identity, whose only purpose is blackmails, theft and control over property and land, with the assistance of the Western countries."[25]

Although denial of the historical reality of Jewish association with Israel is amazing enough, anti-Zionists have gone even further, denying the presence of the Jewish Temple in Jerusalem, despite the fact that part of the temple still survives. PLO chairman Yasser Arafat at Camp David in 2000 claimed that no Jewish Temple ever existed on Temple Mount in Jerusalem, only an obelisk, and that the Jewish Temple was built in Nablus.[26]

International acceptance and United Nations support for Israel was an important element in its creation. Carl von Clausewitz wrote about diplomacy and war, "War is nothing but the continuation of policy with other means."[27] For Arab hostility to Israel, the converse has been also true. Diplomacy has been a continuation of the wars against Israel by other means.

In the history of the existence of Israel, two United Nations votes — the vote on partition of Palestine under the British Mandate and the vote on Israel's admission to the United Nations — loom large. These votes were pillars in the construction of the Jewish state. Part of the work of anti-Zionism has been to try to pull these pillars down.

The General Assembly, by a resolution on May 15, 1947, established a special committee to report on the future of British-mandate Palestine.[28] The committee consisted of representatives of eleven states. The committee heard public hearings and received written submissions. Jewish organizations made submissions to the committee for a separate Jewish state within the boundaries of British-mandate Palestine. They argued that a separate state was needed to save the remnant of European Jewry, then sitting in the refugee camps, and to ensure the future of the Jewish people.[29]

The committee released its report August 31, 1947, with majority and minority recommendations. Eight representatives favoured a partition. The plan of partition stated, "Independent Arab and Jewish States ... shall come into existence in Palestine." Three representatives favoured a federation.

The United Nations General Assembly voted on this report on November 29, 1947.[30] The General Assembly recommended to the United Kingdom, as the mandatory power, to implement the plan of partition in the resolution, which was itself based on the report of the special committee. The vote was thirty-three in favour, thirteen against. The resolution called for the partition of British-mandate Palestine into a Jewish state and an Arab state.

The United Kingdom accepted that recommendation and announced that it would leave the area by midnight on May 14, 1948. The provisional government of Israel declared its independence on that day, and the wars against its existence began.

One year later, on May 11, 1949, the General Assembly voted to admit Israel to the United Nations.[31] The vote was thirty-seven in favour, twelve against, and nine abstentions. The resolution had only two operative paragraphs. One was a decision to admit Israel to the UN. The other was a decision that "Israel is a peace-loving State which accepts the obligations contained in the Charter and is able and willing to carry out those obligations."

Arab states voted against both the partition resolution and the Israeli membership resolution. Over the years, as the membership of the United Nations expanded, the majority support for Israel disappeared. Some states were prepared to go along with the enemies of the State of Israel for the crassest of political and financial reasons. Still other states were of the view that condemnations of Israel might give a push to the Middle East peace process. Then there were the states that abstained out of a desire not to be seen to taking sides.

The foundation for the votes on partition and membership — the notion that Israel is peace-loving and willing to carry out its obligations under the United Nations Charter— became the focus of attack. The strategy was simple and obvious. Since Israel had come into existence with UN support, indeed, some would say because of UN support, they would remove that support. The objective became to have the United Nations endorse — vote by vote, meeting by meeting, organ by organ — resolutions and reports that Israel was neither peace-loving nor respectful of its Charter obligations.

The Charter obligation to respect human rights and fundamental freedoms[32] became the obligation of choice. Since Israel was created in large measure because of the gross violations of human rights of the Jewish people, condemnation of Israel for human rights violations served two purposes at once. By portraying Israel as a perpetrator state, its image as a state for victims was blurred. As well, the notion that Israel respected its Charter obligations was contradicted.

Human rights are bulwarks defending minorities. Minorities must bow to the will of majorities. Majorities, however, are constrained by human rights. To turn the United Nations vote against Israel around, it was not enough for anti-Zionists to get more votes than supporters of the existence of the State of Israel. Anti-Zionists also had to remove the human rights bulwarks that protected Israel once its supporters descended into minority status.

The unending United Nations attempts to condemn Israel as a human rights outlaw, which a later chapter sets out in greater detail, have had little or nothing to do with respect for human rights, and everything to do with laying the groundwork for expelling Israel from the community of nations. The attempt is to delegitimize Israel by taking every international standard at hand and turning it against Israel. The endless, obsessive fixation on Israel at the United Nations is an effort to repeal, through an accumulation of indictments, the legitimacy the United Nations at its inception was seen to have given Israel.

One can see this strategy at work by looking at both United Nations procedures and the content of United Nations resolutions and reports. Israel is accused of the worst crimes known to humanity. The reality of Israeli behaviour becomes a matter of indifference, because the purpose is not to prevent and punish individual crimes, but rather to discredit the State of Israel and those who support it.

The accusations made against Israel are accusations against the state and not against individuals. Because the Jewish community worldwide supports, with few exceptions, the existence of the State of Israel, accusations of criminality against Israel, not for what it does but for what it is, are accusations of support for criminality against the whole Jewish community. The charges are a collective accusation of guilt, rather than individual accusations of crime.

While the charges in the Durban NGO Forum Against Racism's concluding document were bad enough, the purpose of the whole enterprise can be seen in the draft document circulated before the meeting. The working draft circulated before the forum called the State of Israel, not any of its specific practices or policies, "this barbaric and inhumane project."[33]

The Jewish community is all too familiar with collective accusations of guilt, having been told for centuries that the Jewish community, as a community, killed Jesus Christ. The accusations made against the Jewish state of grave breaches of the Geneva Conventions on the Laws of War, colonialism, war crimes, crimes against humanity, genocide, foreign occupation, ethnic cleansing, and acts of apartheid are of the same nature, blaming a whole community for either committing or supporting the most heinous crimes.

Accusing a whole community is a form of incitement to discrimination, hatred, and violence against that community. Discrimination against any ethnic, religious, or cultural group violates the Universal Declaration of Human Rights,[34] the International Covenant on Civil and Political Rights,[35] and the Convention on the Elimination of All Forms of Racial Discrimination.[36] Extreme inflammatory language, accusing Israel of the gravest crimes by virtue of its very existence, and, by implication, accusing the Jewish community of supporting those crimes, is a new antisemitism, an incitement to racial hatred and violence against Jews, both inside and outside of Israel.

The accusation is not just that these crimes happened, but that the commission of these crimes is inherent in the very existence of the State of Israel as a Jewish state. Jewish people worldwide are in turn accused of complicity in these crimes because of the actual or presumed support of the Jewish community for the existence of the State of Israel.

A person who is Jewish does not actually have to support Israel to be the target of this sort of accusation. Because every member of the Jewish community is perceived as a supporter of the State of Israel, every Jewish person is perceived as complicit in these crimes. For enemies of the Jewish state, the Jewish population worldwide, regardless of their views on Israel, is seen as a criminal population.

It is, of course, legitimate to criticize specific Israeli practices and policies. Internationally that criticism should be done in the context of a global survey, country by country, of such practices and policies, using the same standards and language to judge all countries.

However, when Israel, virtually alone, is the target of criticism, the targeting becomes political rather than principled. Selective criticism directed to Israel, when far worse offender countries and non-governmental entities are ignored, is obviously about something else than promoting respect for human rights. That something else is demonization and ultimately destruction of the State of Israel.

A large number of states ganging up on Israel does not make Israel illegal, only unpopular. The Jewish community is all too familiar with this phenomenon. Before and during the Second World War, anti-Jewish bigotry was often blamed on the Jews. It was common to hear that persecution against the Jews was justified by what Jews did or were. Of course, the only thing the Jews did to justify the hatred against them was exist. The only thing that could assuage the hatred against them was genocide.

All this is true of Israel. When states of the United Nations condemn Israel for its failure to recognize the claimed Palestinian right of return, the true quarrel they have with Israel is its existence. What Israel has done to justify the criticism is survive. The only thing that will satisfy anti-Zionist critics is Israel's destruction.

CHAPTER THREE
Accusations of Israeli Human Rights Violations

ANTI-ZIONIST propaganda has been so widespread and sustained that it has assumed a life of its own. Inattentive observers must think that with this much smoke there must be a whale of a fire. So let us consider accusations against Israel one by one — the accusations of genocide, colonialism, terrorism, war crimes, crimes against humanity, apartheid, ethnic cleansing, and racism.

Genocide

The concluding document of the Durban World Conference Against Racism and the Non-Governmental Organization Forum Against Racism accused Israel of genocide. Accusations of genocide against Israel are so commonplace that Yvon Charbonneau, a Canadian, promoted such an accusation, and the government of Canada, in spite of it, did not hesitate to appoint him Canada's ambassador to the United Nations Economics, Social and Cultural Organization (UNESCO) in August 2004. Charbonneau, as head of the Quebec teacher's union in 1983, urged teachers to put posters in schools attacking "the genocidal war of the Israeli government" against Palestinians.[37]

There has been only one Holocaust, but there have been many genocides. There are many false accusations made against Israel, but the strangest and the cruellest is the charge of genocide. It is strange because it has no basis; there is no external reality on which this accusation hangs. It is cruel because it accuses the Jewish state of the very crime of which the Jewish people were victims; it makes a mockery of their victimization. The Jewish community is a survivor community, the remnants of the attempted extinction of the whole Jewish people in the Holocaust. To accuse the Jewish state of genocide, the very crime inflicted on the Jewish community not that long ago, is to ridicule the suffering of the Jewish people.

Why is this anti-Zionist charge of genocide against Israel being made, despite the repugnance and dismay it generates not only amongst the Jewish community, but also amongst the human rights community? One answer is that hate promoters move in an unreal world, a fantasy world of their own making. They generate propaganda for the purpose of instilling hatred, not for the purpose of objective analysis. The more heinous the accusation, the more likely it is that hatred will result. A charge of genocide against Israel, if believed, will undercut support for the existence of the State of Israel. So the charge is made.

Anti-Zionists wallow in mirror rhetoric. Israel has a law of return. So anti-Zionists both reject that law of return as racist and assert a non-existent Palestinian right of return. Israel was built on the ashes of the Holocaust. So anti-Zionists both deny or trivialize the Holocaust and claim that Israel is guilty of genocide against the Palestinian people.

Whatever language is used in support of Israel, anti-Zionists both reject as applying to Israel and adopt for themselves. To a certain extent, this is just bad writing. People do not like what they see, but they cannot articulate their feelings. Rather than reach for words that describe reality, they regurgitate familiar slogans and metaphors.

The global metaphor for evil is Auschwitz. Those who feel hatred but cannot think of words to speak their hatred gravitate to the language of the Holocaust, because those are the words for condemnation that come most readily to mind. In the case of anti-Zionism, this mimicry of the language of the Holocaust is more than just a collapse of the oratorical imagination. It is an indication that anti-Zionism has nothing to say for itself.

The poverty of the schoolyard response to which anti-Zionism succumbs — variations on the theme "So's your old man" — is not, all the same, the ultimate test of its worth. Its worth has to be determined by external reality. The fact that there was a Holocaust inflicted on the Jewish people and that Israel has not committed genocide against any people tells us what an anti-Zionism that denies these facts is: an ideology of hatred against the Jewish state and the Jewish people.

Colonialism

The anti-Zionist contention is that Israel is a colony of the West. Demographically, the charge is strange since the majority of Israelis are either emigrants from other Middle Eastern countries or their descendants. Culturally also the charge is strange, since the language of Israel is not Western. Many aspects of Israeli culture, like the food or the driving habits, are decidedly Middle Eastern.

Historically, the Jewish people are Middle Eastern. The land of Israel has had a Jewish population continuously from pre-historic times. Though the Roman Emperor Hadrian exiled the Jewish population from the land of Israel in 135 A.D. after seventy years of Jewish revolt against Roman rule, the memory of its Israeli roots and history has remained with the Jewish community everywhere in the Diaspora.

Israel is self-governed. It is not governed by the Western states. Israel is certainly not governed by Western Europe. Indeed, many countries of Western Europe have stooped to one-sided criticisms of Israel that both ignore and echo Europe's antisemitic past.

The charge that Israel is somehow Western colonialism at work is so bizarre that it is hard to take seriously. Like other statements of the hate promotion genre, it is not an assertion that bears scrutiny. It is not directed to those who are prepared to consider reality. It is rather propaganda, directed to those the propagandists have trapped or hope to trap into a circular self-referential belief system of anti-Jewish hatred.

Terrorism

In the unending war for the existence and survival of the State of Israel, many innocents have been killed on both sides. However, the killing of innocents does not become terrorism unless those killings are intended, targeted, and have a purpose of intimidation or compulsion.

Anti-Zionist suicide bombings fit the definition of terrorism without question. The suggestion that the State of Israel has a policy of engaging in something similar to suicide bombings, the targeted killing of innocents for a political purpose, is a fantasy. At the same time as anti-Zionists adopt the pretence that the killing of innocent Jews is not terrorism, Israeli self-defence is labelled as state terrorism.

The definition of terrorism, despite all the situational rhetoric, is not a mystery. The International Convention for the Suppression of the Financing of Terrorism defines terrorism as any act "intended to cause death or serious bodily injury to a civilian, or to any other person not taking an active part in the hostilities in a situation of armed conflict, when the purpose of such act, by its nature or context, is to intimidate a population, or to compel a government or an international organization to do or to abstain from doing any act."[38]

Terrorists play to three audiences: the perceived enemy, potential recruits, and the public at large. Against the perceived enemy, terrorism is meant to generate disarray by filling the surviving victims with terror. It is in this sense that Vladimir Lenin said that the purpose of terrorism is terror. In the arena of battle, the more clearly terrorists communicate their message of terror the better it is for them.

Terrorists also seek to gain recruits and publicize their cause. For potential recruits who need to believe in the value of the cause and for the larger public who frown on terrorism, terrorists need to disguise their dirty work. Outside of the arena of battle, they portray themselves nobly, as militants in support of a cause. Terrorists, in order to avoid being labelled terrorists, resort, as one might expect, to terrorism.

To protect themselves, reporters within the reach of terrorist retaliation label terrorists *militants*. These reporters obscure the fact that the militants are targeting innocents, and limit themselves to the suggestion that the violence is done in pursuit of a cause. The attempt by reporters to protect themselves is understandable. But so is correction of these reports by newspaper publishers away from the fray. In Canada, CanWest papers in particular have taken the trouble to remove the obfuscation on a systematic basis and replace the word *militant* with the word *terrorist*, where it belongs.

But there are other outlets who play the terrorist game, repeating the self-serving labels reporters in the field have been intimidated into using. The refusal of many media outlets continents away from the fray to use the word *terrorist* has caused a great deal of unnecessary confusion around the meaning of the word. Today simply calling a terrorist what he or she truly is takes courage.

This obfuscation is pervasive in anti-Zionist propaganda. Anti-Zionists label the killing of innocents through suicide bombers as martyrdom or resistance. *Resistance* is a fine-sounding word, suggesting a legitimate struggle against oppression. The word *martyrdom* conjures up selflessness, idealism.

In the anti-Zionist perversion of any and all language in order to attack Israel and the Jews, *resistance* and *martyrdom* have become code words for killing innocent Jews. The unjustifiable becomes its opposite, the praiseworthy. So anti-Zionists, like the Nazis before them, kill innocent Jews and claim they have done good. And the distortions of scared reporters, left unchanged by faraway editors, mean the public has little idea what is happening.

The debate amongst Islamic states about the meaning of terrorism shows how far the commitment to violating human rights in the name of anti-Zionism has gone. There is a substantial body of opinion amongst Islamic states that killing in the name of anti-Zionism is not terrorism, that the killing of innocents, as long as they are Jewish or perceived to be Jewish, or standing or sitting nearby someone who happens to be Jewish, or frequenting an establishment owned or run by Jewish people, is justifiable.

It is sometimes said that one person's terrorist is another person's freedom fighter. Legally, that statement is without foundation. There are a number of international treaties against terrorism which state that terrorism is under no circumstances justifiable by considerations of a political, philosophical, ideological, racial, ethnic, religious, or other similar nature.[39] Legally, one person's terrorist should be every other person's terrorist. Yet anti-Zionists justify terrorism on political grounds.

This strain of opinion came to the forefront at a special session of the Organisation of Islamic Conference in April 2002. Malaysian Prime Minister Mahathir Mohamad was bold enough to suggest to the conference that all attacks on civilians, including those by Palestinian suicide bombers, constituted terrorism. According to a report from the British Broadcasting Corporation, that suggestion "got little support" from the fifty-three states attending the conference.[40] Iranian Foreign Minister Kamal Kharrazi said that terrorism needed "to be defined delicately. Fighting foreign occupation should not be condemned as terrorism."[41] The conference referred the question of the definition of terrorism to a committee.

Israel is accused of being built on terrorism, on the terrorist acts of Zionists during the war of independence. Anti-Zionist terrorism today is sometimes justified by claimed Zionist terrorism yesterday. Yet on close examination, these charges of terrorism, like every other bit of anti-Zionist rhetoric, just disintegrate.

Take, for example, the bombing of the King David Hotel. The Jewish Zionist fighting force Irgun, under the leadership of Menachem Begin, who later became prime minister of Israel, bombed the King David Hotel on July 22, 1946, killing ninety-one people. Anti-Zionists commonly label this bombing a terrorist act. For instance, one anti-Zionist website calls this bombing "one of the many massacres committed by Jewish-Zionist terrorists."[42]

Though innocents died in this bombing, the attack was not the targeted killing of innocents for a political purpose. The King David Hotel at the time was the site of the British military command. The hotel had a military use; there was a military advantage to be gained by bombing the hotel. Moreover, the Irgun gave three separate advance warnings of the intended bombing — one to the hotel, one to the French consulate, and one to the *Palestine Post* — so that the hotel could be evacuated before the bombing. There was an active attempt to avoid the killing of innocents. The calls were ignored.[43]

War Crimes

Patently fabricated charges of war criminality are made against Israel. The United Nations Commission on Human Rights on April 15, 2002, passed a resolution expressing "its grave concern at the deterioration of the human rights and humanitarian situation in the occupied Palestinian territory, and particularly at acts of mass killing perpetrated by the Israeli occupying authorities against the Palestinian people."[44]

Yet there were no mass killings. Human Rights Watch, on May 3, 2002, released a report stating that the organization "did not find evidence to support claims that the Israeli Defence Forces massacred hundreds of Palestinians in the [Jenin refugee] camp."

The United Nations Commission on Human Rights, in the same resolution, "strongly" condemned the Israeli forces for setting the Church of the Nativity in Bethlehem on fire.[45] Yet the church was not set on fire and remains standing to this day.

The allegation of mass killings, which later was determined to be untrue, at the time was just an unsubstantiated rumour. The continued existence of the Church of the Nativity in Bethlehem was another matter. It was constantly being shown on television, because of the ongoing siege. It was plain for everyone to see that it was not burned down, not on fire. Yet, this resolution, with these phoney charges, passed the commission with forty votes in favour and only five against.

The Palestinian Authority routinely publishes false atrocity stories, many of which are repeated by the Western press. For example, a story was published that the Israeli army shelled the Al Oudah towers in the Um Nasser neighbourhood in the Gaza strip. It turned out that the shelling came from Palestinian mortars aimed at Israel, which fell off target.[46]

False charges of individual criminality can be refuted charge by charge. It is, of course, time-consuming when there are so many of them made for political purposes, without any attempt to conform to reality.

One of the striking features of the antisemitic tidal wave at the Durban governmental and non-governmental conferences was the unwillingness of anti-Zionists to propose anything that might alleviate the wrongs of Israel they claimed to have identified. Anti-Zionist advocates at Durban seemed indifferent to getting specific policies of the government of Israel changed. Rather they wanted the State of Israel, as a state for the Jewish people, to end. The purpose of anti-Zionist war criminal accusations against Israel is not to change the behaviour of Israeli soldiers. It is to condemn the existence of the State of Israel. The worse the claimed behaviour of Israel, the more it suits the anti-Zionist political agenda. The last thing anti-Zionists want is a better Jewish state.

One has to be particularly skeptical of accusations of war criminality made against not just one or a few Jewish soldiers, but against the political leadership of Israel or the state as a whole. It is here that the anti-Zionist agenda becomes most evident.

Though charges of war criminality against Israel are virtually a daily event, reacting to whatever defence activities in which Israeli forces happen to be engaged that day, the charges, by and large, fall into three groups. One is the accusation that the settlements in the West Bank and Gaza violate the prohibition against transfer of civilian populations to occupied territories. A separate chapter in this book deals with that charge.

The second is that Israel sits in illegal occupation of the West Bank and Gaza. A chapter in this book addresses this accusation. It should be noted that even if we assume, contrary to what I argue elsewhere, that this charge is correct, even if we assume that the State of Israel illegally occupies the West Bank and Gaza, no war crime is committed. No person can be prosecuted for the wrongdoing. There is state responsibility only for this assumed wrong, not individual responsibility. Neither the Geneva Conventions on the Laws of War and its Protocols nor the statute of the International Criminal Court makes occupation (or some forms of occupation) a war crime.

The third group of war crimes charges against Israel is that Israel has responded disproportionately to Palestinian attacks. There is a requirement in a protocol to the Geneva Conventions on the Laws of War that prohibits responses that would be "excessive in relation to the concrete and direct military advantage anticipated."[47] Where the response is launched with knowledge that it will cause excessive loss of life, injury to civilians, or damage to civilian objects, the response is a grave breach of the protocol that results in individual criminal responsibility.[48]

Israel is not a party to the protocol and not bound by it. No Israeli could be prosecuted at international law for breach of a treaty by which Israel itself is not bound.

Disproportionateness analysis requires consideration of at least three criteria. One is the concrete and direct military advantage anticipated. If the military advantage of an attack is minor, civilian losses will almost always be excessive. Even where the military advantage is substantial, civilian losses are regrettable. But they may not amount to a war crime. So anyone engaging in disproportionateness analysis must first of all ask, What is the concrete and direct military advantage anticipated? There are two ways to answer that question. One is to ask those who launched the attack. What did they see as the military advantage? The test of disproportionateness refers to anticipation. The anticipation is that of the attackers. So we should know what the attackers anticipated. The other is to attempt to determine in the circumstances what might reasonably be anticipated. The attackers themselves for reasons of military security may not wish to disclose what they saw as the military advantage anticipated. Alternatively, their claims of anticipation may be farfetched, out of touch with reality. Outside independent advice from military experts can tell us what military advantage from the contested operation might reasonably have been anticipated in the circumstances.

The second criterion for assessment of disproportionateness is the alternatives available. Once there is a choice, and either option leads to the same military advantage, the option with the fewest civilian casualties should be chosen. If there is no choice offering the same military advantage as the option chosen, the matter is different. In that situation, it should be more difficult to establish that a war crime has been committed.[49]

The third criterion of disproportionateness is the use by the other side of the civilian population as a shield. The protocol to the Geneva Convention that prohibits indiscriminate attacks also prohibits the use of civilian populations as shields. The protocol states that civilian populations "shall not be used to render certain points or areas immune from military operations."[50] That protocol also states that the use by one side of the civilian population of a shield does not release the other side from the obligation to take precautionary measures to minimize or avoid civilian casualties.[51] Yet the use of civilians as shields is relevant to a determination whether civilian loss consequent on an attack on a military target is excessive. Otherwise the prohibition against use of civilians as shields would be meaningless.

Charges of disproportionateness against Israel are typically made without consideration of any of these criteria. No consideration is given to the anticipated Israeli military advantage from the attack. The accusations that Israel has committed war crimes for responding disproportionately are made by non-military people without military expert advice. People who do not care about Israeli self-defence and have not turned their minds to how it could best be done fling accusations of disproportionateness against Israel with abandon.

Any judgment of proportionality has to consider what is on both sides of the scale, the advantages and disadvantages, the loss to civilians balanced against the military advantage. Anti-Zionists are not prepared to admit that there is anything on the Israeli side of the scale. As far as anti-Zionists are concerned, all attacks against Israel are justified. So, for them, any response whatsoever seems disproportionate.

How Israel could best defend itself is far from the minds of anti-Zionists. So these anti-Zionist charges are not true proportionality judgments, but rather typical anti-Israel nonsense, looking at only one side of the ledger — the side that makes Israel look bad.

A fine example of these sorts of distortions is the criticism of John Dugard, United Nations Special Rapporteur, on the situation of human rights in the Palestinian territories occupied by Israel since 1967. Dugard wallows in anti-Israel discourse, lambasting every effort of Israeli self-defence as a disproportionate response to the threat Israel faces.

His 2003 report had a pretence of balance, criticizing both Palestinians and Israelis for excessive use of force.[52] The criticism was based on statistics of civilian and military casualties only. He wrote, "Neither party to the conflict in the region has paid proper respect" to the principle of proportionality.

But the report quickly degenerated into an anti-Israeli tirade. He stated:

> Israel justifies its policy and practice of assassinations on grounds of self-defence and claims that it is not possible to arrest and try suspects, particularly where they are in areas controlled by the Palestinian Authority. The evidence on this point is inconclusive as there are certainly some instances in which arrests could have been made in the light of Israel's capacity to exercise its jurisdictional power within the areas controlled in theory by the Palestinian Authority. The failure to attempt such arrests inevitably gives rise to suspicions that Israel lacks evidence to place such persons on trial and therefore prefers to dispose of them arbitrarily.[53]

Here there is consideration of an alternative (arrests), but Dugard found against Israel by reliance on inconclusive evidence and suspicions. Furthermore, there is no consideration of the difference in risk to the civilian population or the Israeli military if the alternative were attempted.

Even beyond that, this consideration of an arrest alternative suffers from category confusion. The question of whether to arrest or kill is a human rights law question, not a humanitarian law question. Humanitarian law applies during war. Human rights law applies during peace. There are some basic human rights standards that apply even during war. But the laws of war do not prevent the killing of combatants from the opposing side. Peacetime human rights law prohibits unnecessary or excessive force even against suspects or accused who are avoiding arrest. Wartime humanitarian law prohibits excessive force against only those taking no active part in hostilities, not against combatants for the opposing side.

Even though Dugard used a peacetime human rights standard to criticize Israel for killing rather than arresting, his ultimate conclusion was that Israel had committed war crimes. But the Israeli military cannot have committed war crimes unless its soldiers violated the laws of war.

Dugard, in his conclusion, abandoned any reference to Palestinian disproportionateness and criticized only Israel. Contrary to the laws of war, anti-Zionist terrorists shield themselves from Israeli retaliation for their terrorist attacks by intermingling with the Palestinian civilian population. This shielding has an obvious impact on civilian casualties. But Dugard did not even mention it. He stated:

> The occupation of the OPT [Occupied Palestinian Territory] continues to result in widespread violations of human rights, affecting both civil and socio-economic rights, and of international humanitarian law. Israel's justification for these actions is that they are necessary in the interests of its own national security. As indicated at the beginning of this report, the lawfulness of Israel's response is to be measured in accordance with the principle of proportionality. The Special Rapporteur finds it difficult to accept that the excessive use of force that disregards the distinction between civilians and combatants, the creation of a humanitarian crisis by restrictions on the mobility of goods and people, the killing and inhuman treatment of children, the widespread destruction of property and, now, territorial expansion can be justified as a proportionate response to the violence and threats of violence to which Israel is subjected.[54]

Dugard is not, to my knowledge, a military person. Nor is there any indication in his report that he has sought the advice of military experts. Yet he made judgments that Israeli self-defence efforts were, in the words of the international law standard on which he relied, "excessive in relation to the concrete and direct military advantage anticipated." One-sided judgments against Israel saying that it has used excessive force in armed conflict, made without military expertise or advice, applying the laws of peace rather than war, based on inconclusive evidence and suspicions, without consideration of the use by the other side of civilian populations to shield themselves, are just Israel-bashing.

The note taped to the United Talmud Torahs elementary school library in Montreal justifying the firebombing of April 2004 was signed "The Brigades of Sheik Ahmed Yassin." Yassin was founder and leader of the terrorist organisation Hamas and was killed by Israeli forces shortly before the UTT attack in March. The note said, "If your crimes continue in the Middle East, our attacks will continue."

Obviously it is inappropriate to firebomb a school in Montreal even for acts committed by children attending that school, let alone for an act committed somewhere else by someone else. But was the killing of Sheik Yassin a crime? Does the targeted killing of a terrorist planner and leader violate the laws of war?

Terrorist leaders are not civilians, so their killing cannot be condemned on that basis. The issue here is whether combatants for the opposing side can be killed at a time when they are not engaged in armed combat, but are engaged in preparations for armed combat. The answer to that is yes, they can.

Warring states have a duty not to kill prisoners of war and those who take no active part in hostilities. This includes combatants who are unable to participate in combat. But it defies reality to say that Sheik Yassin was taking no active part in hostilities against Israel at the time he was killed.

Crimes Against Humanity

There are many asymmetries in the wars against Israel, not least the moral. Israeli society goes into elaborate contortions to debate the fine points of the morality of the behaviour of their soldiers.

Anti-Zionism, with its sights set firmly on the goal of destroying Israel, turns every Israeli hesitation to that purpose. The meaning of words and the lives of innocents take second place to that goal. Once the killing of innocents becomes a legitimate means to the anti-Zionist end, there is no morality left.

The internal Israeli debate about right and wrong becomes propaganda fodder in the anti-Zionist cause. Any qualms that Israelis might have become grist for the anti-Israel, anti-Jewish hatred mill.

The massacre of Sabra and Chatilla is a fine example. The massacre was a crime against humanity, but it was a crime perpetrated by Arabs against other Arabs. Yet the State of Israel and the current prime minister, Ariel Sharon, were blamed.

Between September 16 and 18, 1982, eight hundred innocent Palestinians in two refugee camps, Sabra and Chatilla, were massacred in an area of Lebanon then under the control of Israeli Defence Forces. The Israeli government appointed an independent commission to inquire into the massacre. The commissioners were Yitzhak Kahan, President of the Supreme Court and commission chairman; Aharon Barak, Justice of the Supreme Court; and Major General Yona Efrat (Reserve). It was informally called the Kahan Commission.

The commission held sixty sessions and heard fifty-eight witnesses. Staff investigators collected statements from 163 witnesses. The commission published notices inviting both written submissions and testimony from the public and collected evidence both from inside and outside Israel.

The commission concluded that the massacre was inflicted by a Phalangist (Lebanese Christian Arab) unit acting on its own. It observed:

> ... the [Phalangist] forces who entered the area were steeped in hatred for the Palestinians, in the wake of the atrocities and severe injuries done to the Christians during the civil war in Lebanon by the Palestinians and those who fought alongside them; and these feelings of hatred were compounded by a longing for revenge in the wake of the assassination of the Phalangists' admired leader Bashir and the killing of several dozen Phalangists two days before their entry into the camps.

In principle, those conclusions could have completed the commission's work. Nonetheless, in addition to making a finding of direct responsibility against the Phalangist forces, the commission made findings that a number of Israeli officials, including Ariel Sharon, were indirectly responsible for the massacre.

In order to appreciate the conclusion of indirect responsibility, it is important to note what the commission meant by that term. It observed:

> ... the Jews in various lands of exile, and also in the Land of Israel when it was under foreign rule, suffered greatly from pogroms perpetrated by various hooligans; and the danger of disturbances against Jews in various lands, it seems evident, has not yet passed. The Jewish public's stand has always been that the responsibility for such deeds falls not only on those who rioted and committed the atrocities, but also on those who were responsible for safety and public order, who could have prevented the disturbances and

did not fulfil their obligations in this respect. It is true that the regimes of various countries, among them even enlightened countries, have side-stepped such responsibility on more than one occasion and have not established inquiry commissions to investigate the issue of indirect responsibility, such as that about which we are speaking; but the development of ethical norms in the world public requires that the approach to this issue be universally shared, and that the responsibility be placed not just on the perpetrators, but also on those who could and should have prevented the commission of those deeds which must be condemned.

The commission, in assessing indirect responsibility, tried to show moral leadership, imposing on the Israeli government a moral, religious standard not dictated by law. Indeed, the report quoted from the Torah[55] to justify its standard. The commission further applied this standard to Israeli officials and forces only, not to the Lebanese or international forces present at the time or to the United States for failure to use its influence in a helpful way.

The commission found against Ariel Sharon:

> … responsibility is to be imputed to the Minister of Defense for having disregarded the danger of acts of vengeance and bloodshed by the Phalangists against the population of the refugee camps, and having failed to take this danger into account when he decided to have the Phalangists enter the camps. In addition, responsibility is to be imputed to the Minister of Defense for not ordering appropriate measures for preventing or reducing the danger of massacre as a condition for the Phalangists' entry into the camps.

If that behaviour means that Sharon is guilty of a crime against humanity, then so is every Palestinian official who disregards the danger of suicide bombing by Palestinians against the population of Israel, who fails to take appropriate measures for preventing or reducing the danger of suicide bombings. The culture of hatred in the Palestinian community in the West Bank and Gaza against Jews today is every bit as vicious as was the culture of hatred against the Palestinian community within the Lebanese Arab Christian community immediately before the Sabra and Chatilla massacre. It is a double standard for anti-Zionists to charge Sharon with crimes against humanity for his failure to take steps to prevent the Sabra and Chatilla massacre and to remain silent in the face of Palestinian official failure to take steps within their power to prevent suicide bombings against Israel.

Despite the Kahan Commission's condemnation of Sharon, some critics have argued that the commission was too kind to Sharon, that Sharon should have been found directly responsible, as commander of the Israeli Defence Forces in the field. Leslie Green quarrelled with the commission finding that Sharon should not be blamed for failing to order the removal of the Phalangists from the camps when he first got reports about the killing there. According to the commission:

> [Sharon] had heard from the Chief of Staff that the Phalangists' operation had been halted, that they had been ordered to leave the camps and that their departure would be effected by 5:00 a.m. Saturday. These preventive steps might well have seemed sufficient to the Defense Minister at that time, and it was not his duty to order additional steps to be taken, or to have the departure time moved up, a step which was of doubtful feasibility.

Leslie Green wrote that the information Sharon possessed that the operation had terminated and the Phalangists had been ordered to withdraw "should not have affected his responsibility, in the light of the knowledge he possessed, for failing to prevent and, once he knew it had commenced, to terminate, the entire incident ... there was enough evidence to indict Sharon for failure as a commander to prevent the commission of war crimes or crimes against humanity."[56]

The doctrine of command responsibility holds a commander vicariously criminally responsible for the behaviour of his troops. It does not exist in Canadian law, but it does exist in international law. To apply the doctrine to the Phalangists, who were not part of the Israeli army and certainly not under the command of Ariel Sharon, is a stretch.

One can debate the findings of the Kahan Commission. However, in assessing whether any person the Kahan commission found only indirectly responsible for the massacre should be prosecuted today for crimes against humanity, it is not enough to conclude that the Kahan commission was wrong. One must conclude that the Kahan Commission acted in bad faith.

The statute of the International Criminal Court technically does not apply, since it was not in force at the time. However, it does set out general international law principles. The statute provides that a case is inadmissible in the court where "the case has been investigated by a State which has jurisdiction over it and the State has decided not to prosecute the person concerned, unless the decision resulted from the unwillingness or inability of the State genuinely to prosecute."[57]

In the case of Sabra and Chatilla, there was an investigation. If the Kahan Commission had found Sharon directly responsible for the Sabra and Chatilla massacre but Israel had, nonetheless, decided not to prosecute him, one could question the willingness of Israel to do so. However, in light of failure of the Kahan Commission to find that Sharon was directly responsible for the massacre, there is no obligation or, indeed, jurisdiction to prosecute him elsewhere.

When anti-Zionists accuse Sharon of war crimes, bad faith is exactly the accusation they are levelling against Israel. Like other anti-Israel propaganda, the target is not an individual (in this case Sharon) or a practice (in this case the failure to prosecute him), but the Israeli state apparatus. Yet to accuse the Kahan Commission of bad faith, where the chair was Chief Justice of the Supreme Court and one of the other commissioners was a judge of the Supreme Court, defies reality. One has only to read the Kahan Commission report to see the seriousness with which the commissioners undertook their tasks, to note their independence from government.

In sum, the Kahan Commission found Sharon and others indirectly responsible for the massacre using a standard of indirect responsibility that they found in the Torah, but not in international law. Furthermore, the Kahan Commission applied that standard of indirect responsibility to Israelis alone and not to others.

Today, it is hard to find a reference to that massacre without reference to Sharon's "indirect responsibility." Indeed, many references drop the qualification and accuse Sharon of "responsibility." In anti-Zionist lore, this responsibility, particularly since Sharon has become prime minister, has pride of place in the indictment against the State of Israel.

If the State of Israel wants to impose on itself a higher moral standard than it imposes on others, that is its prerogative. If other countries impose a higher moral standard on the State of Israel than on themselves, that is hypocrisy.

Apartheid

Anti-Zionist condemnations of Israel work backwards. Anti-Zionists move from opposition to Israel to charges against Israel rather than from wrongdoings by Israel to anti-Zionism. Their starting point is the vocabulary of condemnation rather than the practices of Israel. Any unsavoury verbal weapon that comes to hand is used to club Israel and its supporters. The reality of what happens in Israel is ignored. What matters is the condemnation itself. For anti-Zionists, the more repugnant the accusation made against Israel the better.

A good example of this phenomenon is accusations of apartheid made against Israel. Apartheid is universally condemned. Its onetime supporters, primarily in South Africa, have long since abandoned it. There was a global coalition opposed to apartheid, which helped to bring about its downfall.

Anti-Zionists saw and remembered this global anti-apartheid effort. They dream of constructing a similar global anti-Zionism effort. The simplest and most direct way for them to do so is to label Israel as an apartheid state. The fact that there is no resemblance whatsoever between true apartheid and the State of Israel has not stopped anti-Zionists for a moment.

Basic to apartheid was the denationalization of all blacks, because they were black, and the allocation of nationality in ten state-created *bantustans*, or home-lands. Blacks assigned to bantustans were subject to influx controls and pass laws. Blacks were forcibly removed from where they lived to their designated bantustans.

Israel has not since its inception taken away vested Israeli citizenship of even one Palestinian for the sole reason that the person is ethnic Palestinian. Israel has not created designated territories within its borders to which it has forcibly removed its own citizens who are ethnic Palestinian. Indeed, when one starts to look at what apartheid really was, any comparison between Israel today and South Africa at the time of apartheid becomes ludicrous.[58]

The charge of apartheid against Israel is so defamatory and harmful that Jean-Christophe Rufin, in a report to the French Ministry of Interior, recommended that it be criminalized.[59] He wrote:

> Certainly, there is no question of penalising political opinions that are critical, for example, of any government and are perfectly legit-imate. What should be penalised is the perverse and defamatory use of the charge of racism against those very people who were victims of racism to an unparalleled degree. The accusations of racism, of apartheid, of Nazism carry extremely grave moral impli-cations. These accusations have, in the situation in which we find ourselves today, major consequences which can, by contagion, put in danger the lives of our Jewish citizens. It is legitimate to require by law that these accusations are not made lightly. It is why we invite reflection on the advisability and applicability of a law ... which would permit the punishment of those who make without foundation against groups, institutions or states accusations of racism and utilise for these accusations unjustified comparisons with apartheid or Nazism.[60]

The ridiculous nature of the charge of apartheid against Israel has not stopped it from being made. For anti-Zionists, the strategy of constructing a new anti-apartheid coalition against Israel is all that matters. The NGO forum held at Durban, South Africa, sets out this strategy plainly. The forum's Declaration includes the phrase "recognizing ... racist methods amounting to Israel's brand of apartheid."[61] The Program of Action states, "We the NGO Forum ... Call for the launch of an international anti-Israel Apartheid movement as implemented against South African Apartheid through a global solidarity campaign network ..."[62]

The accusation made against Israel at Durban of a new form of apartheid was particularly brazen, given that the World Conference Against Racism and the

NGO Forum Against Racism were being held in South Africa, the home of the victims of apartheid. To make a charge of apartheid against Israel, aside from its wild inaccuracy, its obvious political motivation, its incitement to hatred, and its hurtfulness, is disrespectful and trivializes of the suffering of the true victims of apartheid. Palestinians were prepared to bring that disrespect, that trivialization, to the home turf of the victims of apartheid.

The fact that some South Africans were foolish or forgetful enough to accept the comparison between Zionism and apartheid does not validate it. The acceptance is, rather, a testimonial to the relentlessness and dishonesty of anti-Zionist propaganda.

Ethnic Cleansing

Anti-Zionism is an endless mudslinging exercise. If the charge of apartheid does not stick, other insults are tried. One is ethnic cleansing.

The verbal recklessness, mindless opportunism, and venomous reflex of anti-Zionism is highlighted by this label, which anti-Zionists attempt to paste on Israel. The notion of ethnic cleansing became prevalent after the breakup of Yugoslavia, to describe the forced population displacements occurring there. The world watched in horror as the Serbian-dominated government of the former Yugoslavia evicted Muslims from areas of Bosnia that they wanted to attach to a planned greater Serbia and as the Croatian government evicted Serbians from Croatia. When the former Yugoslavian government tried to do the same thing to Albanians in Kosovo, NATO intervened.

Israeli practices have as little to do with ethnic cleansing as they do with apartheid. Not one Israeli citizen has been forcibly evicted from Israel solely because of his or her ethnic origin. By the same token, a connection to reality means as little to anti-Zionists for the charge of ethnic cleansing as it does for the charge of apartheid. To anti-Zionists, the fact that ethnic cleansing is wrong and that there is global support for opposition to ethnic cleansing has been enough to throw the charge of ethnic cleansing against Israel.

Anti-Zionists sometimes refer to events that happened during the war of Israeli independence. However, the flight of Palestinians then cannot be fairly described as ethnic cleansing. There at least three reasons why this is so.

One is that there remains a substantial Arab population in Israel today — hundreds of thousands of people. Many of these Arab Israelis or their ancestors were in Israel from its inception. The demographics of Israel show that Israel is not ethnically cleansed and never has been.

Second, in every armed conflict, civilians flee for their safety. That flight is the fault of the conflict, but not the aim of the conflict. The Israeli war of independence that generated civilian flight was in turn caused by the refusal of Arab states to recognize Israel and their 1948 invasion of Israel. Without the invasion, there would have been no civilians fleeing the conflict. When Arab states call this civilian flight Israeli ethnic cleansing, they are blaming Israel for their own wrongdoing.

Third, the charge of ethnic cleansing ignores that the intention of the United Nations in 1947 and 1948 for British-mandate Palestine, as it was for the British Indian Raj, was to divide the entity ethnically. British-mandate Palestine was to be divided into a Jewish state and an Arab state. The British Indian Raj was to be divided into a Muslim state and a Hindu state. When the British withdrew, there were substantial population movements. In large part, those movements reflected the desires of the moving populations to be in the territory of a state of their own people.

Like many of the charges anti-Zionists level against Israel, the charge is not just wrong. It is hypocritical. At the same time as they denounce non-existent Israeli ethnic cleansing, anti-Zionists call for the ethnic cleansing of Jews from the West Bank and Gaza. Of course, anti-Zionists do not call this ethnic cleansing. Instead, they call for dismantlement of the settlements. But what is the call to dismantle the West Bank and Gaza Jewish settlements if it is not a call for ethnic cleansing? If Israel can host hundreds of thousands of Arabs, then surely the West Bank and Gaza can host Jews.

Racism

It is said that the Israeli Law of Return is racist because it allows Jews admission to Israel on the basis that they are Jewish. The answer to that is that the Holocaust was possible because there was no state to which the Jews could flee. If Israel had existed before the Second World War, the Holocaust would not have happened. Indeed, if Israel had existed before the Second World War, it is possible that the whole war would not have happened. Lucy Davidowicz, in her book *The War against the Jews 1933–1945* writes that, in the minds of the Nazi German leaders, the Second World War was a cover for its planned murder of the Jews.[63]

Even after the war, it was easier for the Nazis who had perpetrated the Holocaust to get out of the displaced persons camps and find resettlement than it was for the Jewish survivors of the Holocaust. Before the creation of the state of Israel, Jewish survivors sat in refugee camps in Europe with no relocation in sight.

A right of refuge is recognized in the Israeli Law of Return. The Israeli Law of Return is more than the righting of a historical wrong, the provision of a haven to survivors of the Holocaust. It has contemporary relevance because of the wave of antisemitism unleashed in the Middle East by the wars against Israel and in Central and Eastern Europe by the collapse of Communism and its replacement by chauvinism. Only Israel offers an escape to every single victim of continuing antisemitism.

The phrase "Zionism is racism" is a blatant form of language distortion. Its repeal did not mean that the desire to obliterate the State of Israel and right to self-determination of the Jewish people has ended. The desire rather takes other, more indirect linguistic forms. At first in addition to, and subsequently instead of, calling Zionism a form of racism, member states of the United Nations have called the Israeli Law of Return racist.

This bandying about of the charge of racism against Israel, the state of the survivor community of the most vicious racism this planet has ever seen, aside from its perversity and cruelty, ignores what racism is. Race has no objective, scientific, anthropological meaning. There are no human races, only one human race. Race exists as a persecutory concept only. The concept of race survives only to identify discrimination and persecution, and to provide protection against it.

The United Nations Convention on Refugees obligates signatory states to provide protection to those who have a well-founded fear of persecution by reason of five listed grounds. One of those grounds is race. To fit within this ground, the person does not actually have to be of a certain race that is targeted for persecution. Such a requirement would be meaningless, since objectively there are no races. Rather, the person has to be perceived by the persecutor to be of a certain race that the agent of persecution has decided to victimize. Race is whatever the persecutory agent thinks it is.

The concept of a race has to be distinguished from the concept of a people. The concept of a people is the exact opposite of the concept of a race. A race is defined by the other, by the persecutory agent. A people is self-defined, by the people themselves. Integral to the right of self-determination of peoples is the right to determine their own membership. Once outsiders can say who is and who is not a member of any given people, the right to self-determination of that people is gone.

The Israeli Law of Return is an integral part of the exercise of the right to self-determination of the Jewish people, because it is an expression by the Jewish people of who are their members. Labelling the Law of Return of Israel as racist is yet another form, like labelling Zionism as racism, of delegitimization and denial of the right to self-determination of the Jewish people.

Just as anti-Zionism is a form of racism, by denying to the Jewish people the right of self-determination, so is opposition to the Israeli Law of Return, by denying to the Jewish people the right to determine their own membership. The right to self-determination cannot exist without the right to self-definition. To say that the Jewish people do not have the right to self-definition is to say that the right of self-determination exists for other peoples, but not for the Jews.

It is also said that the Israeli Law of Return is racist because it is based on ancestry or bloodlines. But the law is not based on blood.

The Israeli Law of Return considers a person as Jewish if the person has become converted to Judaism and is not a member of another religion.[64] Judaism is a religion that anyone can join. Judaism does not proselytize, but it does accept converts. It is impossible to call a law racist when anyone who chooses to convert to Judaism can take advantage of the law.

Race is sometimes identified with colour. Yet Jews come in every colour. There are black Jews, Falashas, who were granted the benefit of the Law of Return and indeed were airlifted from Ethiopia to Israel by the Israeli government. It is impossible to consider a law racist that encompasses all races.

Every citizenship law of which I am aware allows parents to pass on their citizenship to their children. For instance, a child born of a Canadian parent is Canadian, no matter where in the world the child is born. The child can maintain Canadian citizenship throughout his or her life without ever entering Canada, provided that the person establishes a substantial connection with Canada.[65] A citizenship law cannot be racist simply because it is based on birth.

The basic law of Germany allows anyone to become a citizen who is the descendant of a person who was a German citizen and was deprived of that citizenship on political, racial, or religious grounds between January 30, 1933, and May 8, 1945.[66] The person does not have to be a first-generation descendant. This German law is itself informally called a Law of Return. No United Nations resolution has ever suggested that this German Law of Return is racist.

The Israeli Law of Return distinguishes between those who are Jewish and not Jewish, but does not discriminate against those who are not Jewish. Not every legal distinction amounts to discrimination. A prohibition against discrimination does not encompass any law that has as its object improving the lot of the disadvantaged, including those disadvantaged because of race or religion.[67]

The Israeli Law of Return exists as a protection against the racism Jews have suffered and continue to suffer. The law is a form of affirmative action, affirming that Jews who are at risk elsewhere around the world can seek and obtain protection in Israel.

In principle, every person who is the victim of antisemitic discrimination should be considered Jewish under the Law of Return, whether the person has any cultural or religious ties with Judaism or not. If racists target a person as Jewish, then a law and a state created to protect Jews should offer protection to that person. Offering protection to the victims of racism does not make the helpers racist. Acknowledging the existence of racism and the need to defend against it is the antithesis of racism.

The Law of Return encompasses within its definition of a Jew those that had been targeted by the Nazi race laws. The Law of Return includes in its definition of a Jew every person who was born of a Jewish mother.[68] The law further provides that the rights of a Jew are vested in a child and a grandchild of a Jew, the spouse of a Jew, the spouse of a child of a Jew, and the spouse of a grandchild of a Jew, except for a person who has been a Jew and who has voluntarily changed his religion.[69]

The Jewish community has learned through bitter experience which people are likely to be targeted by antisemites for hatred and destruction. The State of Israel, accordingly, through the Law of Return, offers protection to all such people. It confounds logic, language, and common sense to argue that a law designed to protect targets of racist persecution is itself racist.

Calling the Israeli Law of Return racist means rejecting the notion that Jews have been disadvantaged and, in many countries, are still disadvantaged. This sort of labelling is Holocaust denial or Holocaust trivialization in another form.

There is constant criticism that, in Israel, there is discrimination against Palestinians or Arabs or Muslims or non-Jews. Despite that criticism, Israel is committed to equality in principle, and the vocation of Israel as a Jewish state does not change or temper that commitment. The Israeli Declaration of Independence provides that the State of Israel "will establish equal social and political rights for all its citizens without distinguishing on the basis of religion, race or gender." One of the five books of Moses states, "You shall have only one law, the stranger shall be as a citizen."[70]

Israeli Justice Aharon Barak, in a speech given to the Canadian Friends of the Hebrew University in Toronto in June 2000, said, "Zionism was born to negate racism. It learned to know the extent to which racist treatment, dictated by religious or national belonging, can degrade human character. This Zionism is opposed to any patterns of discrimination on the basis or religion or nationality."

The Asian preparatory meeting for the Durban World Conference Against Racism, held in February 2001 in Tehran, said nothing about the imprisonment in Iran of thirteen Jewish community activists for no other reason than that they are Jewish. Nor did it condemn or comment on racism in any of the countries that actually attended the conference. Israel, though physically located within the region from which countries were invited to the Tehran conference, was not allowed to attend. Yet Israel, at Tehran, was criticized as being racist.

Israel is the only Jewish state. For the regional gathering for the area of the world that includes Israel to deny admission to Israel, to condemn racism in Israel, and to say nothing about racism in any other country is blatant discrimination not only against Israel as a state, but against Jews generally.

No state should be judged only by its professed ideals. It should as well be judged by its practice. It is legitimate to criticize discriminatory practices wherever they are found, whether in Israel or elsewhere. However, to criticize racial discrimination only in Israel and in no other country of the world becomes a political act of selective criticism, itself a form of discrimination against the Jewish state and the Jewish people.

CHAPTER FOUR
The Accusation of Occupation

IN Middle East discourse, it is common to hear root cause analysts refer to Israeli occupation of the West Bank and Gaza as the root cause of human rights violations in the region. So, for instance, Rights and Democracy, an agency created by the Canadian Parliament and funded by the government of Canada to promote rights and democracy, wrote that Israeli occupation of the West Bank and Gaza "is the root cause of the Palestinian crisis."[71] Michael Peers, Primate of the Anglican Church of Canada wrote, "The current violence in Palestine has deep roots, but Israeli occupation of Palestinian territory in defiance of United Nations resolutions is at its heart."[72]

Is this so? In discussing root causes, we must distinguish between roots and branches, between roots and fertilizer, and between real fertilizer and imaginary fertilizer.

It is worthwhile to examine root causes in the sense of looking at what violators say as well as what they do. Behind systematic acts of violence there is a discourse of hatred and violence. That discourse is a root cause and must be taken seriously. It is reasonable to assume that perpetrators believe what they say. Their belief systems, no matter how crazed or deranged or silly, motivate their behaviour and are therefore a root cause of that behaviour. When people preach violence against innocents and then act violently against innocents, it is legitimate to draw a connection between what they say and what they do.

However, in the discourse of violence against innocents, not everything the violent say needs to be given equal weight. Some of it is manipulation or hypocrisy. Some of it, in isolation, taken out of context, is inoffensive or well grounded. A lot of the discourse of violence and hatred is neither violent nor hateful. The banal and the sound are interwoven with the incendiary and the spiteful. Hate promoters often, intermixed with their messages of hate, latch on to real grievances, legitimate causes of discontent. The root cause of the violence hate promoters preach is not these grievances, this discontent. It is the determination to turn these grievances into hatred, the willingness to use violence against innocents to act out this discontent. If any popular dissatisfaction to which the violent refer becomes a root cause of violence, then violence can never end unless every dissatisfaction on this planet ends. Root cause analysis that focuses on popular dissatisfaction is an analysis of despair, an appraisal that violence against innocents is an inevitable and unending part of the human condition.

As well, a lot of root cause discourse is projection. People promote worthy causes as the root cause of whatever tragedy has occurred. It is common to hear that the root cause of this or that atrocity is poverty or denial of the rights of some group of people. What violators say is ignored. The rationality of the discourse of root cause analysts displaces the irrationality of the discourse of the violators. This form of root cause analysis is distasteful. By hiding behind violators, those who promote worthy causes tarnish those causes. It should not be necessary to argue against poverty or for human rights to hold out the threat of terrorism.

Root cause analysis that strays from the discourse of the violators is an exercise of imagination, not grounded in reality. It is also presumptuous. It amounts to saying that misbehaviour of others can be explained by what the analyst thinks is right and wrong, rather than what the miscreant says is right and wrong.

If we look at what violators say, it is apparent that it is the existence of Israel that is at the heart of the hatred and violence against Israel and the Jewish community worldwide.

It is no coincidence that all the major Palestinian organizations have called for the elimination of Israel and recourse to violence to do so. Polling indicates that the majority of Palestinians in the West Bank and Gaza believe that Israel should not exist. A whopping 68 percent of those surveyed approve of suicide bombings against Jewish civilians.[73]

The hatred, the antisemitism, the call to kill Jews is direct and explicit. When suicide bombers kill Jewish innocents, there is no need to go any farther than the words of those who organize the killings to explain why they do so. It is silly to wonder what the root causes of violence against Jews are when all one has to do is listen to or read what the violators say.

Root cause analysis that attributes human rights violations in the Middle East to occupation of the West Bank and Gaza is wishful thinking. It confuses roots with imaginary fertilizer. These analysts do not examine the discourse of violators. What they do is project their own rationality on to the violators.

The creation of two states from British-mandate Palestine, one Arab and one Jewish, has been central to any rational solution to the Israeli-Arab wars since their inception. However, realizing that this is so does not make it so. Israel cannot create peace in the Middle East on its own.

Hamas does not even use the word *occupation* in its covenant. It makes no reference to the West Bank and Gaza. The Covenant of Hamas states, "Israel will exist and will continue to exist until Islam will obliterate it, just as it obliterated others before it."[74] The suggestion that Israeli presence in the West Bank and Gaza is the root cause of Hamas hatred against Israel and Jews is a form of wilful blindness, a pretence that Hamas means something different from what it says.

Hezbollah uses the language of occupation, but refers to all of Israel as occupied territory. Husayn Fadlallah, the most senior religious authority of Hezbollah said, "Jews are known as the killers of the prophets; they spread corruption on earth; and they oppress other peoples."[75] As well, Sheik Hassan Nasrallah,

Secretary-General of Hezbollah, said in a TV interview, "I believe that Palestine is an occupied land from the Mediterranean Sea to the Jordan River."

The suggestion that Israeli abandonment of the West Bank and Gaza would somehow quell Hezbollah hatred of Israel and the Jews ignores the plain words of the Hezbollah leadership.

Israel could withdraw unilaterally from part or all of the West Bank and Gaza and leave the Palestinian Authority to declare itself a state. For those who pay no attention to the discourse of anti-Zionist human rights violators in the region and put their own rational thoughts into the minds of these violators, that withdrawal might seem to solve the problem. The two states that the UN called for in 1947 would then exist, and the conflict would seem to have been resolved.

However, it takes only a cursory examination of the discourse of anti-Zionists to realize that this solution is no solution at all. What bothers those who are actually engaged in the violence is not just the presence of Israel in the West Bank and Gaza. It is the existence of Israel.

Anti-Zionists do not distinguish between the West Bank and Gaza on the one hand and the territory of the State of Israel before 1967 on the other. Notable is the charge of occupation found in the constitution of Fatah. Article 22 of that constitution uses the phrase "the Zionist occupation in Palestine." That constitution was written in 1965, before the Six-Day War, before Israeli presence in the West Bank and Gaza.

One response to the suggestion that the occupation of the West Bank and Gaza is the root cause of the current human rights violations is that Jordan and Egypt could have, before 1967, created a separate Palestinian state on the territory of the West Bank and Gaza but chose not to. The issue of boundaries would not have arisen then, since Jordan and Egypt were in possession of all the West Bank and Gaza, including East Jerusalem. Of course, it is too late to do that now. But who in the Arab world now says that Jordan and Egypt should have done that? Where is the expression of regret amongst Arabs or Palestinians that it was not done?

Another example is the violence of anti-Zionists in the face of the peace offers made by the Israeli government under Ehud Barak. The offers by Barak showed unprecedented generosity; before negotiations were suspended in January 2001 because of the Israeli election, Barak offered the Palestinians all of Gaza and, with land swaps, about 97 percent of the West Bank.[76] The offer included control of the Al-Aqsa mosque, the Muslim and Christian quarters of the Old City of Jerusalem, and almost all of Jerusalem's Arab neighbourhoods. The offer further included the admission of several thousand Palestinian refugees to Israel on humanitarian grounds.

Anti-Zionist attacks against innocent Jews increased in volume and ferocity the closer the negotiating parties were to agreement, the more generous Israeli offers became. These attacks showed that what anti-Zionists opposed was not so much Israeli presence in the West Bank and Gaza as any agreement that would frustrate their dream of destruction of the State of Israel.

This attitude had a graphic demonstration in Canada when Barak was invited to speak at Concordia University. He had offered the Palestinians more than any other Israeli leader before or since. Any Palestinian serious about peace with Israel would have welcomed him with open arms. Yet the response of the anti-Zionist group Solidarity for Palestinian Human Rights was that Barak was a war criminal and should not be allowed to speak. The university was afraid of a riot and decided not to allow the speech. Erik Yingling of the Solidarity group said that the university was right to fear a confrontation.[77]

A third example is the aftermath of the Oslo Peace Accords. If the occupation were the root cause of the violence between Israel and Arabs, then surely as the occupation lessened, with the increased autonomy of the Palestinians flowing from the Oslo Accords, the violence too should have lessened. But just the opposite has happened. The less the Israeli presence and power in the West Bank and Gaza, the greater the intensity, the violence, and the inhumanity of attacks from the West Bank and Gaza against Israel.

Increased freedom of Palestinians in the West Bank and Gaza has not meant lessened hostility to Israel. On the contrary, increased freedom has gone hand in glove with augmented hatred. Those who were not free to preach hatred and plan violence from the West Bank and Gaza before 1993 used their newfound freedom to envenom the population, especially the children, against Israel, and to use the territories as staging grounds for attacks against Israel.

There were as many terrorist victims two and a half years after the Oslo Accords as there had been during the ten years before. Five years after the accords, the terrorist toll exceeded that from the twelve years worst years of the pre–Oslo Accords period, 1970 to 1982. From the Oslo Accords to 2002, five times as many Israelis died from anti-Zionist terrorist attacks as during those same years.[78]

The Oslo peace process has been a poor advertisement for ending Israeli presence in the West Bank and Gaza. Unilateral Israeli withdrawal from the West Bank and Gaza, in the absence of a peace accord, is more a question of strategy than a question of principle. All the same, the experience of partial autonomy of Palestinians since the Oslo peace process is a compelling argument for maintaining Israeli presence as long as Palestinians remain committed to using the West Bank and Gaza as a base of operations for attacks on the existence of Israel.

The best example of all is the discourse of the violators. The end of the occupation of the West Bank and Gaza might well satisfy Rights and Democracy, the Anglican Church, and many others. But it would not satisfy Hezbollah, Hamas, or Islamic Jihad. And these groups are the source of the human rights violations against Jews, not Rights and Democracy or the Anglican Church or those other groups that recognize the right of Israel to exist and call for Israeli withdrawal from the West Bank and Gaza.

Prime Minister Ariel Sharon announced his intention to have Israel withdraw unilaterally from Gaza and evacuate the settlements there. If ending of occupation of the West Bank and Gaza were foremost on the minds of the enemies of Israel, this planned withdrawal would have been welcomed. Instead, Hamas responded with rocket attacks.

One of these attacks, in September 2004 from the refugee camp of Jabalya against a civilian target in Israel, the town of Sderot, killed two children. The Israeli defence forces responded with an incursion into Jabalya to counter the attacks. Nizar Rayan, a Jabalya Hamas leader stated, "We begin the fifth year of the *intifada*, and we will keep firing rockets and mortars, we will continue our *jihad* until all of Palestine is returned."[79]

The charge that Israeli occupation of the West Bank and Gaza is the root of all evil is an inflation and simplification. But even those who avoid root cause analysis condemn Israeli occupation of the West Bank and Gaza.

The mantra that Israel sits in illegal occupation of territory is so often repeated that it has become one of those catchphrases that people utter unthinkingly. It is commonplace to hear the West Bank and Gaza referred to as illegally occupied territories. Anti-Zionists refer to all of Israel as occupied territories.

The charge of illegal occupation is, in fact, four separate assertions. The first assertion is that the State of Israel sits in occupation of the land of Palestine. The second is that the existence of the State of Israel, as an occupier state, is illegal. The third is that Israeli presence in the West Bank and Gaza is an occupation, as that term is understood in international law. The fourth is that the occupation of the West Bank and Gaza is illegal, a violation of international standards.

All four of these assertions are wrong. There is no legal foundation whatsoever for the epithet *occupation* for the territory of Israel before 1967. For the West Bank and Gaza, the legal foundation for the charge of occupation is shaky. If we assume that there is an occupation of the West Bank and Gaza, then this occupation would be legally permissible.

Of course, anti-Zionists are more than happy to endorse the notion that the West Bank and Gaza are occupied. What they reject is the notion that only the West Bank and Gaza are occupied. The arguments anti-Zionists have against the occupation of the West Bank and Gaza are the same arguments they have against the presence of the State of Israel in any part of the old British-mandate Palestine.

This anti-Zionist blurring of the distinction between the West Bank and Gaza on the one hand and pre-1967 boundaries of the State of Israel on the other helps the anti-Zionist cause. Any condemnation of Israeli presence in the West Bank and Gaza is generalized and becomes, in anti-Zionist eyes, a condemnation of the presence of the State of Israel in the old British-mandate Palestine.

An obvious response to this blurring is that the legal status of the West Bank and Gaza is different from the legal status of Jerusalem and the territory of Israel before 1967. Intrinsic to the notion of occupation is minority rule. A colony is a territory that is non-self-governing.[80] Not every non-self-governing territory is a colony, but every colony is a non-self-governing territory. Yet Israel outside of the West Bank and Gaza is self-governing.

Because international law recognizes that occupations can be either legal or illegal, the issue of whether Israel is or is not, under international law, in occupation of the West Bank and Gaza looms small. If there is an occupation, as long as that occupation is legal, the occupiers, by the mere fact of being in occupation, have done no wrong.

In everyday language, the word *occupation* is used synonymously with *possession*. The notion of occupying an apartment and having an apartment are interchangeable. In that sense, Israel occupies the West Bank and Gaza simply because Israel is there, in control of the West Bank and Gaza. Even Israeli Prime Minister Ariel Sharon has referred to Israeli presence in the West Bank and Gaza as an occupation. Eugene Rostow has written that *occupation* is a neutral term and has no implication of vileness.[81]

While that may be true for international law scholars, it is certainly not so for anti-Zionist propagandists. When Fatah or Hezbollah call all of Israel Zionist occupied territory, neutrality is the furthest thing from their minds. In political propaganda, occupation is wrong and should cease; the label itself is an accusation.

The charge against Israel of occupation of the West Bank and Gaza has become a tag line. Indeed, the West Bank and Gaza are sometimes even labelled "The Occupied Territories" as if that were their real name. But it is not their name. It is rather a stereotype that has become ingrained in popular culture.

One answer to the accusation of occupation is that this is a misuse of the term *occupation*. But another answer is that there is no occupation, as that term is understood at international law.

Except for basic human rights standards, which require certain minimum treatment of everyone, the Geneva Conventions on the Laws of War apply to international armed conflict. When there is an occupying power, there is also an occupied state. The fourth Geneva Convention uses the phrases "Occupying Power" and "Occupied State."[82] Who, for the West Bank and Gaza, is the occupied state?

The only possibilities are Jordan and Egypt. Before the 1967 war, the West Bank and Gaza were under the control of Jordan and Egypt.

The International Court of Justice, when it gave its advisory opinion on the Israeli security fence, identified Jordan as the occupied power of the West Bank.[83]

The judgment moves on from this legal reasoning to labelling the West Bank as Palestinian occupied territory rather than Jordanian occupied territory. But this labelling is based on the ethnic composition of the West Bank, not on its legal status.

It is wrong, as the World Court did, to consider the West Bank as the occupied territory of Jordan. Jordan and Egypt do not today lay claim to the West Bank and Gaza. They have signed peace treaties with Israel that assert no continuing claim. Even if Jordan and Egypt were once partially occupied states, they are no longer.

The artificiality of the language of occupation was highlighted by the Israeli army incursions into the West Bank in April 2002 in an attempt to dismantle the support for suicide bombings. News reports described Israel forces as occupying Palestinian cities of Jenin, Nablus, and Ramallah. Opponents of the incursions called for an end to the army occupation of the cities.

If you believed that the West Bank and Gaza were already Israeli-occupied territory, these calls would be nonsense. If Israel had occupied the West Bank and Gaza in 1967, the army in April 2002 could not be occupying those West Bank cities. According to the anti-Zionist language of occupation, they were already occupied. The mindlessness of the language of occupation is highlighted by this usage of the label.

The assertion by the International Court of Justice that the West Bank is Jordanian occupied territory is a contortion the law imposed on the court to get to its desired result of slapping the label *occupier* on Israel. The court's shift from legal reasoning that the West Bank is Jordanian occupied territory to labelling the West Bank as Palestinian occupied territory shows that the primary concern of the court was to connect to pro-Palestinian political rhetoric. Outside of the courtroom, the claim made today by those who apply the label "occupied territories" to the West Bank and Gaza is not that Jordan and Egypt are the occupied powers, but rather that the Palestinian people are the occupied power.

However, the Geneva Conventions on the Laws of War do not recognize the legal possibility of the occupation of a people, only the occupation of the territory of a state. A protocol to the Geneva Conventions relating to the protection of victims of international armed conflict does recognize the possibility of the occupation of a people. The protocol encompasses "armed conflicts in which peoples are fighting against colonial domination and alien occupation and against racist regimes in the exercise of their right of self-determination."[84]

The protocol is not as widely ratified as the four Geneva Conventions on the Laws of War. Israel is not a party to the protocol, though it is a party to the Conventions. A treaty binds only signatory states. Because Israel is not a party to the protocol, it is not bound by its terms.

The legal principles behind the charge that Israel sits in alien occupation of the West Bank and Gaza are not consistently applied. If you condemn China for occupying Tibet, that does not mean that you are right to condemn Israel for occupying the West Bank and Gaza. After all, Tibet never invaded China. Tibet never sought to destroy China. Tibetan organizations do not deny China's right to exist. Tibetans have not been launching armed terrorist attacks against China from Tibetan soil.

But the converse is certainly true. If you do not condemn China for occupying Tibet, you have no business condemning Israel for its occupation of the West Bank and Gaza. Silence on Tibet and condemnation of Israel show a double standard. They show that the true enemy is not occupation, but rather Israel.

If the accusation of occupation of the West Bank and Gaza is now made against Israel, it should have been made earlier against Jordan and Egypt. Yet it never was. The Protocol on International Armed Conflict post-dates the 1967 war,[85] but the concepts of colonial domination, alien occupation, and racist regimes were hardly new to that protocol. If Israel is in alien occupation of the West Bank and Gaza, occupying it against the Palestinian people, why were not Jordan and Egypt before Israel also in alien occupation of the West Bank and Gaza, also occupying the territories against the Palestinian people?

The only answer that would allow Jordan and Egypt to be distinguished from Israel is that Israel is alien or foreign to the region, but Jordan and Egypt are not. In other words, the distinction depends on a belief in anti-Zionism. If you believe in anti-Zionism, then it follows that Israel is an alien occupier of the West Bank and Gaza, even though Egypt and Jordan were not alien occupiers. With this distinction, alien occupation is not something Israel is doing wrong; the label "alien occupation" is just another way of saying to believers that the existence of Israel is wrong.

The position of the government of Israel is that, though the West Bank and Gaza are not occupied territory as that term is understood in the Geneva Conventions on the Laws of War, they are prepared to accept and apply voluntarily the obligations set out in those conventions that bind occupying powers. David Kretzmer has argued that because the State of Israel is applying those obligations, it is tacitly admitting that the West Bank and Gaza are occupied territory.[86]

If it were not for the anti-Zionist propaganda swirling around the issue, the debate would be pointless. What difference does it make what something is called, as long as the behaviour remains the same? The difference is that the label "occupation" has become a club that is used to attack the very existence of Israel.

The Geneva Convention on the Protection of Civilians in Time of War sets out rules that must be followed when there is an occupation. It does not set out rules for judging which side is right and which is wrong in resorting to the use of force. It does not tell us when an occupation is illegal.

Nonetheless, international law tells us that any occupation that is the fruit of a war of aggression is illegal. By that standard, if Israel was in occupation of the West

Bank and Gaza before the peace treaties with Jordan and Egypt, that occupation was legal. Jordan and Egypt were the aggressors in the 1967 war, and Israel seized the West Bank and Gaza when defending itself against that aggression.

The Security Council of the United Nations, despite its many resolutions passed and words uttered on Israel, has never once labelled the Israeli presence in the West Bank and Gaza illegal. Indeed, resolutions calling on Palestinians and Israelis to negotiate an end to the Israeli presence in the West Bank and Gaza imply the opposite, that the Israeli presence in those territories is legal until such time as the negotiations succeed. George Fletcher of Columbia University wrote, "Because it [UN Security Council resolution 338, passed in 1973 after the Yom Kippur War] insisted that the Palestinians negotiate an end to the Israeli presence, the Security Council could not have thought the occupation itself violated international law … It is not illegal for victorious powers to occupy hostile territory seized in the course of war until they are able to negotiate a successful peace treaty with their former enemies."[87]

United Nations Secretary General Kofi Annan in March 2002 characterized the Israeli occupation of the West Bank and Gaza as illegal. However, his office, in April 2002, issued a clarification stating, "the Secretary General was not addressing the legality of Israel's original action in occupying territory during the war of 1967." Rather, he was "calling attention to Israel's failure to accept the legal obligations that the status of an occupying power carries with it, and its actions that run contrary to those obligations." This statement gave no indication what the Secretary General thought those failures and actions were.[88]

There is an obligation to negotiate in good faith the end to Israel's presence in the West Bank and Gaza. But Israel can hardly be accused in negotiating in bad faith, given the generosity of its last offer in January 2001 in Taba before negotiations broke down.

Michael Lynk has argued that international law requires that an occupation be as brief as possible and that it end when it ceases to be justifiable in self-defence.[89] The international law treaties on the laws of war do not set out time limits for occupation or criteria for determining time limits for occupation. Let us suppose, all the same, that Israel is, indeed, an occupying power within the meaning of international treaties. Let us further assume that the interpretation Lynk has given of international law is correct.

In that case, the occupation of the West Bank and Gaza by Israeli forces ceases to have a military justification and should end once all organizations representative of the Palestinian people within the West Bank and Gaza renounce the use of force, in word and deed, to destroy Israel. Alternatively, the occupation should end when those Palestinian forces who are exercising authority over the West Bank and Gaza are both able and willing to prevent the use of the West Bank and Gaza for armed attacks against Israel.

It is apparent that nothing like that has happened. The existence and power of the Palestinian Authority since the Oslo Peace Accord in 1993 can be seen as a test to determine whether Israeli military presence in the West Bank and Gaza could end. It is a test that the Palestinian Authority has failed miserably. The Palestinian Authority has shown neither the ability nor even the willingness to protect Israel from armed attacks originating from the West Bank and Gaza.

Indeed, there is substantial evidence that they have been complicit in these attacks. Yasser Arafat's Fatah movement has taken part in attacks on Israel through Tanzim and the al-Aqsa Martyrs Brigade.[90] What is worse, these armed attacks are not just against Israeli military targets, but against innocent civilians.

Anti-Zionists create a situation where an Israeli military response is necessary in self-defence. For that situation, it is not anti-Zionists who are blamed, but Israelis. Israeli self-defence is labelled and condemned as occupation. The only response that would satisfy anti-Zionists would be an Israeli renunciation of self-defence, or auto-destruction.

What should the West Bank and Gaza be called, if not occupied territories? Dore Gold, a former Israeli ambassador to the United Nations, suggests the name "disputed territories."[91] The trouble with that label is that, for anti-Zionists, all of Israel is disputed territory. Israel is free to determine its own position. But it cannot determine what others want to put in dispute.

Another set of possibilities is the names that Judge Koojmans of the International Criminal Court gives to West Bank in his separate reason, which forms part of the advisory opinion on the Israeli security barrier. He calls the West Bank before 1967 Jordanian controlled territory, or territory under the authority of Jordan.[92] Similarly, one can call the West Bank and Gaza today Israeli controlled territory, or territory under the authority of Israel.

Judge Koojmans endorsed a shift in terminology, calling the West Bank "controlled territory" when Jordan was in possession and "occupied territory" when Israel is in possession. The struggle for the gold medal for hypocrisy amongst the judges of the court is hard fought. It is difficult to know whether to give the award to Judge Koojmans, whose hypocrisy is explicit, or to the majority, whose hypocrisy is hidden by omission.

Judge Koojmans wrote that he failed to understand why the court in its majority opinion omitted consideration of the legal status of the West Bank before 1967, though they purported to engage in a legal historical review of the West Bank.[93] But Judge Koojmans' own reasoning, which filled in its gap, should explain the court's omission.

The legal status of the West Bank both before and after 1967 is essentially the same. Only the state in control has changed. If Israel is going to be considered the occupier of the Palestinian people after the 1967 war, then Jordan must be considered the occupier of the Palestinian people before the 1967 war. If the latter is not considered true, then neither can the former. The court avoided and presumably wanted to avoid either of those conclusions. So the court just did not discuss the subject.

Labelling or categorizing the West Bank and Gaza in any way is difficult because a category is a generalization, and the situation of the West Bank and Gaza is unique. In the history of the United Nations, Israel is the only member whose very existence has been widely contested. Israel is the only member whose existence today other members oppose and denounce.

In a general sort of way, one can say that the West Bank and Gaza are territories won from aggressor states by an attacked state responding in self-defence. The aggressor states have abandoned their claim to the territories. The territories are populated by a belligerent population hostile to not just the presence of the victor state in the territories but to the very existence of the victor state. The status of the territories remains unsettled both under the domestic law of the victor state and at international law. What do you call that?

One possibility is "unsettled status territories." That label, albeit clumsy, asserts no position on the legal status of the West Bank and Gaza. As well, it distinguishes those territories from Israel.

Wᴴᴬᵀ is wrong with the settlements? Though the complaints against Israel are never-ending, there is one that looms over all others: the complaint about the settlements in the West Bank and Gaza.

The settlements are often described as the major obstacle to peace in the Middle East. B'Tselem called the presence of settlers in Hebron "the primary cause of grave violations of Palestinian human rights" within the city.[94] Virtually every peace plan has as a component the abandonment of the settlements and the eviction of the settlers. Alternatively, the boundaries of Israel and the West Bank and Gaza are re-jigged so that some settlements would become part of Israel, and Israel would give up in exchange part of its own territory.

Yet, in principle, the settlements seem innocent. Why do people get so worked up about what is in essence nothing more than Jews living in the neighbourhood? Outside of the West Bank and Gaza, hostility to Jews living in any neighbourhood would be seen for what it is — bigotry and antisemitism.

In Canada and many other countries, it is legally possible for a person selling land to impose a restriction on a purchaser preventing the purchaser from using the land in a certain way or from selling the land to a certain type of buyer. Years ago, Drummond Wren bought land in Ontario with such a restriction attached, stating, "Land not to be sold to Jews or persons of objectionable nationality." He asked the Ontario courts to have the restriction declared invalid. Justice Mackay did so in a judgment of October 1945.[95] Mackay wrote:

> Nothing could be more calculated to create or deepen divisions between existing religious and ethnic groups in this province, or in this country, than the sanction of a method of land transfer which would permit the segregation and confinement of particular groups to particular business or residential areas, or conversely, would exclude particular groups from particular business or residential areas ... It appears to me to be a moral duty, at least, to lend aid to all forces of cohesion, and similarly to repel all fissiparous tendencies which would imperil national unity ... That the restrictive covenant in this case is directed in the first place against Jews lends poignancy to the matter when one considers that antisemitism has been a weapon in the hands of our recently defeated enemies, and the scourge of the world.

All that could be said of opposition to the settlements. Nothing could be more calculated to create or deepen divisions between Jews and Arabs in Israel and the nascent Palestinian state than the sanction of a method of land transfer that would exclude Jews from those territories. It is a moral duty to repel opposition to the settlements. That opposition is poignant when one considers that anti-semitism has been the scourge of the world.

The principle of the *Drummond Wren* judgment eventually became statutory law. Ontario legislation states that every covenant that "restricts the sale, ownership, occupation or use of land because of the race, creed, colour, nationality, ancestry or place of origin of any person is void and of no effect."[96] Yet that is all opposition to the settlements is: opposition to the sale, ownership, occupation, or use of land because of the race, creed, colour, nationality, ancestry, or place of origin of the occupier. Why do so many people who would oppose restrictive covenants forbidding sales of residential properties to Jews everywhere else in the world endorse the notion in the West Bank and Gaza?

One argument against the settlements is that they may lead to or reinforce territorial claims made by some Israelis. However, there is no necessary connection between the two. Territorial positions should be expressed directly, rather than indirectly through hostility to the presence of individual Jews or Jewish settlements.

Another argument against the settlements is that the presence of Jewish settlements in a Palestinian state in the West Bank and Gaza will lead to Israeli extra-territorial attempts to protect those settlements against anti-Jewish attacks. This argument is reflected racism, succumbing to the prejudice of others. It is discrimination to say to a person, "You cannot live there," on the basis that the person would be subject to violent racist attacks.

If Jews in a Palestinian state in the West Bank and Gaza are going to be subject to racist attacks, then the Palestinian state should defend them, not evacuate them. Israeli extra-territorial attacks to defend Jewish settlements in a Palestinian state in the West Bank and Gaza would occur only in response to a failure of the Palestinian state to defend those settlements. The true culprit in this hypothetical situation is neither the settlements nor the Israeli efforts to defend the settlers, but the anti-Jewish attacks and the failure of the future Palestinian state to protect its own residents.

Israel has been accused of violating the human rights of Palestinians in the West Bank and Gaza by allowing Jews to settle there. Anti-Zionists have focused their charges on the obligation in the Geneva Convention relative to the Protection of Civilian Persons in Time of War not to transfer civilian populations to occupied territories.[97] The charge is that the Israeli government, through encouraging the settlements, has transferred civilians to the West Bank and Gaza and thereby committed a war crime.

The Geneva Convention's obligation not to transfer civilian populations, according to the International Committee of the Red Cross, was included to prevent a practice adopted during the Second World War, in which certain powers transferred portions of their own populations to occupied territory for political and racial reasons, or in order, as they claimed, to colonize those territories. Such transfers, the Red Cross observed, worsened the economic situation of the native population and endangered their separate existence as a race.[98]

Nazi Germany inflicted two sorts of transfers of its own civilian population to occupied territory. One was the transfer of its ethnic Jewish population to the death camps in occupied Poland. The other was the transfer of parts of its ethnic German population to places the Nazis occupied in order to solidify that occupation.

Both sorts of transfers were forced. The first was obviously more serious than the second. However, the prohibition in the Geneva Convention appears to apply to both sorts of transfers.

Transferring civilian populations to occupied territory is not a grave breach of the Geneva Convention. The obligation falls on the states parties to respect the prohibition. There is no individual liability, and there is no duty on states to penalize violations. However, a protocol to the Geneva Convention imposes that duty but does not otherwise change the prohibition. The transfer of civilian populations *is* a grave breach of this protocol.[99] The protocol requires the contracting parties to provide penal sanctions for those committing grave breaches and those ordering grave breaches to be committed.[100]

The protocol offence also penalizes, in the same subsection, the transfer of civilian populations to, from, and within occupied territories. No distinction is made amongst the various forms of transfer. The assimilation of the various forms in the same subsection emphasizes that the primary victim of the offence of transfer is the person transferred. It would be ludicrous to see the word as having different meanings within the same subsection depending on the direction of the transfer, to see transfer from or within occupied territory as meaning forced movement only and transfer to occupied territory as including induced movement.

However, if the word *transfer* is to mean induced movement from or within occupied territory as well transfer to occupied territory, then induced movement of a civilian population from one part of an occupied territory to another becomes a breach of the Geneva Convention and a grave breach of the protocol. Applied to the West Bank, Israel would be guilty of a breach of the Geneva Convention for inducing Palestinians to move from one part of the West Bank to another, a decidedly peculiar result and one that not even the most rabid critics of Israel have advocated.

If encouraging the settlements violates international law, then the person doing the inducing is an offender, but the person being induced is not. That interpretation defies the ordinary understanding of criminal responsibility, where the person committing the act is the primary wrongdoer and the person inducing the act is only an accessory. How can there be a crime when the person committing the act induced has done nothing wrong?

Making encouragement of settlements into a war crime trivializes the very idea of war crimes. War crimes are meant to be great wrongs. Yet an inducement to settle may be nothing more than a tax cut, or the construction of a road, or the collection of garbage. Criminalizing the settlements would mean that mass murderers and those who organized garbage collection would sit side by side in war crimes jails.

Turning the creation of settlements into a war crime creates unsolvable problems of causality. When a person moves voluntarily, the inducements offered to the person to move may have little or nothing to do with the move. Many of the Israelis who moved to the West Bank moved out of religious conviction. They would have gone there whether the state encouraged settlement or discouraged it. Is the imagined offence of which those who encourage settlements are accused one of strict liability, so that the inducer is guilty even if the inducement had no causal relationship to the act performed? Or would a court have to determine from each settler the impact the inducement had on his or her own motivation?

Turning the creation of settlements into a war crime creates equally unsolvable problems of responsibility. The responsibility for an order lies with the person giving the order. The responsibility for an inducement is less clear.

A Red Cross commentary highlights the confusion by stating, "The fact that the transfer must be done by the occupying power appears to require government involvement. With respect to individual criminal responsibility, this offence seems to presuppose that the conduct of the perpetrator must be imputable to the occupying power. Therefore, individuals acting in their private capacity would not be criminally responsible." However, it is impossible to prosecute an occupying power. A court will prosecute individuals, not states. But which individuals will they be? Will they be the civil servants in the ministry that proposed the inducement to the government? Will they be the cabinet members that proposed the inducement to the whole cabinet? Will they be the government members that proposed the inducement to parliament? Will they be the members of the governing party that proposed the inducement to the electorate? Or will they be the members of the electorate that voted for the party proposing the inducement?

Of course, even laws that violate fundamental standards of humanity can proceed through a democratic process. At the level of international law, these local laws are manifestly unlawful. The defence of superior orders is not available to a person committing a wrongful act when the order is to comply with a local law that is manifestly unlawful at international law. However, for the offence being discussed here, there would be no order, only an inducement. The person committing the act would commit no wrong, only the person offering the inducement. So the law of superior orders provides no answer to the conundrums posed by the Red Cross commentary.

The notion that Israel has violated the Geneva Conventions by allowing Jews to settle in the West Bank is as zany, in its own way, as the equation of Zionism with racism. There is all the difference in the world between forcible transfer, the offence in the Geneva Conventions, and voluntary settlement, even where that settlement is encouraged. Transfer is something that is done to people. Settlement is something people do. People choose to settle. Others choose when civilians are transferred. To equate the crime of transfer with Jewish settlements in the West Bank is yet another example of how far anti-Zionists can drift from the moorings of reality when attacks on Israel are their destination.

There is a fundamental distinction between being forced to do what you do not want to do and being allowed to do what you want to do — between tyranny and freedom. To equate the two is sophistry, rejecting a distinction fundamental to the respect for human rights. Israeli settlers in the West Bank and Gaza were neither transferred nor deported. They all settled of their own free will. If the settlers commit no crime by acting freely, then those who guarantee that freedom also commit no crime.

It is, of course, legitimate to assert, as a matter of public policy, that people should be prevented, in some ways, from being free to do what they want. But that is far different from an assertion that the exercise of this freedom violates international law. Equating the Israeli respect for the freedom of the West Bank settlers to the real Nazi tyranny of forced transfer and deportation of civilian populations during the Second World War is just anti-Zionist propaganda.

There is a fundamental human right to freedom of movement; however, that right is not absolute and must be balanced with other rights.[101] In particular, it has to be balanced against the right to self-determination of peoples. The right to freedom of movement cannot justify a mass influx that would turn a majority into a minority and deny the majority its right to self-determination as a people. That is why the claimed Palestinian right of return cannot be justified under the principle of freedom of movement.

However, there is no such influx with the settlements. There are, according to recent population estimates, about 187,000 Jewish residents and 2.3 million people total in the West Bank. There are 177,000 Jewish residents of East Jerusalem and 20,000 Jewish residents of the Golan Heights. Gaza has about 8,000 Jewish residents and a total population of 1.3 million. The total Israeli population, including Israelis living in the West Bank, Gaza, East Jerusalem, and the Golan Heights, is 6.2 million. 80 percent of Israelis are Jewish.[102]

The size of the Jewish settlements in the West Bank and Gaza does not even come close to threatening the continuation of Palestinian majority in those territories. Jewish residents of the West Bank and Gaza both in absolute and percentage terms are far fewer in number than non-Jewish residents of Israel within the pre-1967 boundaries.

It makes no more sense to say that Jews should not live in the West Bank and Gaza than to say that Arabs should not live within Israel's pre-1967 boundaries.

Amnesty International, in a September 2003 report, called for the forcible evacuation of Jews from the West Bank and Gaza, without calling for Arabs to be forcibly evacuated from pre-1967 Israel.[103] Evacuation of Arabs from Israel would be a violation of human rights, and I do not suggest that there should be such an evacuation. But evacuation of Jews from the West Bank and Gaza would be just as much a violation of human rights.

What threatens the viability of a Palestinian state in the West Bank and Gaza is not the existence of the settlements or their size, but rather anti-Zionist intolerance of them. As long as having Jews living in the neighbourhood is considered in the West Bank and Gaza to be a capital crime, it is impossible to conceive of a Palestinian state living side by side in peace with Israel.

Contrary to what B'Tselem says, the presence of Jews in Hebron is not the primary cause of grave violations of Palestinian human rights within the city. The primary cause is the anti-Zionist murderous hatred of Jews in their midst.

There is nothing in international law that says that the West Bank and Gaza must be *judenrein*, or "free of Jews." Jews have as much right to live in the West Bank and Gaza as Arabs have to live in Israel. Israel protects Arabs living in Israel. But the Palestinian Authority offers no protection to Jews living in the West Bank and Gaza. Anti-Zionists attempt to kill Jews living in the West Bank and Gaza, and have, in fact, killed many.

Why was the construction that was variously called a fence or wall or security barrier built around some of the settlements in the West Bank? It would seem obvious to anyone not blinded by anti-Zionist propaganda — to protect those who live in them. Antisemites want to kill Jews. Israel builds a barrier around Jewish neighbourhoods to protect the Jews who live in them.

Anyone who truly does not want the security barrier to be there should focus on preventing the killing of Jews simply because they happen to live in the neighbourhood. If Palestinians in the West Bank were prepared to accept the presence of Jews in their midst and offer them protection, the security barrier would not be necessary.

Canada has signed, ratified, and legislated the Protocol on International Armed Conflict.[104] The protocol offence of transferring civilian populations to occupied territories, as far as I am aware, has not led to even one prosecution against Israelis in Canada or elsewhere. If the anti-Israeli rhetoric about West Bank settlements is correct, then the Canadian provincial Attorneys General have not only the power, but indeed the duty, to prosecute any Israeli visiting Canada who was involved in these settlements.[105] Even though not every country in the world has ratified and implemented the Protocol on International Armed Conflict, many have, and any country can. The fact that no country has launched such a prosecution shows, if any further demonstration is needed, that charges that the settlements violate the prohibition against transfer of civilian populations to occupied territories are just so much hot air.

The offence of transferring civilian populations to occupied territories in the statute of the International Criminal Court has a seemingly insignificant addition to the prohibition found in the Geneva Convention and the offence found in the Protocol on International Armed Conflict. The court offence adds the words "directly or indirectly."

The International Committee of the Red Cross, in a working paper of June 1999 on the elements of the crimes in the court statute, wrote, "The inclusion of the word 'indirect' seems to indicate that the population of the occupying power need not necessarily be physically enforced or otherwise compelled. Therefore, acts of inducement may fall under this war crime."

The fact that the Red Cross could propose this interpretation shows the anti-Israel sentiment floating underneath the surface of the neutral language of the statute of the International Criminal Court. The statute applies to acts committed after the statute comes into force by nationals of states parties or on the territories of states parties. The Red Cross interpretation, if true, would mean that, should Israel ratify the court treaty, encouraging settlements in the West Bank and Gaza would be an offence.

General Assembly resolutions show that anti-Israeli states are of the view that all the settlements are illegal. A 1999 General Assembly resolution reaffirmed that "all illegal Israeli actions in Occupied East Jerusalem and the rest of the Occupied Palestinian Territory, especially settlement activities and the practical results thereof, remain contrary to international law and cannot be recognized, irrespective of the passage of time." If that view holds sway, then not only would inducements to establish new settlements be a war crime, but inducements to maintain existing settlements would also be a war crime.

There is a small comfort that can be drawn from the Red Cross commentary. The commentary reinforces the argument, if reinforcement is needed, that the prohibition of transfer of civilian populations to occupied territories in the Geneva Convention and Protocol could not possibly apply to Israel. According to the Red Cross, while the World Court statute goes beyond forcible transfer, the Geneva Convention and Protocol certainly do not.

Though there is no obligation to defer to the Red Cross, their opinion deserves consideration. When it comes to their interpretation of the statute of the International Criminal Court, I suggest that the anti-Israel rhetoric and motivation of a few states led the Red Cross to misinterpret an offence in the statute that was not intended to criminalize inducements to settle. The Red Cross uses the phrase "seems to indicate." If one were to listen only to the anti-Zionist states, the wording in the statute would indeed seem to indicate what the Red Cross wrote. However, it is a mistake to base any interpretation of the statute on the anti-Israel animus of a few vocal states.

The addition of the word *indirectly* does not change the crime of transfer from a crime of force only to a crime of inducement as well. There was a provision in the draft statute of the International Criminal Court, used for negotiating purposes throughout the conference, which had as an option that the definition of war crimes include "the establishment of settlers in an occupied territory and changes to the demographic composition of an occupied territory."[106] This option was rejected by the conference and is not in the statute as approved. It would be strange that an option which the conference rejected should resurface as an interpretation of a general word.

The Red Cross interpretation defies the ordinary meaning of words. An indirect transfer of people or goods or money from one place to another ordinarily means a roundabout transfer, where the people or goods or money transferred go from the place of origin to an intermediate place or places and then to the place of destination, rather than going straight from the place of origin to the place of destination. Literally, the words *indirect* and *direct* refer to direction, the place to which you are heading, not to the vehicle that got you there; they refer to the route of transfer, not the means of transfer.

The Red Cross interpretation contradicts the court statute's interpretative clause. The statute provides that the definition of a crime should be strictly construed and should not be extended by analogy. In case of ambiguity, the definition of a crime must be interpreted in favour of the person being investigated or prosecuted.[107] This interpretative provision is placed in the statute under the general heading "*Nullum crime sine lege,*" meaning "no crime without law."

The Red Cross interpretation is not a strict construction. It is an extension of the offence by analogy. In my view, the Red Cross is unambiguously wrong. However, even if there is an ambiguity in the statute, the Red Cross, erroneously, resolves that ambiguity against those potentially accused. The Red Cross interpretation would create a crime without a clear, specific law, in violation of the statute.

The Red Cross interpretation has no external support. The states parties to the Geneva Convention relative to the Protection of Civilian Persons in Time of War held a conference on "the Occupied Palestinian Territory, including Jerusalem" in Geneva in December 2001, which asserted the illegality of the settlements. That conference could not have asserted the settlements to be illegal if states hostile to the settlements shared the views of the Red Cross. There is a difference of opinion about the meaning of the Geneva Convention prohibition, about whether it includes inducements or is limited to forcible transfer. Critics of Israel take the position that both the Geneva Convention prohibition and the court offence include inducements. Israel and its friends take the position that both are limited to forcible transfer.

However, the global community is agreed that there is no substantive difference between the Geneva Convention prohibition and the court offence. That is the position of the government of the State of Israel.[108] It is also the position of the governments hostile to the settlements. No state, to my knowledge, takes the position of the Red Cross that the Geneva Convention prohibition is limited to forcible transport but that the court offence includes inducements to settlement. At international law, the opinion of states about what the law is, accompanied by supporting practice, is constitutive of that law.

The Red Cross interpretation is a discredit to the International Criminal Court. To read the statute of the court to include an anodyne act committed by a politically unpopular state makes the statute appear to be a home for special pleadings, vendettas, and selective prosecution. The court can have credibility only if it is independent from ephemeral political disputes. The Red Cross interpretation puts one of these disputes, Israeli settlements in the West Bank, at the heart of one of the court offences. That sort of interpretation may today give some psychic satisfaction to those opposed to the settlements. However, it undercuts the International Criminal Court not just today, but forever.

The statute of the court provides that the Assembly of States Parties must adopt elements of crimes to assist the court in its interpretation and application of the crimes.[109] There were four state proposals for the elements of the crime of transfer of civilian populations to occupied territories.[110] An American proposal referred to the transfer as compulsory but did not state forthrightly that it had to be compulsory. A joint proposal of Costa Rica, Hungary, and Switzerland avoided the issue of whether transfer must be compulsory and just repeated the language of the statute. A Japanese proposal stated that crime is committed if the transfer violated the Geneva Convention relative to the Protection of Civilians in Time of War, but did not say whether, for the Geneva Convention to be violated, transfer had to be forcible. Seventeen Arab states proposed that the crime is committed if the perpetrator "induced, facilitated, participated or helped in any manner in the transfer of civilian population of the occupying power into the territory it occupies."

An anti-Israeli agenda was apparent from the Arab state proposal. The question became, what would other states do about it? In the end, the Japanese proposal and the joint proposal of Costa Rica, Hungary, and Switzerland were adopted, just repeating the language of the Court statute. However, there was one significant addition. A footnote was added to the word *transferred*. The footnote said, "The term 'transfer' needs to be interpreted in accordance with the relevant provisions of international humanitarian law."

In other words, the statute was not meant to create law. It was restating existing law. The position of the Red Cross that the statute changed the law was, in effect, rejected.

The International Court of Justice, in its advisory opinion on the Israeli security barrier, found the settlements to violate international law. The court stated that the prohibition against transfer of civilian populations to occupied territories found in the Geneva Convention relative to the Protection of Civilian Persons in Time of War covers "not only deportations or forced transfers of population such as those carried out during the Second World War, but also any measures taken by an occupying Power in order to organize or encourage transfers of parts of its own population into the occupied territory."[111]

Judge Buergenthal, the lone dissenter, agreed with the majority on this point.[112] The majority court opinion gave no reason for coming to this conclusion and cited no authority. Judge Higgins, in a separate opinion, complained about this absence. Showing a mastery of understatement, she described the court's treatment of the issue as "somewhat light."[113] "Completely weightless" or "defying gravity" would have been more accurate. Regrettably, she did not show the same mastery of international law. Without any analysis or citations of her own to fill the gap she decried, she ended up agreeing with the court on this point anyways.

The sole reasoning of the court on transfer of civilian populations to occupied territory related to Israel, its intended target. The court reasoned that the combination of the settlements and the security barrier generated fears of annexation by Israel of the territory on the Israeli side of the barrier.[114] They considered the settlements plus the barrier a de facto annexation.

This reasoning is tied up with the court's prior reasoning that the West Bank is Jordanian occupied territory, discussed in another chapter of this book. One obvious question from the court statement of de facto annexation is, Annexation from whom? The answer the logic of the judgment of the Court leads us to is annexation from Jordan.

Another obvious question is, Annexation of what? Because the court has tied itself in a legal knot, feeling compelled to find that the West Bank is Jordanian occupied territory in order to apply the label of occupier to Israel, the answer is: the annexation of all territory between the Israeli security barrier and the Israeli boundaries before 1967. All this territory was under the control of Jordan before the 1967 war.

Even if one puts aside the breathtaking silliness of the reasoning that the West Bank is today Jordanian occupied territory, the conclusion of annexation is untenable. It is based on fears alone. The court stated that it "cannot remain indifferent to these fears." In other words, fears of annexation became annexation. Prejudice becomes reality. Because anti-Zionist propagandists portray Israel as a land-grabbing, expansionist state, the court held that Israel is such a state. Anti-Zionist propaganda became to the court both fact and law.

The court's reasoning on the security barrier follows the standard logic of anti-Zionist propaganda. Anti-Zionists attack Israelis. Israel defends its population, in this case the settlers, by building a security barrier. Israeli efforts at self-defence are decontextualized, judged in the absence of the attacks that precipitated them. The security barrier is condemned in the abstract, as if the attacks that generated the barrier never occurred.

Though this was presumably not the intention of the court, their reasoning supports the position put forward earlier in this chapter. The phrase "directly or indirectly," added by the Rome Statute of the International Criminal Court to the crime of transferring civilian populations to occupied territories, must mean something. It is not mere surplusage. When drafters want to the say the same thing in two different texts, they use the same words. When drafters want to say different things, they use different words. The Rome Statute refers at several points to the Geneva Convention relative to the Protection of Civilian Persons in Time of War and must be interpreted to be compatible with it.[115]

But, if, as the International Court of Justice concludes, to "encourage" transfer of civilian populations to occupied territories is already a violation of the Geneva Convention relative to the Protection of Civilian Persons in Time of War, to what do the words "directly or indirectly" in the Rome Statute refer? They cannot refer to encouragement, since that, according to the World Court, is already covered by the Geneva Convention. So they must refer to something else. What is that something else?

The only plausible explanation is the one given earlier in this chapter. The phrase "directly or indirectly" must mean transfer either directly from the territory of the occupying power to the territory of the occupied power or indirectly through the territory of a third power.

The court has abandoned the possibility that the phrase prohibits encouragement of transfer, since the court has found that prohibition absent that phrase. So what is the possible legal basis for the conclusion that encouraging transfer is a violation the Geneva Convention relative to the Protection of Civilian Persons in Time of War? In the absence of reasons or citations, one is hard-pressed to guess.

But this much is certain. The issue of legality of encouraging transfer must, according to the reasoning of the court, stand or fall on the Geneva Convention relative to the Protection of Civilian Persons in Time of War alone. The Rome Statute does not create the prohibition.

Yet if one looks at Geneva Convention alone, the conclusion of the court cannot possibly stand. Indeed, one can use the court's own reasoning elsewhere in the judgment to come to this conclusion.

The court elsewhere in the judgment was quick to trumpet in support of its conclusion that the West Bank and Gaza are occupied territory, a Red Cross opinion that the Geneva Convention applied to the West Bank and Gaza.[116] The court, in a typical piece of distortion, referred to a provision of the Geneva Convention that states, "The International Committee of the Red Cross in this field shall be recognized and respected at all times."[117] The "field" to which the phrase in the Geneva Convention refers is relief. But the court opinion drops reference to the "relief" qualifier and is bold enough to assert, despite the plain wording, that the Geneva Convention requires states parties to defer to the Red Cross in the legal interpretation of the Geneva Convention.

However, as noted earlier, the Red Cross holds the view that encouraging transfer of civilian populations to occupied territories is not a violation of the Geneva Convention relative to the Protection of Civilian Persons in Time of War and that the Rome Statute of the International Criminal Court creates the prohibition. When the Red Cross legal interpretation disagrees with that of the court, as it does here, the court just ignores the Red Cross opinion. The notion of deference to the Red Cross legal interpretation of the Geneva Convention is thrown out the window.

I do not suggest we defer to the Red Cross legal opinion any more than we defer to the court's advisory opinion. But the court cannot have it both ways. They cannot promote deference to a Red Cross opinion on the meaning the Geneva Convention relative to the Protection of Civilian Persons in Time of War when the Red Cross agrees with the court and ignore the Red Cross when they disagree.

Either the court's deference to the Red Cross opinion that the West Bank and Gaza are occupied territory is wrong, or the court's disregard of the Red Cross opinion that the Geneva Convention does not prohibit encouraging transfer of civilians to occupied territories is wrong.

Either one of these errors is enough to undermine the conclusions of the court. If the West Bank and Gaza are not occupied territory, the conclusions of the court cannot stand. If encouraging transfer of civilians to occupied territory is not a violation of the Geneva Convention relative to the Protection of Civilian Persons in Time of War, the conclusions of the court also cannot stand. So no matter which way one looks at the reasoning of the court, it is unsustainable.

The advisory opinion of the International Court of Justice on the Israeli security fence, though an attempt to sully Israel, in the end sullied far more international justice. If the International Court of Justice could get so far off legal base for the crassest of political reasons, what hope is there for the International Criminal Court?

Jews who live in the West Bank and Gaza and those who encourage them to do so may be as innocent as newborns. But if the International Criminal Court behaves like the International Court of Justice, innocence will not matter. All that will matter is that Israel is the target.

There is hope that the International Criminal Court will be less political than the International Court of Justice because of differences in structure. The International Court of Justice is an organ of the United Nations. The International Criminal Court is not.

Judges of the International Court of Justice are chosen by the United Nations General Assembly. Judges of the International Criminal Court are chosen by the states parties to the statute of the court.[118] The most rabid anti-Zionist states, including Iran, Syria, and Libya, are all not parties to the statute of the court and have no say in choosing judges. They have not joined and are not likely to join soon, because adherence would put their own human rights record under the jurisdiction of the court.

The General Assembly does not have the power to refer to the International Criminal Court a situation in which crimes appear to have been committed that are within the jurisdiction of the court. Only states parties, the prosecutor acting on his own initiative, and the Security Council have this power.[119]

At the time of the Rome conference, Israeli opposition to the court focused on the fact that the statute of the court included the offence of "directly or indirectly" transferring civilian populations to occupied territories.[120] By the time of the Rome conference, accusations against Israel for violating the Geneva Convention relative to the Protection of Civilian Persons in Time of War because of the settlements were old hat.

Elyakim Rubinstein, the then Israeli Attorney General, observed after the Rome conference that the Geneva Convention prohibition had become a stick with which to beat the Jewish settlements in Judea, Samaria, and Gaza. (Judea and Samaria are ancient Biblical names for the West Bank.) Israel voted against the court for fear that the court would use this stick against Israel.[121]

Esther Efrat-Smilg, speaking for Israel in the General Assembly Sixth Committee, said that a basic element of the crime of transfer of civilian populations must be that the transfer was in violation of the Geneva Convention relative to the Protection of Civilian Persons in Time of War. She added that the addition in Rome of the phrase "directly or indirectly" had no basis in the established framework of international law. It could be only explained as politically motivated.

It is easy to sympathize with Israeli suspicions of the court, given the cloud of anti-Israeli rhetoric surrounding the offence of transfer of civilian populations to occupied territory. Indeed, events subsequent to the Rome conference, including the convening of the Geneva Convention conference and the commentary by the Red Cross, have reinforced those suspicions.

The United Nations has treated Israel so badly that the confidence of Israel and its supporters in United Nations institutions has been destroyed. Israel and its supporters can legitimately ask whether the Court will launch perverted political attacks against Israel, as so many other UN institutions have done.

It is understandable that criminalizing an act of which the State of Israel has been falsely accused under international law would lead the Israeli government to suspect an attempt to lay the groundwork for politically motivated criminal charges against Israelis. Israelis have been bitten so many times by multilateral institutions, they did not want to see another one created.

The Israeli position conceded both too much and too little. The Israelis conceded too much by stating that the offence in the court must equate to the offence in the Geneva Convention. Since the United Nations had already voted the settlements to be in violation of the Geneva Convention, surely the position should be not only that the two prohibitions equate, but also that both proscribe forcible transfer only and not inducements.

They conceded too little by rejecting the phrase "directly or indirectly" as anti-Israeli. The problem is with the interpretation of that phrase by anti-Israeli states rather than with the plain meaning of those words. Indeed, to use the metaphor of Elyakim Rubinstein, it seems strange that the government of Israel would direct so much criticism to the stick and so little to those wielding the stick. What is relevant in understanding the meaning of crimes is what the words actually mean.

The forcible transfer of populations is an awful crime. That is true whether the forcible transfer is directly to occupied territories or indirectly through other territories. That sort of crime should be penalized by an international criminal court. The fact that some states are prepared to turn language on its head to accuse Israel of anything and everything should not change the reality of the criminal nature of population transfers.

If someone tries to hit you with a chair, of course, you want to fend off the attack. However, it is a mistake to blame the chair, to decide you will never sit on a chair again. Surely, the blame must be put on the attacker. The chair is wholly innocent. Refusing to sit on a chair again because of such an attack does nothing to prevent further attacks. It is just a self-inflicted harm.

The same is true of the offence of transfer of civilian populations. If states accuse Israel of violating the obligation not to transfer civilian populations, the fault lies with the states that make this frivolous accusation, not with the offence of transfer of populations. Blaming the offence or the statute of the court because it includes the offence shifts the blame from the wrongdoers to the wholly innocent. It does nothing to prevent further frivolous accusations. It weakens an institution that will benefit the global community and Israel once it gets going.

We can draw an analogy with the UN resolution that Zionism is a form of racism. There were two possible reactions to that resolution. One was that Zionism is not a form of racism. The other was that, because of the equation of Zionism with racism, anti-racism standards should be dropped from international instruments. The first possibility was obviously the more sensible reaction. Why should the position be any different for a prohibition against transfer of civilian populations to occupied territories?

The controversy about settlements in the West Bank and Gaza could end overnight, if Palestinians in those territories were just prepared to accept the notion of Jews living in their midst. The International Criminal Court is meant to be a permanent institution.

It would be naive to think that anti-Zionism and antisemitism will disappear once there is a final agreement with the Palestinian Authority, but the settlements themselves could cease to be an issue. To use the phrase of Elyakim Rubinstein, anti-Zionists may find another stick. It would have been a mistake for the Rome conference to be influenced by an ephemeral political controversy around settlements in the West Bank to exclude from a permanent institution deterrence of a great wrong.

The clause criminalizing transfer of populations to occupied territories was promoted by Arab states. However, that promotion was more hindrance than help to the insertion of the clause in the statute of the court. Israel, for one, would likely have had no objection to the anti-transfer clause and may well have had no objection to the court itself if Arab states had just kept their mouths shut about the clause both before and at the Rome conference. With friends like the Arab states, the anti-transfer clause did not need enemies.

The Rome conference should not be condemned for succumbing to Arab pressure on the anti-transfer clause. Rather, the conference should be commended for not being spooked by flimsy Arab accusations against Israel into abandoning deterrence to a great wrong.

Israel could have been legitimately concerned if the International Criminal Court statute criminalized only this violation of the laws of war, which does not amount to a grave breach of the Geneva Conventions, and no other. That would have been evidence of anti-Israeli bias in the statute. However, there are all together twenty-six different clauses penalizing violations of the laws of international armed conflict that do not amount to grave breaches of the various Geneva Conventions and a further twelve clauses penalizing violations of the laws of internal armed conflict that do not amount to serious violations of common article three of the Geneva Conventions.

The Geneva Conventions provision about transfer of civilian populations to occupied territory is a legacy of the Holocaust. It is to the credit of the Rome conference that it kept its hold firmly on this legacy in the face of Arab distraction and that it did not fumble this legacy away.

Let us suppose the Rome conference provided for no penalty for the transfer of civilians to occupied territories. Let us suppose further that, long after the West Bank settlements cease to be an issue in the Middle East, there are real transfers of civilians to occupied territories. The diplomats at Rome would then have that war crime on their consciences. They could be blamed for allowing it to happen, by doing nothing to prevent it. The conference acted responsibly, by seeing through the flim-flammery of Arab accusations against Israel and basing its decision on what was truly at stake.

Lawmakers should not drop offences from criminal law statutes solely because there are false accusations of the commission of these offences. For instance, there have been false accusations of child sexual abuse based on claimed recovered memory. The offences of incest or child sexual abuse should not be dropped from the Canadian Criminal Code because of these false accusations. The Rome conference behaved correctly by paying scant attention to the argument that the offence of transfer of civilian populations to occupied territory be dropped from the statute of the International Criminal Court because of false accusations against Israel.

The International Criminal Court is an institution in the making. The Protocol on International Armed Conflict is the here and now. The International Criminal Court, once established, will have a power, but not a duty, to prosecute. States parties to the Protocol on International Armed Conflict have a duty to prosecute, if they do not extradite.

A person who accepts that there is no substantial difference between the Geneva Convention, the protocol, and the statute of the court and who argues against Israeli ratification of the statute because of the inclusion of the offence of transfer of civilian populations to occupied territories would also have to argue for renunciation of the Protocol on International Armed Conflict and repeal of its legislation by every country that has adopted the protocol. Yet such an effort would be pointless in protecting Israel and harmful generally to international peace and security.

All the same, caution is wisdom. Both the International Court of Justice and the International Criminal Court are in The Hague, Netherlands. The International Court of Justice advisory opinion on the security barrier showed that The Hague's air is poisoned with anti-Zionism. The International Criminal Court will be breathing the same air.

Absent a referral by the Security Council, the court has jurisdiction over only nationals of states parties and crimes committed on the territory of states parties.[122] The International Criminal Court will have no jurisdiction over Israelis in Israel, the West Bank, and Gaza as long as Israel refrains from joining the Court. Given the contamination of the legal environment of The Hague on issues relating to Israel, an Israeli reluctance to adhere to the statute is understandable.

Mrs. Teasdale: "Your excellency, I thought you left."
Chicolini: "Oh no. I no leave."
Mrs. Teasdale: "But I saw you with my own eyes."
Chicolini: "Well, who are you going to believe, me or your own eyes?"[123]

EVERY time a court gives judgment, justice itself is on trial. The court judges the parties, and the public judges the court.

The General Assembly of the United Nations in December 2003 asked the International Court of Justice for an advisory opinion on the legal consequences of the fence being built along the length of the West Bank to protect Israel from the infiltration of suicide bombers. That request was the most formidable challenge to the international justice system the world has seen.

The wording of the question asked by the General Assembly was this:

> What are the legal consequences arising from the construction of the wall being built by Israel, the occupying Power, in the Occupied Palestinian Territory, including in and around East Jerusalem, as described in the report of the Secretary-General, considering the rules and principles of international law, including the Fourth Geneva Convention of 1949, and relevant Security Council and General Assembly resolutions?

The General Assembly made that request by resolution dated December 8, 2003, with ninety votes in favour — less than half of the membership of the United Nations. There were eight votes against, nineteen states not voting, and an amazing seventy-four abstentions. On balance, 101 states did not support the request for an advisory opinion, far more than did.

The breakdown between democratic and non-democratic states is even more stark. The request was supported mainly by non-democratic states; democratic states were overwhelmingly opposed.

The court replied on July 9, 2004, by agreeing to answer the request. By doing this, the court failed the test of justice in spectacular fashion.

The answer the court gave was that "the construction of the wall" is "contrary to international law." The court added that Israel is under an obligation to dismantle that part of the structure located in the territories that Jordan used to control before 1967, which the court labels Palestinian occupied territory.

The United Nations General Assembly's request for an advisory opinion, though in form a request for a legal opinion, in reality raised the question of whether the World Court would become corrupted by the anti-Zionist lobby, whether the anti-Zionist cancer would spread to this United Nations organ. The answer, regrettably, is that anti-Zionism has metastasized to the court.

In principle, the court did not have to answer the question asked. Canada, though abstaining on the resolution vote in the General Assembly requesting the opinion, filed a brief with the court stating that the legal issues surrounding the fence "would be more effectively addressed in a broader negotiation context rather than within the procedural limitations of a judicial hearing." Thirty-two other countries took a similar position.

But the court demurred. A majority of the court first decided to answer the question and then embraced the United Nations General Assembly anti-Zionist agenda with gusto.

As the Israeli Supreme Court itself has noted, there are legitimate criticisms that could be made of the route of the fence, where the disruption to the lives of the people affected by the chosen route outweighs the security value.[124] The Israeli Supreme Court was the appropriate venue to question the route of the fence, and the judgment was reasoned. But the advisory opinion of the International Court of Justice was a different matter.

There have been no requests for advisory opinions on the legality of the anti-Israel behaviour of Arab states, the Palestinian Authority, or the various anti-Zionist terrorist groups against Israel, nor are there likely to be. Israel is one of several countries with security fences traversing contested territory. India has a fence through Kashmiri territory claimed by Pakistan; Saudi Arabia has a fence through territory claimed by Yemen; Turkey has a fence through territory claimed by Syria.[125] There have been no requests for advisory opinions on the legality of these other security fences, nor are there likely to be.

The image of justice is a blindfolded woman holding scales. In the case of Israel, the General Assembly and the court peeked, saw Israel, and put their thumbs on the scale.

The advisory opinion is a shoddy piece of legal workmanship. It denies the right of self-defence against terrorism. It makes assumptions of fact against Israel about Israeli de facto annexation of parts of the West Bank, without making findings of fact.

It is self-contradictory, treating the West Bank and Gaza sometimes as having international status and sometimes not, depending on whether it suits the ultimate outcome against Israel the judges want. For the purpose of denying Israel the right of self-defence, the court asserts that the West Bank and Gaza have no international status.[126] For the purpose of asserting that the West Bank and Gaza are occupied, the court asserts the international status of these territories.

As noted in the earlier chapter on settlements, the court equates freedom with tyranny by equating the exercise of the right to freedom of movement of the settlers with forcible transfer of the settlers. As noted in the earlier chapter on occupation, though it calls the West Bank Palestinian occupied territory, the court's application of the label "occupied territory" to the West Bank depends on its having determined the West Bank to be Jordanian occupied territory.

The opinion of the court is a complete legal washout; it does not deserve to be taken seriously. It is already being used as fodder for anti-Israel propaganda, but that is all that it is good for.

The judgment is such a mess that any lawyer familiar with international law would have to wonder how a group of judges could have been so far off the mark. For all but one of the judges, the explanation is political.

The question as posed by the General Assembly was hardly neutral. It adopted terminology that Israel rejects. It calls a fence a "wall," though the barrier when complete will be a fence for more than 97 percent of its length and a wall for less than 3 percent.[127] It refers to Israel as "the occupying Power." It refers to the West Bank as "occupied Palestinian territory." It defines this territory to include East Jerusalem.

The notion that the fence is a wall is a contested issue of fact. The notion that Israel is an occupying power, that the West Bank is Palestinian occupied territory, and that this territory, insofar as it exists, includes East Jerusalem, are all contested issues of international law.

This was not a request for an opinion. It was a statement of an already formed political opinion with a request for endorsement of that opinion. This is an abuse of the power to request an opinion and a bad faith exercise.

Questions posed to the World Court that attempt to answer questions of international law are not truly requests for advisory legal opinions but just statements of political opinion for which the General Assembly is seeking outside support. However, the court does not exist to put a legal rubber stamp on political opinions of the General Assembly. The court undermines its own existence by consenting to being used for that purpose.

The power of the World Court to give an advisory opinion is derived from the Charter of the United Nations[128] and from the Statute of the International Criminal Court.[129] Both instruments require that the question forming the subject matter of the request should be a legal question. Yet the question submitted by the General Assembly was a political question. The court, accordingly, was not empowered to answer it.

Superficially, the question looks legal. In form it asked, "What are the legal consequences arising from a certain state of events, considering the rules and principles of international law?" However, when one looks at the description of the events about which a legal opinion was asked, it is apparent that something else was going on here.

Judge Koojmans wrote, "The request is phrased in a way which can be called odd to put it mildly."[130] He nonetheless sided with the majority in favour of answering the question. He reasoned that, although the question was political and so a decision to answer to the question would also be political, so would a decision not to answer the question. The fault for the politicization of the court, so his reasoning went, lay with the General Assembly for asking the question rather than with the court for answering it.[131]

The logic is that of a rape victim who reasons that she might as well enjoy the experience and cooperate with her rapist, since she is going to be raped anyways. The most effective way to say no to politicization is to refuse to go along. By going along, the court obscured whatever objection it might have had to its abuse.

The World Court is an organ of the United Nations, and there is no doubt what opinion the General Assembly wanted the court to give. The General Assembly resolution requesting the advisory opinion was an anti-Israel diatribe. The resolution did not ask the court to determine whether or not Israel was in violation of international law. In substance, the question the General Assembly posed was, "What are the legal consequences of Israel's blatant violations of international law?" Given the tendentious nature of the question, for the court to have held Israel in compliance with international law would have meant thumbing their noses at the General Assembly.

Judges of the World Court are elected by the General Assembly, that is to say, by the very body posing the question. Members are elected for nine years and may be re-elected. This system creates a bias. For the judges to have held that the Israel security fence conformed to international law would have been rejecting the firmly held views of those who had put them on the court and who would be deciding whether or not they stay on the court.

The General Assembly elects judges from candidates nominated from regional groupings. All the judges in the court but one were nominated from states or regions that had already declared that the fence was illegal. Even the European Union, long before the advisory opinion, had expressed the view that the fence violated international law. For many of the judges, a pro-Israel opinion would have been a career-ending move.

For one judge, the bias was not just institutional; it was explicit. Shortly before he was appointed to the court, Judge Elaraby of Egypt had expressed his personal view in a newspaper interview that the presence of Israel in the West Bank and Gaza was an occupation in violation of international law. He further decried what he called Israel's policy of "establishing new facts," a criticism that was subsequently levied against the fence. Israel asked the court to remove the judge from the case, but the court, with only one dissenting vote, refused.[132]

Judge Buergenthal, the American, was the only judge in the court expressing an independent view, one not tainted by a prior expression of legal opinion by those who would decide on the judge's future legal career. The American government, to my knowledge, has not expressed an opinion on the legality of the fence. Buergenthal dissented, reasoning that the court should have declined to answer the request for the advisory opinion on the basis that the court did not have before it the requisite information and evidence to answer the question.

But even the judgment of Buergenthal was not all that it should have been. He made some gratuitous legal comments about the illegality of Jews living in the West Bank and Gaza that are surprising and unfounded.

The problem with the Buergenthal opinion, though it is untainted by the bias from which every other opinion suffers, is that it is undermined by the failure to respect the rule that both sides must be heard. Buergenthal himself, when criticizing the opinions of his colleagues, took note of the fact that Israel had not participated fully in the advisory court proceedings.

Given the stacking of the court against Israel, Israel's less than full participation in the proceedings was wise. Israeli participation would have given a veneer of legitimacy to a kangaroo court. But the absence of that full participation meant that none of the judges, including Buergenthal, had a fully argued case before him. In that situation, though the comments by Buergenthal against Israel were a good deal fewer and farther between than the adverse comments of the other judges, even his comments should not be given legal weight.

Superficially, it would seem that the General Assembly can ask an advisory opinion about absolutely anything. The Charter of the United Nations has conferred on the General Assembly a competence relating to any question or matter within the scope of the Charter.[133] The Charter further gives the General Assembly a competence to consider the general principles in the maintenance of international peace and security.[134] The Charter also provides that the General Assembly shall initiate studies and make recommendations for the purpose of encouraging the progressive development of international law and its codification.[135]

Nonetheless, this general power is constrained by the obligation to avoid circumventing the powers given exclusively to the Security Council and denied to the General Assembly. In particular, the Security Council has exclusive powers to decide what measures are to be employed to maintain or restore international peace and security.[136]

The General Assembly cannot, either on its own or in combination with the World Court, decide what measures are to be employed to maintain or restore international peace and security. Any attempt to do so would be a perversion of the United Nations system. Yet that is exactly what this advisory opinion sought to do: to circumvent the exclusive powers to decide what measures are to be employed to maintain or restore international peace and security in the Middle East.

One can see that the answer that the court gave is a determination very much like what the Security Council might make under its powers to maintain or restore international peace and security. It is an answer only the Security Council could give. It corrupts and defies the UN system for the World Court to be able to say, on the request of the General Assembly alone, that states are under an obligation to do anything on matters of peace and security, without any involvement whatsoever of the Security Council.

The question asked by the General Assembly should have been answered, but only in a procedural way. The procedural legal consequence arising from the construction of the wall/fence and the General Assembly request is that the substantive legal consequences must be decided by the Security Council. The court should have said only that it could provide to the Security Council substantive advice on legal consequences if requested to do so.

The UN Charter provides that any question relating to the maintenance of international peace and security on which action is necessary shall be referred by the General Assembly to the Security Council.[137] The request to the World Court for an advisory opinion is a form of action. But in this case, the General Assembly did not refer the request for an advisory opinion to the Security Council, and so the request was invalid.

In the *South West Africa* case, though a request for an advisory opinion was made by the General Assembly, it was a request for an opinion on the legal consequences of a Security Council resolution. That resolution had determined the continued presence of South Africa in Namibia to be illegal. The resolution was passed consequent on a referral by the General Assembly.[138] The General Assembly made that referral because it lacked the necessary powers to ensure the withdrawal of South Africa from Namibia.

In the Israeli fence/wall case, there was no comparable Security Council resolution. The only Security Council resolution passed subsequent to the commencement of the construction of the fence/wall to which the General Assembly request resolution referred was a resolution that simply endorsed the road map and called on all parties to fulfil their obligations under it.[139] There was no mention of the fence/wall. In that earlier resolution the West Bank was not called Palestinian occupied territory; Israel was not called an occupying power. There was, unlike in the *South West Africa* case, no obvious connection between what the General Assembly did through its advisory opinion request resolution and what the Security Council had done.

In the *South West Africa* case, the World Court reasoned that the precise determination of acts permitted and forbidden by member states consequent on the illegality of South Africa's continued presence in Namibia was a matter that lies within the competence of the appropriate organs of the United Nations acting within their authority under the Charter. That is easy enough to say when both the General Assembly and the Security Council had wanted South Africa to withdraw from Namibia. Each had made the necessary political decision. All that was left was enforcement.

For the security barrier, there was no comparable decision by the Security Council. There is little doubt that enforcement of a decision of the World Court on matters of international peace and security rests with the Security Council. But when the Security Council has not asked the question, has no apparent interest in the answer, and has made no prior determination of illegality or opposition, any determination by the World Court becomes more than just empty air. It is an affront to the Security Council and its exclusive powers over matters of international peace and security.

The World Court in its reasons acknowledged the structure of the United Nations, the limited role of the General Assembly, and the exclusive responsibility of the Security Council in dealing with peace and security. The court nonetheless noted an exception carved out during the Korean War. When North Korea invaded South Korea, the Security Council authorized UN intervention on the side of South Korea at a time when the Soviet Union had walked out and was not voting. But the Soviet Union returned and began, through its veto, to hamper UN conduct of the war. So the Security Council passed a procedural resolution[140] allowing the General Assembly to trench on matters of international peace and security provided only two conditions were met. One was that there was a persistent veto stymieing the Security Council. The second was that there was a threat to peace and security relevant to the issue being considered.

The trouble is that in this case, there was neither. The Security Council had never been presented with a resolution asking for an advisory opinion from the World Court on the fence. So no such resolution was vetoed. Nor, objectively speaking, is the fence a threat to peace and security. The threat to peace and security comes from suicide bombers who precipitated the building of the fence. In any case, the court never determined that the fence created a threat to peace and security. The court relied on only a General Assembly resolution that the fence was a threat to peace and security.[141] In other words, a contested legal dispute was resolved by reference only to a political vote. Because Israel was on the losing side of a vote, because Israel is politically unpopular, it is legally wrong. It is hard to imagine any court being more blatantly political than that.

The permissive character of the Statute of the International Court of Justice on advisory opinions[142] gives the court the power to examine whether the circumstances of the case are of a character that should lead it to decline to answer the request for an advisory opinion. Even if the question asked is a legal one that the court is competent to answer, it may nonetheless decline to do so.

In this case, the arguments just given about the constraints on the power of the General Assembly to request the advisory opinion, even once rejected on legal grounds, should have provided compelling reasons why the question should not have been answered on discretionary grounds. There were other compelling arguments as well.

The Charter of the United Nations calls on all states to pursue in good faith the peaceful settlement of disputes. The dispute between Israel and her neighbours, including the Palestinian Authority, about which the question asked by the General Assembly forms part, is best resolved by negotiations. Legal wrangling over rights and wrongs in the World Court does nothing to move the parties towards negotiations. By casting the issues as matters of right and wrong, each side became entrenched in its own position. Attitudes became hardened. The litigation moved the parties away from a negotiated settlement to their disputes.

The Palestinian Authority is not a state party to the statute of the World Court. Israel, which is a state party by virtue of being a member of the United Nations, opposed the request for an advisory opinion. Israel has not accepted the compulsory jurisdiction of the court. The question asks the court to give an opinion on a matter in dispute between the Palestinian Authority and Israel, which legally could not be brought before the court under its compulsory jurisdiction.

In 1923, in the *Eastern Carelia* case, the Permanent Court of International Justice declined to render an advisory opinion requested by the League of Nations. The request concerned a dispute between Finland and Russia, and Russia was not a member of the League of Nations. The court applied the principle that no state can, without its consent, be compelled to submit its disputes with other states to any kind of judgment or opinion by the court.

In the 1950 advisory opinion *Interpretation of Peace Treaties with Bulgaria, Hungary and Romania*, the World Court agreed to comply with the request of the General Assembly for an advisory opinion despite the opposition of all three concerned states — Bulgaria, Hungary, and Romania. In doing so, the court noted that it was considering only the applicability of a procedure for the settlement of disputes and was not pronouncing on the merits of these disputes. The implication of that reasoning is that the court in that case may well have refused to answer the request for an advisory opinion if it had been asked to pronounce on the merits of a dispute amongst the states concerned.

But here there was no doubt that the court was asked to pronounce on the merits of a dispute between Israel, the Palestinian Authority, and other states. The reasoning in the 1950 opinion militated against answering the question in this case.

The World Court in the *Western Sahara* case of 1975 also agreed to comply with a request of the General Assembly for an advisory opinion, this time on the legal status of the Western Sahara, despite the objections of Spain. At the time there was a dispute between Spain and Morocco on the attribution of territorial sovereignty of that territory.

The court, in agreeing to comply with the request, observed that the purpose of the reference was to assist the General Assembly in its own functions of decolonization and not to bring before the court a dispute between states, and that the legal position of Spain could not be compromised by the court's answer to the questions submitted. The court in that case, it is apparent, would have declined to answer the question asked if the answer could have compromised the legal position of Spain.

That was certainly not true with the Israel fence/wall reference. The legal position of Israel was compromised by the answer the court gave to the question submitted. So the question should not have been answered.

As set out in an earlier chapter, one of the many anti-Zionist slurs against Israel is that Israel is, like South Africa before it, an apartheid state. Anti-Zionists have attempted to mimic the anti-apartheid campaign in a variety of ways. It is no coincidence that the request for an advisory opinion copied so closely a question directed against apartheid South Africa in the *South West Africa* case.

At the time the *South West Africa* advisory opinion request was before the World Court, South Africa argued that the court should decline to answer the request for an advisory opinion on the basis that the question was contentious, relating to an existing dispute between South Africa and other states. The court held that the fact that, in order to give its answer, the court might have to pronounce on legal questions upon which divergent views existed between South Africa and other states did not convert the case into a dispute between states.

The Palestinian Authority is not a state, but for the purposes of the advisory opinion it was treated like one. The World Court, by order dated December 19, 2003, allowed the Palestinian Authority to both submit a written statement and take part in the oral hearing on the same terms as states. No entity representing Namibia participated in the *South West Africa* case. It would have been inconsistent with the order the court had already made to allow the Palestinian Authority to submit both written and oral pleadings, as well as completely out of touch with reality for the court to agree to answer the question asked on the basis that the dispute that Israel has with the Palestinian Authority over the legality of the fence is merely an abstract question of international law on which there are divergent views amongst states, and in fact, the court rejected this basis for assumption of jurisdiction.[143]

As well, in the *South West Africa* case, the formal dispute was between the United Nations and South Africa, not amongst states. The League of Nations had mandated South Africa to administer South West Africa. The United Nations General Assembly terminated this mandate. The Security Council adopted resolutions declaring the continued presence of South Africa in Namibia illegal. The court was asked to determine the legal consequences of the termination of the mandate. In the course of answering the question, the court held that the United Nations was the successor to the League of Nations for the purpose of the mandate.

In the Israeli fence/wall case, unlike the *South West Africa* case, the dispute rests amongst member states and the Palestinian Authority, not between a United Nations organ and the State of Israel. It may well be that the court can and should give advisory opinions in the context of legal disputes between states and the United Nations. However, that does mean that the court either can or should give advisory opinions on disputes amongst states or between a state and a non-state entity.

In this case, as well, unlike the *South West Africa* case, there is no referral of the underlying issue by the General Assembly to the Security Council. There is no Security Council endorsement of an underlying position of the General Assembly. It may well be that the court can and should give an advisory opinion on a matter of international peace and security on the request of the General Assembly where the Security Council approves of the request or approves of the underlying political position on which the request is based. But the matter is different where the Security Council says nothing either on the request or the underlying political position on which the request is based.

One has to keep in mind the large number of anti-Israel resolutions at the General Assembly. This reference is just one question. But now that the court has accepted jurisdiction, there is every possibility that it will at some point be over-whelmed, as other organs of the United Nations have been, by the anti-Zionist lobby.

The fence/wall is just one of a wide variety of defensive tactics Israel has used to try to combat terrorism, and one of the most anodyne. In the construction of the fence, as far as I am aware, no one has died, and no one was injured.

Virtually all of Israeli's means of self-defence have been condemned by anti-Zionists as violations of international law. Now that the court has agreed to answer this advisory question, the court can expect, seriatim, one Israeli defensive tactic after another brought before them for a determination of its "legal consequences."

The United Nations has lost credibility because it has allowed itself to be hijacked by anti-Zionist states. The World Court's acceptance of jurisdiction in this case is a signal that the defences of the court are down, that it is susceptible also to an anti-Zionist hijacking.

The risks to the court, though, go far beyond that. If the court is prepared to answer a question on the rights and wrongs of armed conflict posed by only the side in that conflict that has the most votes at the General Assembly, there are potentially many more such questions that can be asked. The court could end up being dragged into many armed conflicts, not in a neutral way, not in a way to help resolve the conflict, but, as here, by being asked to answer a biased, one-sided question, asked to condemn the behaviour of one side.

The World Court should do everything possible to avoid being caught up in anti-Zionist institutional abuse of UN organs. Answering the substantive international law questions in the way the Israel proposed would have been one way of doing that. But a simpler and more direct way would have been simply to refuse to allow the processes of the court to be abused by those with illegitimate ends.

It is in the very nature of any political dispute that one side is more popular than the other. There is no doubt that right now at the United Nations the Palestinian cause can muster many votes, and the Israeli cause can muster only a few. It is apparent from the way the question was asked that the anti-Israel United Nations majority wanted the court on its side. But the political unpopularity of Israel was no reason for court involvement in the disputes Israel has with the Palestinian Authority or with neighbouring states. Once the World Court agreed to answer the question asked and stuck its head into a political dispute, it undermined both the court itself and the cause of international justice.

There are all sorts of legal questions that the General Assembly could have asked the World Court about the behaviour of anti-Zionist states and the Palestinian Authority. The General Assembly could have asked:

> What are the legal consequences of the failure of states and the Palestinian Authority to:
>
> **a)** prevent the activities of suicide bombers directed against Israel;
> **b)** prohibit the incitement to hatred against the Jewish people and war propaganda against Israel;
> **c)** repress and eliminate terrorism in all its forms and manifestations against Israel;
> **d)** ban and seize the funding of anti-Zionist terrorist organizations including but not limited to Hamas, Al Aqsa Martyr's Brigade, the Palestinian Popular Liberation Front, and Hezbollah?

But these questions were not asked. The armed conflict in the Middle East raises many questions about compliance with international law. The side that has the greater number of votes in the General Assembly, the politically more popular side, got to ask the court in its questions in the most tendentious way imaginable; the side with fewer votes was not able to ask the court its questions.

In the end, the World Court had the option of holding only one side at fault or blameless. But, because it was never asked, it did not have the option of holding the other side at fault. The court was able to spell out its views on the legal consequences of the violations of international law by one side, but it could not spell out the legal consequences of the violations of international law by the other side.

This form of questioning was inherently imbalanced. The problem was not just the answers that were given. It was the very asking of the question.

The General Assembly, as is apparent, has no built-in restraints. It is a tyranny of a majority. The only restraint is the World Court itself.

The court should have declined to answer a question posed in the context of armed conflict which raises the culpability of only one side in that conflict. Otherwise the court ends up taking sides in the conflict, which it has so obviously done here.

Peace is, of necessity, a reciprocal affair. It is impossible to have peace if only one side wants peace, if only one side is prepared to lay down its arms and accept a settlement. For the General Assembly to ask and the court to answer questions about the culpability of only one side in the Middle East conflict ignores the need for reciprocity for peace to occur.

Setting out the legal obligations of one side of an armed conflict decontextualizes the acts of the side under legal scrutiny from the armed conflict of which the acts form part. This is standard anti-Zionist fodder, treating the Israeli acts in isolation from their context, so that they are made to seem like gratuitous acts of cruelty rather than a measured response to the worst sort of violence.

Although setting out legal obligations of both sides is not necessarily the best way to achieve peace, at least it is a possible contribution to peace. It may make sense to hold that legally each side should engage in certain behaviour. Resolutions of the Security Council, or of the General Assembly before the automatic anti-Zionist majority seized control of it, have called on Israel to engage in certain acts provided Palestinians and states are willing to live at peace with Israel. But it makes no sense even to consider what one side should do in isolation, without considering any legal constraints on the other side.

The question, in the form that it was asked, was a provocation and an insult, not just to Israel, but to justice, to peace, to the Security Council and the Court. The Court should not have swallowed this insult whole and demeaned both itself and the cause of justice by agreeing to answer it.

Israel can survive yet another piece of anti-Zionist propaganda labelling its every effort of self-defence a crime against humanity. What is less certain is whether the cause of international justice and the World Court itself can survive its politicization.

Once the court has become so obviously political, which states, except the politically popular, would want to submit to its judgments? Now that the court has been stripped bare of any pretense of impartiality, how can we ever think of it as clothed in the robes of justice? Now that the court has been shown to be eager to abandon reason for politics, which of its past judgments can be taken seriously?

For Canada, for Israel, for the majority of the countries of the world, the World Court gave advice it was not asked to give, and like all unwanted advice, it should just be disregarded. For the sake of peace, the advisory opinion should be ignored. But for the sake of justice, it should be mourned.

CHAPTER SEVEN
The Claimed Palestinian Right of Return

THE claimed Palestinian right of return is not a right, since it is recognized in neither Israeli law nor international law.[144] Nor is it about return, since it is applied to millions of people who have never set foot in Israel.

There are 6.5 million Palestinians around the world who trace their descent from the 1.4 million Arabs who lived in Palestine before 1948 and who identify themselves as Palestinians. Potentially all of these 6.5 million people would benefit from the asserted right of return.

As of December 30, 1999, according to Israel's Central Bureau of Statistics, the population of Israel was 6.2 million people, of which 4.9 million were Jews. To introduce into that population a potential 6.5 million non-Jewish Palestinians would mean that the Jewish character of the State of Israel would end, the preservation of the cultural identity of the Jewish people would be threatened, and the right to self-determination of the Jewish people would be defeated.

International human rights law allows for restriction on freedom of movement in order to preserve the cultural identity of a people.[145] If for no other reason, Israel is justified in preventing the entry of 6.5 million non-Jewish Palestinians into Israel.

A policy of entry into the Jewish state of Israel of 6.5 million Palestinian Arab Muslims, coupled with denial of the right of Jewish refugees around the world to seek protection from persecution in Israel, should be seen for what it is, a naked attempt to end the right to self-determination of the Jewish people. The massive influx of a population that shares neither the language nor the culture and religion of the Jewish people would mean the end of that state as a state for the Jewish people.

When the Nazis propagandized against the Jews, they did not advocate gas chambers and roving death squads. Instead, they argued, euphemistically, for a final solution to the Jewish problem. There was no Jewish problem, only a problem of antisemitism. The Nazis created the problem of antisemitism, not the Jews. Nazis fabricated a problem for which they blamed the Jews, and then proceeded to kill the Jews to "solve" their manufactured problem.

Today, we can see through the euphemism of the final solution. The euphemism itself has become discredited. After 6 million deaths, we are now able to pierce through its obfuscation to see what lies beneath. No member state of the United Nations today calls for a final solution to the Jewish problem.

Something similar has happened to the phrase "Zionism is a form of racism." It became apparent over time that the phrase was nothing more than an anti-Israel and anti-Jewish ploy. Labelling Zionism as racism, though not dropped, has lost favour with antisemites and the enemies of Israel. Instead, new euphemisms are used, asserting the right of return of the Palestinian people and labelling as racist the Israeli Law of Return.

There may be some who assert the right of return for Palestinians without any awareness of the impact it would have on the Jewish people. Others are aware but either do not care or, worse, support that impact. For those in support, "the right to return of the Palestinian people" is today what "the final solution to the Jewish problem" was in the days of Hitler — a mask of words obfuscating the end result: destruction of the Jewish people.

In support of the claimed Palestinian right of return, it is sometimes argued that every person has a right of entry to his own country. The argument goes on to say that because Israel is the country of the Palestinians, Palestinians have a right of entry to Israel.

It is true that the Universal Declaration of Human Rights asserts a right of return. However, the treaty that followed up this provision, the International Covenant on Civil and Political Rights, does not. The closest is the right of entry. The Universal Declaration of Human Rights provides, in article 13(2), that everyone has the right "to return to his country." The International Covenant on Civil and Political Rights provides, in Article 12(4), "No one shall be arbitrarily deprived of the right to enter his own country."

The General Comments on Freedom of Movement of the Human Rights Committee, established under the International Covenant on Civil and Political Rights, state as a general principle that a country is a person's own country where the person, because of his or her special ties to or claims in relation to a given country, cannot be considered to be a mere alien.[146] The Committee gives three examples. Of the three, the first two are presented with a good deal more certainty than the third. The comment says of the first two examples that "this would be the case, for example, ..." For the third example, the Committee says only that the language of the Covenant "permits a broader interpretation that might embrace other categories of long-term residents, including but not limited to ..."

The three examples are these:

a) The person has been stripped of his or her nationality in violation of international law.

b) The country of nationality has been incorporated in or transferred to another national entity, whose nationality is being denied them.

c) The person is stateless, a permanent resident of the country, and arbitrarily deprived of the right to acquire the nationality of that country.

Neither the examples nor the general principle apply to Israel. Israel has not stripped Palestinians of their nationality in violation of international law. The country of nationality of the Palestinians has not been incorporated in or transferred to Israel. Stateless Palestinians are not permanent residents of Israel who have been arbitrarily deprived of the right to acquire the nationality of Israel.

More generally, Israel is not the country of stateless Palestinian refugees. These refugees do not have special ties to or claims in relation to Israel that make them more than mere Israeli aliens.

In support of the claimed right of return, it is said that Palestinians have been stripped of their nationality in Israel in violation of international law. However, Palestinians who claim a right of return to Israel never had nationality in Israel to be stripped of. There are alive today some Palestinians who had the nationality of British-mandate Palestine. However, British-mandate Palestine no longer exists.

Alternatively, supporters of the claimed right of return argue that the country of nationality of Palestinians, British-mandate Palestine, has been transferred to Israel, whose nationality is being denied them. In reality, according to United Nations General Assembly resolution of November 29, 1947,[147] there were to be two states created out of British-mandate Palestine, not one. The details of the plan of partition were superseded by United Nations Security Council Resolutions 242 and 338 of 1967 and 1973. However, the principle that there would be two states in the land of Palestine, one Jewish and one Arab, was not.

The suspended animation of the future Arab state on the territory of British-mandate Palestine has prevented the application of the principles of state succession. The Arab state, once created, may and certainly should allow Palestinian refugees to acquire the nationality of that state.

The Draft Articles on Nationality of Natural Persons in Relation to the Succession of States, adopted by the International Law Commission in July 1999, deal with the situation where a state ceases to exist and the various parts of the territory of the predecessor state form two or more successor states. One article attributes nationality based on habitual residence.[148] Another article grants a right of option.[149]

The trouble with using these provisions is that, even though the predecessor state, British-mandate Palestine, has dissolved and ceased to exist, there are not now two successor states on the territory of the old Palestine. It is impossible for the International Law Commission Draft Articles on Nationality of Natural Persons in Relation to the Succession of States to operate according to their terms until the Arab state is created, its law of nationality is legislated, the choice between the Arab and Jewish state is put to those Palestinian refugees who have the choice, and the option is exercised. Some of those Palestinians who, before its creation, left the territory of what has now become Israel may have left because they wanted to live in an Arab Palestinian state rather than in a Jewish state.

Today, presumably some of the Palestinian refugees would prefer to live in an Arab Palestinian state and not a Jewish state.

As explained later, it is not altogether apparent that the principles set out in the International Law Commission Draft Articles on Nationality of Natural Persons in Relation to the Succession of States should apply to British-mandate Palestine. However, even if these principles are applied, the delayed creation of an Arab state in British-mandate Palestine cannot create a right to nationality in the Jewish state. If the Arab state, once created, would be the country of Palestinian refugees, the delay in its creation cannot now make Israel their country.

Supporters of the claimed right of return say that Palestinians are stateless; they or their ancestors were permanent residents in what is now Israel, and they have been arbitrarily deprived of the right to acquire Israeli nationality. The answer to this is that Palestinians are not now permanent residents of Israel. Most of them have never been permanent residents of territory that is in Israel. They have not been arbitrarily deprived of the right to acquire Israeli nationality.

Israel has signed the Convention on the Reduction of Statelessness but has not yet ratified it. The Vienna Convention on the Law of Treaties provides that a state is obliged to refrain from acts that would defeat the object and purpose of a treaty when it has signed the treaty subject to ratification unless and until it has made its intention clear not to become a party to the treaty.[150]

The denial of Israeli citizenship to stateless Palestinian refugees would not defeat the object and purpose of the Convention. Palestinian refugees never had the citizenship of Israel. So the provisions of the Convention obligating states not to deprive certain persons of nationality do not apply to Israel and the Palestinian refugees.

There is nothing in the Convention on the Reduction of Statelessness dealing with the dissolution of a predecessor state and its succession by two new states. The general rule in the Convention is that a contracting state shall grant its nationality to a person born in its territory who would otherwise be stateless.[151] By now, many of the Palestinian refugees have been born outside Israel; this general rule would not apply to these Palestinians.

Even for those born before the creation of Israel in the territory of what later became Israel, the problem caused by the delay in creation of the Arab state arises. When that Arab state is created, would Palestinian refugees "otherwise be stateless"? In principle, they should not be, because the new Palestinian state should give all Palestinian refugees an option of acquiring nationality in that state. Insofar as statelessness has resulted from the failure of the Arab state to come into existence, the remedy for that statelessness must be the creation of the Arab state and not the creation of nationality in the state of Israel.

Another tack that defenders of the claimed Palestinian right of return take is this: a country with which a person has genuine and effective links is the person's own country. Israel is the country of the Palestinians because that is the country with which Palestinians have genuine and effective links: their ancestors came from there; they are attached to the territory; and that attachment is inculcated in their children.

The answer to that argument is that there are people who have links with countries of which they are not nationals that are far stronger than the Palestinian refugees' links with Israel. Anyone who accepts the principle that a country with which a person has genuine and effective links is the person's own country must apply that principle first to these other people.

The notion that a country is the person's own country because the person has genuine and effective links with that country most commonly arises when a Western country attempts to deport a Third World national who has lived in the West for many years, without having national status in the West. It is common for a deportee from a Western country to argue that, at international law, the deportation is illegal, even though the deportee is not a national of the country from which the person is being deported, because the country is his or her own country due to his or her genuine and effective links with it.

These deportees may have been born in the country and spent their whole lives there. They may know the language of the country and not that of the country of their nationality. They may be acculturated to the country of deportation and alienated from their country of nationality. All their immediate family may be resident and even nationals in the country of deportation. It is impossible to call for recognition of a right of return of Palestinians because of genuine and effective links of Palestinians to Israeli territory without first calling for an end to Western deportations of Third World immigrants and visitors.

Even if you accept that many non-nationals ordered deported have a right to remain in the country trying to deport them, it does not necessarily follow that Palestinian refugees have a right of entry to Israel. The ties of Palestinian refugees to Israel are more akin to those of emigrants to their country of emigration than to those of deportees to the country that wants to deport them.

Accepting in a general sort of way the right of entry asserted for Palestinian refugees would mean unscrambling history. The consequence would be that descendants of émigrés would have a right of entry to their ancestral countries.

A right of return based on genuine and effective links would apply to virtually everyone in the Americas. Except for its aboriginal population, everyone in the Americas has an ancestor born abroad. Many people in the Americas show an attachment to the country of their ancestors and inculcate that attachment in their children. There are as well many millions of people who fit this description in the rest of the world. It would create havoc to grant all those people a right of return to the country of their ancestors.

The non-governmental organizations Human Rights Watch and Amnesty International have both endorsed the claimed right of return of Palestinians to

Israel.[152] In doing so, they have abandoned their human rights mandates and called for a human rights violation. The organizations have been led astray, in part, by a misreading of the *Nottebohm* case in the International Court of Justice.[153]

Friedrich Nottebohm was a German national carrying on business in Guatemala from 1905. He took out Liechtenstein nationality in 1939, after the beginning of the Second World War. Guatemala was at war with Germany, but not with Liechtenstein. In 1943, Guatemala, as a result of war measures, removed Nottebohm and refused to readmit him.

Liechtenstein claimed before the World Court that Guatemala had acted towards Nottebohm in a manner contrary to international law. The court ruled that, if a person has only one nationality, then other countries must recognize that nationality. If a person has two nationalities, then the nationality of one of the states can be invoked against a third state only when that nationality corresponds with a factual situation. The ties of Nottebohm to Liechtenstein were so tenuous that Liechtenstein was not entitled to invoke Nottebohm's nationality against Guatemala.

In order to determine whether ties are tenuous or whether there are genuine and effective links with a country, the court proposed specific criteria: habitual residence of the individual concerned, the centre of his interests, his family ties, his participation in public life, attachment shown by him for a given country and inculcated in his children. Those criteria, applied to Nottebohm, did not point to Liechtenstein.

Human Rights Watch and Amnesty International have drawn from this case support for the claimed Palestinian right of return. The organizations argue that Israel is the country of the Palestinians because Palestinians have genuine and effective links with Israel. Palestinians have genuine and effective links with Israel because at least some of the *Nottebohm* criteria apply. Palestinians have an attachment to territory within the boundaries of Israel, and that attachment is inculcated in their children.

This argument fails to note that the World Court in the *Nottebohm* case did not deal with the situation where a person has no nationality. It is a stretch to apply the *Nottebohm* case to the situation of the Palestinians who have no nationality rather than two nationalities.

However, if one does so, one can see that the *Nottebohm* case does not support the position argued by Human Rights Watch and Amnesty International. On the contrary, the case supports the completely opposite position, that Israel is not the country of the Palestinians.

The court observed that at the time of his eviction from Guatemala in 1943, Friedrich Nottebohm had been settled in Guatemala for thirty-four years. Guatemala was the centre of his interests and business activities. If the reasoning of Human Rights Watch and Amnesty International were correct, then the court would have considered Nottebohm to have effective nationality in Guatemala.

Guatemala could not have removed him, not because they were obliged to recognize Liechtenstein nationality, but because, in reality, he was Guatemalan.

The court did not condemn the Guatemalan ejection of Nottebohm as an enemy alien. By the time the case was decided, the war with Germany was long since over. Yet the court did not rule that Nottebohm had a right of return to Guatemala.

Even if we put aside the question whether Guatemala was the country of Nottebohm and consider only Liechtenstein and Germany, here too the reasoning of the court undercuts, rather than supports, the position of Human Rights Watch and Amnesty International. Between Liechtenstein and Germany, Nottebohm chose Liechtenstein. Yet the court held that this choice should be disregarded and that the matter should be viewed objectively.

Palestinian refugees may well want to go to Israel. However, if we are to follow the *Nottebohm* reasoning, then this choice must be disregarded. Viewed objectively, Palestinian refugees who have never set foot in Israel and are not Jewish either by culture or religion have far more genuine and effective links with the Palestinian state in the making than with Israel. Those links must be viewed in combination with the right to self-determination of the Jewish people and the large number of stateless Palestinian refugees. The result is that stateless Palestinian refugees who have never set foot in Israel would have a right of entry to a new Palestinian state only, not to Israel.

An old chestnut pulled out whenever the Palestinian right of return is asserted is the argument that the 1948 United Nations General Assembly Resolution 194 recognizes the claimed Palestinian right of return. For instance, the Asian preparatory meeting for the World Conference Against Racism, held in February 2001 in Tehran, referred to Resolution 194 in support of the claimed Palestinian right of return. It was the sole reference in the document to support the right.

An examination of that resolution shows that it asserts no such right. Rather it resolves, "the refugees wishing to return to their homes and live at peace with their neighbours should be permitted to do so at the earliest practicable date."[154]

The resolution registers support, from some of the nations of the world, for granting permission to Palestinian refugees to return, not for a right of return. The language of rights was neither used nor intended. The support for permission to return was also subject to a precondition: the refugees must be willing to live at peace with their neighbours. Yet many of the countries in the Arab world that host Palestinian refugees remain at war with Israel. Granting permission to return, according to the resolution, should follow peace with Israel, not precede peace.

The resolution also supports permission to return for the refugees alone, not their descendants. Of course, in 1948, the nations of the world may well have not anticipated that the Palestinian refugee problem would remain unresolved fifty-seven years later. Nonetheless, that resolution cannot be read as support for the proposition that those who have never set foot in Israel, adult descendants of the original refugees, should be granted permission to enter Israel.

The use of the word *permission* has its own special significance. The word acknowledges that the right to allow or to deny entry rests with Israel. The resolution recommends to Israel that its admitted power of entry to its own territory be exercised in a particular way.

Reliance on Resolution 194 in support of the claimed Palestinian right of return is a form of Orwellian doublethink, saying two opposites at one time and believing in both with equal fervour. No anti-Zionist state would accept that non-nationals have a right of entry into that state's territory simply because of historic links to the territory. Every anti-Zionist state would assert that entry into its own territory is a sovereign right of the state, subject to its permission, and not the right of the foreign national. Yet these same states rely on a General Assembly resolution that accepts and recognizes this same sovereign right in Israel as somehow creating a right in individuals that Israel must respect.

Resolution 194 was not passed unanimously or by consensus. In particular, the Arab states voted against it. There is an obvious hypocrisy for the Arab states who voted against Resolution 194 to say to states that voted for the resolution, "You are bound by your vote, but we are not bound by ours."

Even if Resolution 194 could be read as an endorsement of the claimed Palestinian right of return, that endorsement should be disregarded because it does not respect the rights of the Jewish people. Human rights standards invalidate the vote, when it's read in that way.

There are many United Nations General Assembly resolutions that assert, up front, the Palestinian right of return.[155] It seems puzzling that the 2001 Tehran declaration would cite a UN resolution that does not endorse the claimed Palestinian right of return and pretend it does, rather than cite UN resolutions that do endorse a Palestinian right of return. It is also, at first blush, strange that Arab states would invoke a resolution they had earlier opposed and pass over resolutions they had always supported.

The answer presumably lies in the date of Resolution 194. The resolution was passed on December 11, 1948. It followed closely upon the creation of the State of Israel on May 14, 1948. The resolution was passed by a General Assembly not in the thralls of the reflex anti-Israel majority that subsequently developed. Later resolutions asserting up front the Palestinian right of return were passed around the time of the resolution equating Zionism with racism.

Enemies of the State of Israel rely on Resolution 194, which does not say what they want and which they voted against, rather than later resolutions, which do say what they want and which they shepherded through the United Nations, because they see the earlier resolution as a sort of admission by the then friends of

Israel. Reliance on Resolution 194 should be seen for what it is, a cheap debating trick rather than a serious argument.

Sometimes it is said that the claimed Palestinian right of return to Israel, because of its repeated acceptance by the international community, has become customary international law. Customary international law is custom or practice by states, which they consider binding upon themselves. Once a customary international law exists, it binds the whole international community, not just those who have been instrumental in establishing the law.

In order for there to be customary international law, there must be law (that is to say, a general principle), it must be customary, and it must be international. The claimed Palestinian right of return meets none of these criteria. It is first of all not a general principle. It is a particular situational assertion. The general principles invoked in support of the claimed right of return (the right to enter one's own country or the right to nationality) do not give Palestinians a right of return to Israel. Second, it is not customary. A general principle on which Palestinians could rely to give them the right they assert is the principle that descendants have the right of entry into the country of their ancestors. Yet there is no general practice around the world of giving non-national descendants the right of entry into the country of their ancestors. A custom of this nature simply does not exist. Third, it is not international. Those states that support the right of return claimed for Palestinians are asserting a claim against one state only, Israel. They are not accepting any principle as binding upon themselves.

Defenders of the right of return claimed for Palestinians argue that the right has been recognized elsewhere in other situations. But analogies with other situations are never exact.

The Palestinian Liberation Organization put out a Factfile dated April 2000 with a section titled "The Right of Return and of Compensation in Other Selected Cases." The cases listed are the former Yugoslavia, Abkhazia/Georgia, Cyprus, Namibia-South Africa, and Iraq-Kuwait. In none of these cases is the situation the same as that in Israel. Except for the former Yugoslavia, all are single-state situations. The division of Cyprus has not been recognized by the international community.

On the breakup of the former Yugoslavia, there was no acceptance by the international community of its division into ethnic or religions components to parallel the international acceptance of the partition of British-mandate Palestine into an Arab state and a Jewish state. The genocide in Bosnia followed the breakup of the former Yugoslavia; there was no genocide prior to the breakup prompting the international community to assert the right to self-determination of any one of its religious or ethnic communities.

The closest one can come to a historical parallel to the creation of Arab and Jewish state out of British-mandate Palestine is the partition of the Indian subcontinent in 1947 and the creation of two states, one predominantly

Muslim (Pakistan), and one predominantly Hindu (India). After partition, there was a mass movement of Hindus from Pakistan to India and of Muslims from India to Pakistan, in the midst of wide-scale armed combat. The international community does not now assert a right of return of those who moved after that partition, whether they relocated voluntarily or out of fear. This silence about the Indian subcontinent speaks volumes about the claimed Palestinian right of return.

The Palestinian people are a population of stateless refugees without a durable solution. Both statelessness and failure to find a durable solution for a refugee population are human rights violations from which the Palestinian people suffer.

There is a real problem, but the existence of the state of Israel is not the cause. Its destruction is not the solution.

The preferred solution at international law to the problem of statelessness is not nationality in a state in whose territory ancestors have lived, but rather nationality in the state where the descendants have been born. The United Nations Convention on the Reduction of Statelessness has, as mentioned, a general rule that contracting states shall grant nationality to a person born in that territory.

The Convention is not widely accepted, having only twenty-one states parties. So it cannot be considered customary international law. Because the United Nations Convention on the Reduction of Statelessness has not been signed and ratified by most of the states where stateless Palestinian refugees have been born, these states cannot be held to account for violation of the Convention. Nonetheless, the Convention provides a useful guide or standard.

The solution to the problem of statelessness of Palestinian refugees is the grant of nationality by the states in whose territories Palestinians have been born. It is the failure of these states to grant nationality to Palestinians, as well as the failure to reach a peace agreement that would establish a Palestinian state, that created the problem of statelessness of Palestinians — not the existence of the State of Israel.

The solution to the Palestinian refugee problem is not relocation to Israel. The Office of the United Nations High Commissioner for Refugees (UNHCR) promotes three durable solutions: local integration, third-country resettlement, and voluntary repatriation. These durable solutions are not part of any treaty. However, their support by the Office of the United Nations High Commissioner for Refugees and its executive committee does give them an international status.

The notion of voluntary repatriation of stateless refugees is an oxymoron. Stateless refugees, by definition, have no country of nationality. There is no country to which stateless refugees can be repatriated.

Some of the stateless Palestinian refugees once had nationality in a state that no longer exists, British-mandate Palestine. Other stateless Palestinian refugees never had nationality anywhere. It is legitimate to ask whether either Israel or the

Palestinian state in the making should become, for the first time, the country of nationality of stateless Palestinian refugees. However, in answering that question, we must keep in mind that what we are talking about is patriation, not repatriation.

In general, the community of nations should share the responsibility for resettlement of refugees. Israel has done more than its fair share of resettlement of the world's refugee population because of its Law of Return and the protection it has given to Jewish refugees fleeing antisemitism. There are other countries that have done a good deal less than Israel in resettling refugees and who could provide a durable solution to the problems Palestinian refugees face.

Advocates of the claimed Palestinian right of return argue that, even if there is no Palestinian right of return while the war against Israel continues, the right arises once there is peace. A final peace agreement with Israel must include a Palestinian right of return.

Yet, in general, a peace agreement should be settled between the parties to the agreement. It is inappropriate for outsiders to say what should or should not be in a peace agreement. For outsiders to insist that one provision or another should be in a peace agreement creates an obstacle to the peaceful settlement of disputes by emboldening one of the parties to the dispute.

There is, nonetheless, an exception to the general principle that a peace agreement should be left to the parties. No peace treaty should bargain away human rights. Indeed, some human rights values are peremptory norms of international law, which no treaty can bargain away. The Vienna Convention on the Law of Treaties provides that a treaty is void if it conflicts with a peremptory norm of international law.[156]

The claimed right of return of Palestinians to Israel is not a right, let alone a human right. The relevant human right is a right to nationality. The Universal Declaration of Human Rights provides that every person has the right to a nationality.[157] The Declaration, however, does not assert the right to any particular nationality. The wrong, the human rights violation, that the Declaration seeks to combat is statelessness. The remedy for the wrong is the grant of nationality. No human rights instrument states that the sole acceptable remedy for the wrong of statelessness is the grant of nationality in the state now encompassing the territory in which ancestors resided.

The closest one can come to finding an instrument recognizing a right that stateless Palestinians could invoke is the International Law Commission Draft Articles on Nationality of Natural Person in Relation to Succession of States. The Draft Articles have yet to be approved by the United Nations General Assembly. In its 2000 session, the General Assembly simply invited governments "to take into account, as appropriate, the provision contained in the articles." A paragraph in the resolution's preamble referred to the Draft Articles as "a useful guide for practice in dealing with this issue."[158]

The Draft Articles repeat what is in the Universal Declaration of Human Rights: everyone has a right to a nationality in at least one state.[159] The Draft Articles make proposals to ensure that this happens, but do not suggest that the right to nationality is violated if nationality is granted in one state and not another.

As indicated previously, the Draft Articles propose that, in a situation where a state has dissolved and various parts form two successor states, each successor state should attribute its nationality to persons who have their habitual residence in its territory, with an option of nationality in the other state. The International Law Commission puts forward this proposal as a solution to the problem of state-lessness, but not as the only acceptable solution. Nationality in either state that succeeds the predecessor state, or indeed any state, is a solution to the problem of statelessness consistent with human rights.

The removal of statelessness is not the only human rights value one has to keep in mind in assessing the acceptability of a Middle East peace agreement. There is also the right to self-determination of the Jewish people and the right to preserve their cultural identity. Any provision of a peace agreement that denies or threatens these rights is unacceptable in human rights terms.

The problem of statelessness of Palestinians can be resolved in two ways by a Middle East peace agreement: by granting statehood in the new Palestinian state that would be created by the peace agreement, or by granting statehood in Israel. Either of these grants would resolve the Palestinian problem of statelessness. Only the first, however, would be consistent with respect for the right of the Jewish people to self-determination and the right to preserve their cultural identity. The other solution would violate the human rights of the Jewish people. There is no other Jewish state through which the right to self-determination and right to preservation of the cultural identity of the Jewish people can be respected. The choice is Israel or nothing.

In support of the claimed Palestinian right of return, it is sometimes said that international law prohibits forcible exile or expulsion of any one based on their group identity or ethnic origin. The argument continues that Israeli law has forcibly exiled or expelled Palestinians in violation of international law.

The answer to that argument is that there is no Israeli law stating that Palestinians are exiled or expelled. Nor is there any Israeli law that can be considered in substance to be a measure exiling or expelling Palestinians.

The Israeli Nationality Law requires that a person who, immediately before the establishment of the state, was a Palestinian citizen and did not become an Israeli national by return must have been in Israel from the day of the establishment of the state to the day of the coming into force of the Nationality Law to have the right to Israeli citizenship.[160] Alternatively, the person must have entered Israel lawfully during that period.

In other words, every person who was a Palestinian citizen immediately before the establishment of the state but who left Israel before the coming into force of the Israeli Nationality Law is not an Israeli national. This provision, coupled with the Immigration Law of Israel, means that a Palestinian who left the territory of what is now Israel immediately before or after Israel was created cannot now come back.

Whether those who lived in the territory before the creation of the State of Israel or the coming into force of the Israeli Nationality Law were forcibly exiled or expelled in violation of international law is entangled with the question of whether Israel is their own country. At international law, every country has a right to deny entry to foreigners. If Israel is not the country of the Palestinians, then the State of Israel has the same right to deny them entry as any country does to deny entry to any foreigner.

Even if Israel were now completely empty territory with no inhabitants, it is impossible to describe those who never set foot in Israel as forcibly exiled or expelled from Israel. If the land of Israel were empty, the right of return of Palestinian refugees, at its strongest, would exist only for those who had once lived in what is now Israel, their spouses, and their minor children.

Of course, the land of Israel is not now empty. A country is not just land. It is also, indeed it is primarily, people. The Jewish people who are now in Israel have rights that compete with the rights of those who once lived in what is now Israel. These competing rights are the right to self-determination and the right to cultural preservation that would be threatened or lost by the mass entry of Palestinians into Israel.

Because Israel already has a minority Palestinian Arab-speaking Muslim population, Israel could admit and integrate a small number of Palestinian refugees without changing its character or purpose, its *raison d'être*. However, the number of Palestinian refugees is not small.

The notion that Israel is the country of the Palestinians focuses on the territory of Israel to the exclusion of its people. It is a rejection or denial of the Jewish reality of the State of Israel. It is impossible at the same time to accept that reality and to assert that Israel is the country of the Palestinians.

T HAT anti-Zionism is just one more form of bigotry is apparent from the patterns of prejudice it follows. These are patterns of both discrimination and of incitement to hatred. The patterns of discrimination are double focus, charges of dual loyalty, a double standard, blaming the victim for the victimization, transferring blame from the perpetrator, and deference to the prejudice of others. The patterns of incitement to hatred are a wealth of unverifiable detail, supposed admissions by members of the target group, decontextualization, stereotypes, assumption of bad faith, and abuse of religious discourse.

Patterns of Discrimination

First, double focus. One would think, if a person is attacked because the person is Jewish, that the person is a victim of racism and antisemitism. However, elements of the anti-Zionist movement, when they do not attempt to appropriate or ignore the notion of antisemitism or to adopt Nazi anti-Jewish propaganda, distinguish between forms of antisemitism. The antisemitism of the Nazis, according to this line of thought, is real antisemitism. Attacks on Jews worldwide grounded in anti-Zionism are not antisemitism, but merely criticism of Israel–Middle East politics. Criticism of Israel is legitimate, so this argument goes; therefore, attacks on the Jewish community as actual or perceived supporters of Israel are also legitimate.

There is a meaningful distinction between criticism of the existence of the State of Israel as a Jewish state and criticism of the practices and policies of the state of Israel. However, the distinction anti-Zionists make is not between criticism of Israeli practices and Israeli existence, but between antisemitism and anti-Zionism.

One form of antisemitism denies Jews access to goods and services because they are Jewish. Another form of antisemitism denies the right of the Jewish people to exist as a people because they are Jewish. Anti-Zionists distinguish between the two, claiming the first is antisemitism, but the second is not. To the anti-Zionist, the Jew can exist as an individual as long as Jews do not exist as a people.

To anyone grounded in human rights, that distinction has to be nonsense. The full realization of human rights requires respect for both individual and collective rights. Respect for the dignity and worth of the human person requires respect for every person's right to full membership in a people that freely pursues its own economic, social, and cultural development.[161] Taking a racial slur or stereotype directed against someone who is Jewish and replacing the word *Jew* with the word *Zionist* does not change the slur into acceptable discourse.[162]

Another indicator of antisemitic prejudice is the charge of dual loyalty. Before and during the Second World War, it was common for the loyalty of Jews to their home countries to have been suspect because they were Jews. The myth of the world Jewish conspiracy is the most egregious form of the antisemitic canard that Jews are not true citizens of the countries where they reside.

Anti-Zionism has its own variation on this dual loyalty libel, the slander that Jewish non-governmental human rights organizations are neither working for human rights nor non-governmental, but rather agents and unconditional defenders of the government of the State of Israel. At non-governmental meetings in Durban, South Africa, in August 2001 representatives of Jewish organizations were asked to leave on the ground that they represented a government rather than the non-governmental community.

I myself have been the target of this particular form of bigotry. Because I have been an outspoken critic of anti-Zionism, an anti-Zionist campaign was organized to have me ejected from my positions in Amnesty International.

Hanna Kawas, Chairperson of the Canada Palestine Association, sent e-mails to Amnesty International in January and February 2002, criticizing AI for allowing me to work in the organization. The January e-mail said, "We do NOT think Mr. Matas should be involved in the work of Amnesty International in any capacity."

Amnesty International responded, "Mr. Matas always makes it clear when he is speaking or acting on behalf of AI and when he is doing so on behalf of other organizations. Mr. Matas has no role in developing or presenting Amnesty's policies or actions in relation to the Middle East."

Kawas replied in February, "We urge AI Canada to stop working with people like David Matas."

Annie C. Higgins, PhD, sent an e-mail to Amnesty International in January 2002 that went even further, asking AI to expel me from the membership. She wrote, "Matas is a member of AI? How? Why?"

It was not just the request for exclusion that was troubling. It was the language as well. I am described in the February e-mail from Hanna Kawas as "a self-declared violator of Palestinian human rights." Of course, all that I have declared is my support for the existence of the State of Israel, admittedly, even before this book was written, in great detail. According to Kawas, if you defend the existence of the State of Israel, you do not just support the violation of human rights; you are yourself violating human rights. If we are to apply her logic, support for the existence of the State of Israel is not just wrong-headed, it makes the supporter a human rights violator.

With this brush, Kawas tars not only me, but also the whole organized Jewish community worldwide. The whole community, according to the standards invoked by Kawas, is one of human rights violators. Here we have the secular human rights equivalent to Jews as Christ-killers, Jews as the anti-Christ.

Today, we do not see, as we did before the Second World War, Jews excluded from educational institutions, facilities, and services throughout the world. But when it comes to human rights organizations, Jews are still victims of an exclusionary animus. What happened to me is an example of what happens to Jews everywhere who are so bold as to attempt to defend the existence of the State of Israel.

This form of slander could not be uttered unless the attackers made no distinction between the existence of the State of Israel and its behaviour. Unconditional support for the existence of the State of Israel is the expression of a human right that one would expect Jewish organizations to articulate. Jewish human rights organizations, if they are to remain true to their human rights mandate, should be calling for the preservation of the human rights of the Jewish people, including the right to self-determination. They should be defending the State of Israel against criticisms that are at bottom criticism of the existence of the State of Israel rather than of its behaviour.

What is at work here is moral blindness. Anti-Zionists see no distinction between criticism of the State of Israel and its delegitimization. The only purpose of anti-Zionist criticism of the behaviour of the State of Israel is its demonization, delegitimization, and destruction.

Some attacks on claimed Israeli behaviour are attacks on the existence of Israel. When Israel is accused of atrocities it did not commit and for which there is no evidence, that accusation is not an attack on policies or practices. It is an attack on existence. For instance, when Israel is accused of mass killings in Jenin, without evidence and in spite of the evidence, in form that accusation may seem be to a criticism of a practice or policy. In substance, it is an attempt to demonize and delegitimize the existence of the State of Israel.

Someone who denies the right of Israel to exist does not make the distinction between criticism designed to end the existence of the State of Israel and criticisms designed to end specific practices and policies of the State of Israel. More than that, the anti-Zionist does not even grasp the distinction, because for the anti-Zionist, the distinction is pointless. When someone defends Israel against delegitimizing criticism of alleged Israeli behaviour, the anti-Zionist sees only a defender of the behaviour of the State of Israel.

As well, it is a standard debating technique, when you have no answer to the argument of the other side, to attack the character and personality of your opponent. Anti-Zionists have no rational arguments to rebut the responses of those who assert the right to self-determination of the Jewish people. Instead, the characters of those who defend the rights of the Jewish people are attacked. Supporters of the existence of the State of Israel are accused of bias, of lacking perspective, of being unconditional apologists for a government.

Another hallmark of prejudice is the use of a double standard. It is a common feature of distorted justice systems. In the United States, for instance, blacks who kill whites historically have been more likely to receive the death penalty than whites who kill blacks. Both the black person who kills and the white person who kills have done something wrong. The issue is not only innocence or guilt, but also punishment. Equal wrongs must be treated equally. Wrongdoing cannot become an excuse for excessive punishment of a member of a minority group. This sort of double standard, overreacting to wrongdoing, is common when it comes to criticism of Israel.

Intergovernmental forums are wrapped up in politics. The one-sidedness of the criticism against Israel when governments meet can be dismissed as a reflection of Israel's unpopularity. The reaction of independent human rights organizations to Israeli behaviour demonstrates even more vividly than UN behaviour the prejudice that has developed against Israel.

The Canadian organization Rights and Democracy, in a letter of April 2, 2002, to the Canadian Minister of Foreign Affairs, attacked Israel at length but said not a word about Tanzim or al-Aqsa or Fatah or Hamas or Hezbollah or suicide bombers. The letter is explicable only as the expression of a double standard so widely accepted that the author, Warren Allmand, then president of a human rights organizations, did not even recognize it.[163]

To take another example, Amnesty International produced reports on Palestinian suicide bombings[164] and Israeli retaliatory behaviour in Jenin and Nablus.[165] The Palestinian report used the impossibly high standard of certainty to determine culpability of the Palestinian Authority. The Israel report used the much lower standard of clear evidence to determine the culpability of the Israeli Defence Forces. The Palestinian report stated that it was not possible to determine "with certainty" that the Palestinian Authority was responsible for the attacks. The Israel report stated there was "clear evidence" that some of the acts committed by Israeli Defence Forces were war crimes.

A standard form of evasion one finds in virtually every situation where there are human rights violations is blaming the victims for their victimization. Israel and the global Jewish community are no exception.

This phenomenon of blaming the victim even goes so far as to blame Israel and the Jews for the deaths from anti-Zionist suicide bombings. According to this logic, it is Israel and the global Jewish community, because of its support of Israel, that have driven the bombers to commit their dastardly deeds.

So, for example, Sa'id Ghazali writes an article in the British newspaper the *Independent* under the title "Suicide bombers are the appalling but inevitable result of decades of despair."[166] In an article supposedly dedicated to determining the causes of the killings, the author says nothing about the persistent incitement to hate. Instead he blames Israel for its occupation of the West Bank and Gaza.

He also blames the international community, in particular America, Britain, and again Israel, for not implementing justice in the region. He does add, "We [Palestinians] should blame ourselves for not working hard to have a good rule in Palestine," but immediately undercuts that statement with the assertion, "Yasser Arafat has been forced by the Oslo Accords to behave like a dictator."

Another form of this phenomenon of blaming the victim is a false symmetry between Palestinian attacks on innocent civilians and Israeli responses in self-defence. The phrase "the cycle of violence" is often used as if the suicide bombings and the attempt to respond to those bombings are on the same plane. United Nations resolutions, in their more benign paragraphs on the Middle East, call on all parties to the conflict to respect international standards, as if Palestinian attacks on civilians and Israeli responses were equivalent.[167]

If people who used the phrases "cycle of violence" or "attacks on civilians on both sides" just paused for a moment to think about what they were saying, they would realize what nonsense it was. There are no Israeli suicide bombers responding to anti-Zionist suicide bombers. Israeli forces do not aim to kill innocent Palestinians simply because they are Palestinian.

False Middle Eastern symmetries are reminiscent of traditional antisemitic slurs that the Jews must have done something to justify all the hatred against them. Just as, in the days before and during the Holocaust, Jewish character and the behaviour of individual Jews were blamed for the hatred and the ravages the Jewish community faced, today the character of the State of Israel and the behaviour of the government of the State of Israel are blamed for anti-Zionist attitudes and attacks.

Not every Jew before the Holocaust was a perfect angel. The misbehaviour of individual Jews, all the same, was no excuse for the Holocaust. Today, not every action of the State of Israel is beyond reproach. Those reproaches, even when well grounded, are no excuse for anti-Zionism.

A phenomenon related to blaming the victim is blame transference. Perpetrators of human rights violations in a conflict situation blame victimization of both sides on their opponents. So those violations of human rights that Palestinians suffer, for which Arab governments are responsible, are blamed not just on Israeli behaviour, but on the existence of Israel and its support by the global Jewish community.

The State of Israel, like the Jewish population in the days of Hitler, has become the scapegoat for a problem whose cause lies elsewhere, the accused for a violation whose perpetrators are elsewhere. Like the Jewish problem in the days of Hitler, the Palestinian problem today is created by enemies of the Jewish people in order to justify their destruction. The victimization of the Palestinians comes from the very people who call the Law of Return of Israel racist, who call for the right of return of the Palestinian people.

Leaders in the support of anti-Zionism are Tunisia, Algeria, Libya, Iran, Syria, Saudi Arabia, and Yemen, all countries with abysmal human rights records. When these countries attack Israel, it should be obvious that their primary concern is not respect for human rights. Indeed, while these countries condemn Israel for their violations of Palestinian rights, these very same countries violate the rights of Palestinians with gusto.

The Arab world has victimized Palestinians, denying them statehood, failing to resettle them, and then transferring blame. The article by Sa'id Ghazali, which is far from the worst of its genre, refers to fifty-four years of displacement, as if Palestinians today, most of whom were born where they now live and have not moved at all, were somehow in the wrong place.

Many states in the Arab world want Israel to end. In order to get sympathy for that goal, these states victimize their Palestinian populations and shift the blame to Israel. One can sympathize with the plight of the Palestinian people without faulting the existence of the State of Israel.

Equating the creation of the State of Israel to the suffering of the Palestinian people is yet another euphemism for denial of the rights of the Jewish people, a rejection of their right to self-determination and cultural preservation, a masked form of racism. The suffering of the Palestinian people flows from their stateless-ness, the failure of the global community to provide a durable solution to the refugee population, and the continuation of the war with Israel, not from the existence of the State of Israel.

The suffering of the Palestinian people is caused by their refusal to recognize the reality of Israel and not that reality itself. Arab insistence on a non-existent right of return, not Israeli rejection, has led to Palestinian misery. If there were peace, if Palestinians were given nationality in the new Palestinian state to be established by the peace agreement or in the territories of the states where they are now living or in refugee resettlement countries around the world, their suffering would end.

One example of blame transference is the article written by Sa'id Ghazali. He blames Yasser Arafat's dictatorial behaviour on the Oslo Accords and not on Arafat himself. The suggestion is that if the Oslo Accords were different, giving the Palestinians more of what they want, the Palestinian Authority would then be democratic.

Another example is the Palestinian child intifada phenomenon. Normally, the fault for the victimization of child combatants is placed on the shoulders of those who recruit them and use them in combat. In the case of the Palestinian children victimized in the intifada, that would be the Palestinian anti-Zionists. Ambassador Alan Baker, then legal advisor to the Foreign Ministry, in a talk at Montreal's Concordia University on January 21, 2002, reported that the Palestinian Authority would pick up children in buses and hand them rocks to attack Israeli soldiers. Behind the young children were older children with Molotov cocktails. Behind the older children were Palestinian Authority military with machine guns.[168] Matthew Kalman reports that Palestinian Authority security cars collected children from the street to El-Khadouri at the western entry to Tulkarm in the West Bank to throw stones at Israeli troops. Parents who protested were condemned as fifth columnists and threatened.[169] Nonetheless, in the anti-Israel world the blame for the use of children and their victimization has been placed not on the Palestinian Authority, but on Jews worldwide.

One of the most astonishing forms of blame transference is the accusation that Israel and the Jews are responsible for the attacks on the World Trade Center. This slander is astonishing not merely because of its divergence from well-known facts, something that every antisemitic slur shares, but also because of its widespread acceptance in the Arab world. A Gallup Poll conducted for *USA Today* in February 2002 in a variety of Muslim nations indicated a common belief that the perpetrators of the attacks on the World Trade Center were not Arabs. The most prevalent theory was that the attack was planned by Israel and that Jews were forewarned to stay away from the World Trade Center the day of the attacks.[170]

Prejudice flourishes not just because of the bigotry of the few, but also because of the deference of the many. The line "Some of my best friends are Jewish" has become, in the Jewish community, a comic punchline. It leads to laughter even when it is spoken alone. It is shorthand for the hypocrisy of which the Jewish community has been victim. It telegraphs the attitude that the speaker does not consider himself or herself prejudiced, despite discriminatory behaviour, because of personal friendship with one or two Jews. The attitude is, in a sense, real, in that the speaker does not share the prejudices of the truly bigoted and discriminates out of deference to the bigoted, rather than out of belief. However, for the Jewish community, the result is much the same.

All that can be said of Zionism. Since anti-Zionism is an attack on Jews as a people, deference to anti-Zionism occurs in the international arena. Some states vote to condemn Israel for crimes it did not commit, not out of anti-Zionism, but rather out of deference to anti-Zionist states. These deferring states pretend to be balanced when there is no balance to be drawn. They draw false parallels between Israeli and anti-Zionist behaviour and fabricate phoney symmetries so as not to offend their anti-Zionist colleagues.

There are fifty-six states in the Organization of the Islamic Conference. For the most part, they vote as a bloc on anti-Israel issues, and that bloc vote is heavily influenced by the views of the Palestinian Authority. There is, of course, only one Jewish state. If there were fifty-six Jewish states and only one Islamic state, votes in the international arena by states that are neither Islamic nor Jewish would be far different from what they are.

The same phenomenon happens to a lesser extent with human rights non-governmental organizations. Human rights organizations are more grounded in reality and less buffeted by politics than governments. Yet they too have a constituency — people interested in and involved with human rights. When a large group of people, including many of their own members, attack the existence of the State of Israel in the name of human rights, human rights organizations are put in an awkward position. They do not want to alienate this constituency.

Human rights organizations must realize, if they are to remain true to their human rights principles, that this anti-Zionist constituency and sympathy are profoundly mistaken. So they develop evasive techniques. One is to suggest that the discussion move on to other issues, that there be less talk about Israel and more talk about other matters. That was a response of the major international human rights organizations at the 2001 Durban non-governmental Forum Against Racism.

The international NGOs disassociated themselves from the attacks on the Jewish community, but refused to condemn those attacks. At a press conference, they all urged the media to move on to other issues. All of them refused to sign the petition of the Eastern and Central European Caucus, though they were asked to do so.

Irene Kahn, Secretary General of Amnesty International said, "There is language in the [NGO] document that AI doesn't agree with." She then outlined some areas the documents did address, including "human rights violations in the Middle East against Palestinians and Israelis," and said, "We agree with the issues even if the language in the document is not that we would use." She added, "There are many human rights violations in the Middle East and it is wrong to cite only those in one country."

Michael Posner, of the Lawyers Committee for Human Rights, said, "There are serious human rights violations in the West Bank and Gaza that need to be condemned and we find the language [in the NGO document] inaccurate and reject it ... The zeal of one group on behalf of victims to make their point should not infringe on the rights of others. But I agree with Irene that there is much of value in this document." Human Rights Watch said, "We have participated in many NGO caucuses ... we cannot agree with some of the language used ... but this document is better than the government document in that it names the victims, countries, perpetrators ... it is a voice for those outside the governmental process." The International Service said, "It is impossible to endorse such a document, but in our monitoring of the conference, we see this document as part of an important long term process ..."

In response to a question from National Public Radio, Michael Posner said the Lawyer's Committee rejected the idea that "Zionist is racism language. That language doesn't have a place at this conference, as Mary Robinson said. But it's time to move on …" Human Rights Watch said that governments have used the Middle East language in the NGO document as a convenient scapegoat to "avoid issues NGOs have come here to address."

Deference is also a Canadian phenomenon. Stung by criticism that two New Democratic Party Members of Parliament, Pat Martin and Judy Wasylycia-Leis, had visited Israel in August 2004, NDP leader Jack Layton announced that he would consult with Muslim members of the party before MPs are allowed to visit Israel in the future.[171] He required no similar consultation for visits to other countries — none with Kashmiri party members for MPs visiting India or Pakistan, nor with Tibetan party members for MPs visiting China, nor with Sahrawi party members for MPs visiting Morocco, nor with Chechen party members for MPs visiting Russia.

Another evasion is to characterize anti-Zionist diatribes as the feelings of victims, perspectives they are entitled to express, even if those feelings are not ones the organizations would endorse. That was the position of both Human Rights Watch and Amnesty International at the Durban World Conference Against Racism and its non-governmental forum.

Irene Kahn, the Secretary General of Amnesty International, speaking at the forum on behalf of the International Non-governmental Organization (INGO) Caucus, proposed that there be no votes and that the Drafting Committee document just be accepted and forwarded to the intergovernmental World Conference in its entirety as the various perspectives and views of the victim groups. She proposed that there be an introductory paragraph explaining that the document had not been adopted by everyone and that there was language in the document that not everyone agreed with. The proposal was defeated by the plenary.

The Jewish Caucus voted against that proposal, even though it was a prefer-able alternative to what was then likely to happen and later did happen, deletion of the Jewish Caucus protests against anti-Zionism. It was the position of the Jewish Caucus that the anti-Zionist clauses in the draft declaration and program were not just a point of view, a differing perspective. They were an incitement to discrimination, hatred, and violence against the Jewish people, in violation of human rights standards. Wording that calls for human rights violations and is itself a human rights violation should not be allowed to stand in any document, let alone a document that purports to promote respect for human rights.

Patterns of Incitement to Hatred

Anti-Zionism fits the mould of hate speech. Hate messages often succeed by the detail they contain. The use of references to sources which may be seen as credible, statistics and so on, give the messages a persuasive force. The overall impression of the messages is one of research and reflection, normally by reference to sources that either are difficult or impossible to track down or verify.[172] Hate promoters also resort to arcane arguments that a layperson would find difficult to decipher.

One of the appeals to promoters of antisemitism of *The Protocols of the Elders of Zion*, a Czarist Russian forgery attempting to show a Jewish plan to control the world, is its detail. Unless the reader knew that *The Protocols* were a forgery, they might indeed persuade the gullible or reinforce the prejudice of someone predisposed to antisemitism.

Anti-Zionist propaganda is both highly generalized and highly detailed. Anti-Zionist slurs against Israel are not just overblown general accusations of genocide, apartheid, and so on. They are also very specific detailed accusations of alleged wrongdoing.

Human rights organizations, which are understaffed and not in a position to investigate every allegation, become easily bamboozled by the anti-Zionist lobby. This lobby, acting out of an obsessive, frenzied hatred of the Jewish state and its supporters, throws up a cloud of accusations that human rights organizations don't have the time, the energy, the staff, or the funding to penetrate. Faced with histrionic, persistent anti-Zionist allegations of human rights violations against Israel, human rights organizations have a tendency simply to go along, to endorse these allegations, without thinking them through or checking them out.

Human Rights Watch and Amnesty International are better than most, because they do a lot of independent research. But even they got lost when it came to endorsing a non-existent Palestinian right of return. The organizations were led astray, in part, by a misreading of the *Nottebohm* case in the International Court of Justice,[173] which they seemed incapable of fathoming.[174]

Anti-Zionist slanders of Israel are a particularly dangerous trap for human rights organizations who do not do their own investigations and rely on the investigations of others. So, for instance, the Canadian organization Rights and Democracy released a statement on April 2, 2002, which states: "We have watched in horror the carnage suffered by the Palestinian people in the territories occupied militarily by Israel since 1967 and the destruction of infrastructures, in particular, sanitary infrastructures (drinking water mains) and medical infrastructures (hospitals, birth centres and ambulances, etc.) destruction that seems more and more to be a systematic and premeditated policy."

The letter cites no sources either oral or written. There is lots of detail, but it is impossible to verify. It is inappropriate for a human rights organization to make unsubstantiated, unsourced, unverifiable allegations of human rights violations. Allegations of human rights violations should be grounded in verifiable fact.

Similarly, the letter throws out legal hocus-pocus that, as long as no one looks at the texts being cited, might seem persuasive. For example, the letter says, "Israeli occupation is contrary to Article 2 of the Geneva Convention relative to the Protection of Civilian Persons in Time of War." Yet Article 2 does not set out any obligations that could be violated. It is an article setting out the scope of the Convention only. It is no more possible to violate a treaty scope provision than it is possible to violate a definition section. The letter has several other legal howlers like that.[175]

Traditional antisemitism is bad form in polite society. The pattern of fraudulent accusations against Israel as a means of delegitimizing the existence of the State of Israel is not widely appreciated. But contrarily, the new antisemitism that is anti-Zionism has almost become *de rigueur* in polite society. Even those who should have a human rights sensibility cannot avoid sinking into the anti-Zionist quagmire.

Another tactic hate promoters use to make their propaganda seem credible is to refer to supposed admissions by members of the group attacked. These admissions are meant to give the hate messages a persuasive force.[176]

These "admissions" are another form of the personal fallacy. It is wrong to reject or accept any statement simply because of the source. Anti-Zionist attacks are no more credible because they come from Jews rather than non-Jews, from Jewish or Israeli organizations rather than Palestinian, Arab, or Islamic organizations.

Not all Arabs or Palestinians or Muslims are anti-Zionists. Not all Jews support the existence of Israel. Certainly not all Jews are sensitized to the connection between the campaign to delegitimize the State of Israel and the survival of the Jewish people.

Although, in the end, it did not do them much good, some Jews before and during the Holocaust, in a vain attempt at self-protection, mimicked the prejudices of the persecutors. Other Jews fell prey to the same ideas that non-Jews around them had adopted, the then pervasive ideology of antisemitism.

The Jewish community sees that same phenomenon today. Though the bulk of the Jewish community does not side with anti-Zionists, some individual Jews and organizations do. Their "admissions" then become fodder for anti-Zionist propaganda.

So, for instance, the organization Solidaire du peuple palestinien ("Solidarity with the Palestinian people") has on its website today information from a report published in 1998 by B'Tselem, an Israeli organization, titled "Routine Torture: The Methods of Interrogation of the [Israeli] General Security Service." The Palestinian National Authority has on its website reference to a host of B'Tselem statements and reports. One goes under the heading "Israeli Illegal Settlement Policy like Apartheid Regime in South Africa." Another is titled "B'Tselem Criticizes Israeli Occupation Army's Unjustified Gunfire." A third is "B'Tselem Research: Another Stillborn Palestinian Baby." A fourth is "B'Tselem Issues Report on Israeli Disregard of Palestinian Lives." A fifth is "B'Tselem Exposes Israeli Army Lies." A sixth is "B'Tselem report Refutes Israeli Allegations on Beit Rima Massacre."

When the Palestinian National Authority quotes with such generosity an Israeli source, the reason is not just the content. The reason is also that the source is Israeli. That is meant to add to the persuasiveness of the material. Yet objectively it should not; only the accuracy of the material should matter.

Decontextualization is a common facet of war propaganda interlaced with hate propaganda. Take the activity of almost anyone out of context and it can become blameworthy. Activities, like words, can be twisted beyond recognition. A photographer, with a carefully chosen focus, can show you anything.

If a photographer or a TV cameraman shows a person being shot, but does not show the shooter, the shooting can be blamed on anyone. If the police arrest a person who has committed a crime, the arrest, out of the context of the crime, will appear to be baseless. If a search is considered without reference to its search warrant, the search will appear to be arbitrary. If a court sentence is assessed without reference to the crime, the sentence will appear cruel. If a person defends himself against an attack and we turn a blind eye to the attack, the self-defence will seem like aggression.

Much of the anti-Zionist criticism of Israel is of this nature. The enemies of Israel launch violent attacks against Israel, and Israel, in response, defends itself. Anti-Zionists then criticize Israel for acts of self-defence, ignoring the attacks that precipitated them and portraying them instead as spontaneous eruptions of violence towards innocents. What, with the proper focus, would be understandable, excusable behaviour becomes, out of context, atrocious, abhorrent behaviour.

Decontextualized criticism of Israel is such a standard feature of anti-Zionist rhetoric that it seems hardly worthwhile citing examples. It is at its most blatant where the target audience is the population of the Arab world living in countries without ready access to alternative sources of information. What is striking is the extent to which human rights organizations have bought into this anti-Zionist screed.

So, for instance, Rights and Democracy, in its statement of April 2, 2002, criticized Israel for its incursions into the West Bank and Gaza without any recognition that the presence of Israeli troops had been prompted by the attacks against Israel coming from the West Bank and Gaza. There is no reference in the letter to the suicide bombers and to the Israeli incursions as a reaction. A reader relying on only this letter for information would think that the Israeli behaviour was gratuitous cruelty.

The government of Canada, in a rare moment of lucidity in the Middle East, voted against a 2002 UN resolution at the Human Rights Commission that criticized Israel alone. The resolution had the all the anti-Zionist vitriol that has become a UN trademark. The resolution requested Mary Robinson, the United Nations High Commissioner for Human Rights, to make findings and recommendations to deter Israeli human rights violations.[177] Palestinian human rights violations were not mentioned.

Rights and Democracy, not satisfied with its own one-sided focus on Israel, condemned the government of Canada for the fairness it showed. Warren Allmand, president of Rights and Democracy, wrote that he was "shocked to hear" of the Canadian vote in opposition.

Human Rights Watch and Amnesty International, in reports critical of Israel, are insensitive to sequence. Human Rights Watch, in May 2002, put out a report of an investigation into the Israeli military operation in Jenin in which they found no evidence of a massacre but some evidence in support of charges of other violations of the laws of war. At the time of the release of the report, Human Rights Watch said it was also investigating suicide bombings.[178] Amnesty International had a similar sequence. It put out a report on Israeli behaviour on April 12, 2002.[179] In that report, it wrote that the abuses perpetrated against Israeli citizens by armed Palestinian groups would be addressed in separate statements and reports.

This sequence is all wrong. Suicide bombers attack. The Israeli government responds. A report on suicide bombers should either precede or coincide with a report on the Israeli response. To examine the Israeli response first and put off the report on the suicide bomber attacks gives the impression of a double standard, that Israeli behaviour in response is being examined more carefully, more closely, more urgently than the attacks that precipitated it. Criticism of Israel comes first. Criticism of those who attack Israel, no matter how viciously, comes second.

The misplaced sequence reinforces misplaced criticism of Israel. The out-of-sequence reports feed into the myth of spontaneous Israeli cruelty.

In the International Covenant on Civil and Political Rights, the obligation to prohibit hate propaganda and the obligation to prohibit war propaganda sit side by side, and for good reason.[180] Hate propaganda is often a form of war propaganda, and in the Israeli context that is certainly so. Anti-Zionists use hate propaganda against the Jews and the Jewish state as a weapon of war. Human rights organizations and institutions should be sensitive to the abuse of their own vocabulary and mechanisms to undermine their goals. Yet when it comes to Israel, they seem oblivious, pouring fuel on an already raging fire.

Another facet of incitement to hatred is the use of stereotypes. Stereotypes of intent permeate racism. Conclusions are formed about what a person thinks or feels or intends based on the colour of his skin, his ethnic origin, or his religion. There are stereotypical fears that a person intends to steal or to rape or to cheat, even though the person has said or done nothing to justify that fear.

Stereotypes reject the assumption of good faith and replace it, instead, with an assumption of bad faith. The behaviour of the person is viewed and interpreted through the prism of the bad faith assumption. Innocent activities are reinterpreted to be consistent with the assumption. For the bigoted, the target is not to be taken at his word; his real intent lies elsewhere.

One can see this form of racism at work with anti-Zionism. It would seem obvious that Israel is present in the West Bank and Gaza first because of the attacks of Egypt and Jordan in 1967 and subsequently because of the absence of a peace accord and the continued commitment of the populations of the West Bank and Gaza to use those territories as a staging ground for attacks of Israel. The Oslo negotiations showed that Israel was willing to give up land for peace.

Yet for anti-Zionists, only what tarnishes the existence of Israel is obvious. Only a motivation attributed to Israel that makes no distinction between the West Bank and Gaza on the one hand, and the territory of Israel before 1967 on the other hand, serves their purpose. Anti-Zionists say that Israeli motivation for its presence on the West Bank and Gaza and all of British-mandate Palestine territory is occupation, colonialism, and imperialism.

The letter of Rights and Democracy states, "The building and expansion of settlements in the Israeli-occupied territories reveals the policy of Israel to control and colonize areas of occupied territories." Note the use of the words *colonize* and *reveals.* Israel has not stated that it has a policy of controlling and colonizing areas of occupied territories through the building and expansion of settlements. The letter does not quote or cite any such policy. The letter just imagines such a policy based on its twisted observations of reality. The letter assumes bad faith on the part of the Israeli government.

To take another example, Derrick Pounder, an investigator for Amnesty International, commented following autopsies he carried out in Jenin Hospital in April 2002, "What was striking is what was absent. There were very few bodies in the hospital. There were also none who were seriously injured, only the walking wounded. Thus we have to ask: Where are the bodies and where are the seriously injured?"[181]

The implication of Pounder's question, something that was stated explicitly in anti-Zionist propaganda, was that Israel was engaged in mass killings of civilians and then burying the bodies in unmarked graves to hide their dirty work.

The obvious, good faith answer to the Pounder question, one that subsequently turned out to be true, was that there were so few bodies because there were so few dead. The absence of civilian casualties should have led Pounder to commend Israel for the caution and care with which it fought, to congratulate Israel for avoiding civilian casualties. Instead, it led him to suggest mass crimes and a cover-up.

Pounder has done a number of reports for Amnesty about Israel. Amnesty has quoted these reports in support of its own conclusions on Israel. Pounder's reflex assumption of Israeli bad faith puts into question all the work he has done for Amnesty about Israel.

The letter from Rights and Democracy and the quote from Derrick Pounder are taken as examples not so much because they are egregious as anti-Zionist diatribes, but rather because they come from a human rights organization, in the case of Rights and Democracy, and a human rights investigator, in the case of Derrick Pounder — both of whom should know better.[182]

For anti-Zionists, what comes first is not the events, but their own anti-Zionism. If the facts do not fit the prejudice, then it is the facts that must be changed. Derrick Pounder and Rights and Democracy have not bought the steak — they have not called for the destruction of the State of Israel — but they have bought the sizzle.

Anti-Zionism has corrupted Islamic discourse even more than it has corrupted human rights discourse. Historically, Islam has not been an antisemitic, suicidal religion preaching the killing of innocents. Calls for a holy war against Israel and recruitment of suicidal killers of innocent Jews by indoctrinating them into thinking of themselves as Islamic martyrs have their origins in anti-Zionism, not the Islamic religion.

Muslim intellectual Tareq Ramadan says, "Nothing in Islam can legitimize xenophobia."[183] Dalil Boubakeur, rector of the Grand Mosque of Paris in a speech in April 2002, quoted a passage in the Koran that condemns attacks on Jewish temples and Christian churches.[184]

Regrettably, piety, not just in Islam but in every religion, has all too often become a mask for prejudices that intrinsically have nothing to do with religion.[185] Religion is not the cornerstone of the hatred. Rather, the conceptions of a religion have been construed and twisted to condone the prejudice.[186] Conflicts often give rise to propaganda that use religious grounds to justify attacks. Violence is initiated by conflict entrepreneurs with their own political agendas who, to further their quest for power, make use of the religious feelings of the public at large.[187]

The political distortion of Islam to feed the anti-Israel agenda is evident in the Palestinian mosques, media, and education system. The Palestinian Authority exhorts through its official television channel, PATV, and its newspaper, *Al Hayat-Al Jadidi*, that young children become martyrs. Literature glorifying attacks against Israelis as martyrdom is taught in Palestinian schools.[188]

Examples of abuse of the Islamic religion by antisemitic, anti-Zionist Muslim clerics are legion. For instance, Sheikh Osama Abdullah Khayyat, during the 2002 annual pilgrimage to Mecca, Saudi Arabia, uttered a prayer in the Grand Mosque that included the phrase "Lord ... defeat those tyrant Jews."[189] Media reports describe this incantation as "traditional." Although one Canadian newspaper reported this prayer under the headline "Millions at Mecca pray for Israel's defeat,"[190] as one can see, the prayer is not directed against Israel; it is directed against Jews. It combines both an incantation and a slur against Jews. It says Jews are tyrants. It says I, being Jewish, am a tyrant.

The ideology of Nazism was buttressed by the antisemitism of a perverted Christianity. There are still today some extreme right-wing fringe antisemites who

127

latch on to Christianity to justify their bigotry. All too late, mainstream Christianity took substantial steps to purge itself of antisemitism.

It is unfair to blame Christianity for the Holocaust, to suggest that the Holocaust was inherent in Christianity. Yet there was a direct link between Christianity and the Holocaust. Christianity presented an ideology, a theology of antisemitism, by portraying the whole Jewish community, including Jews living in the modern era, as Christ-killers.

Today's killing of Jews is supported both by a distorted Islam and a corrupted human rights ideal. However, it is as unfair to blame Islam itself for the attack on the World Trade Center, the suicidal killings in Israel, and the attacks on the Jewish community worldwide as it is to blame Christianity for the Holocaust.

Human rights has become the secular religion of our times. Respect for human rights has become the secular equivalent of good and violations of human rights have become the secular equivalent of evil. Perversions of human rights have become the secular equivalent of religious distortions to fuel prejudices and political agendas.

When Israel, because of its very existence, and the Jewish people, because of their active or presumed support for Israel, are accused of complicity in massive violations of human rights, that is the secular equivalent to the antisemitic Christian myth of Jews as Christ-killers or the antisemitic Islamic myth of Jews as tyrants. Just as Christianity after the Holocaust had to purge itself of its anti-semitic theological strains, today both Islam and human rights have to cleanse themselves of their very own anti-Jewish elements.

Though pointing to the reality is useful, it is not a complete answer to this promotion of hatred. Hatred does not stop just because it is factually wrong. Hatred is quasi-theological, founded on belief rather than reason. Like the Christian myth that the Jews killed Christ, which could not be dispelled by hard information that Jews almost two thousand years after the death of Christ bore no responsibility whatsoever for Christ's death, the myth that the State of Israel is guilty of gross violation of human rights cannot be dispelled by hard information alone. What is needed is a renunciation of the core belief that the State of Israel must not exist.

ONE would have thought, given their common parentage and common inspiration, that the United Nations human rights system and the government of the State of Israel would have worked together hand in glove. One would have expected that the human rights system would have supported the state of Israel.

However, just the opposite happened. Like two rival siblings, these two children of the Holocaust have turned against each other. Perversely, Israel became, for the UN human rights system, the primary target of its condemnations. The United Nations human rights system has attacked Israel relentlessly.

The cancerous growth of anti-Zionism has spread from one organ of the United Nations to another. For many organs of the United Nations, anti-Israel denunciation has become the principal item of business. That is certainly true of the United Nations Commission on Human Rights, which has abandoned its human rights vocation to focus on Israel, spending more time and energy on Israel than any other country, passing one resolution after another on Israel and ignoring real violations by countries with abominable records of human rights violations.

In the early years, the United Nations Human Rights Commission focused on themes to the exclusion of countries. Once the system shifted to countries, it shifted to Israel almost immediately. The first target of the Human Rights Commission was South Africa, in 1967. Second was Israel, in 1969. For six years, the Commission considered only these two countries and no others. In 1975, the Commission added Chile to its list.

Even after the UN human rights system broadened its scope beyond its initial trio of Israel, South Africa, and Chile to other countries, the time spent on Israel was disproportionate. For the last forty years, almost 30 percent of country-specific resolutions and 15 percent of the Commission's time have been directed against Israel.[191] For years, fully one-third of the time of the Human Rights Commission was spent on Israel alone.

As well, the invective against Israel by far exceeds the language used against other countries with much worse violations. The United Nations has been so blatantly one-sided in its opposition to Israel for so long that to pick one example is gratuitous. One-sided attacks on Israel have so consumed the United Nations that these attacks have become the first order of business. Libraries could be filled with demonstrations of the imbalance and the double standard of the United Nations against Israel.[192]

For instance, in 1989, a resolution on Israel before the United Nations Commission on Human Rights used such language as "noted with severe disapproval," "strongly condemns," and "deplores." The resolution referred to Israeli practices as "inhuman treatment," "terror," and "flagrant violation of human rights."

That same year, the Commission passed a resolution about Guatemala at the height of its civil war, when disappearances and arbitrary executions were widespread. By any objective standard, the human rights violations in Israel that year paled in comparison with the human rights violations in Guatemala. Yet the language used in the Guatemala resolution was far milder. The resolution stated only that the Commission was "seriously concerned" about the climate of violence and the human rights situation. The Commission stated that it "recognizes that the Government is committed to promoting the protection of human rights" and "urges the Government to intensify its efforts."

Even Iran, suffering from the ravages of the Ayatollah Khomeini, was treated more kindly in 1989 than Israel. The Commission expressed "its deep concern" to Iran at reports of human rights violations and urged the government of Iran to respect human rights.

Rather than being a haven from antisemitism, the United Nations has become a forum for antisemitism. Statements are made within UN precincts that would not have been tolerated within any democratic parliament. For instance, in 1997, the Palestinian representative to the UN Commission on Human Rights, echoing the traditional antisemitic blood libel, claimed that Israeli doctors had injected Palestinian children with the AIDS virus.

Each year matters get worse. The UN Human Rights Commission, at its annual six-week session in 2002, spent a good half of its time on Israel, far more than the time it spent on all other countries of the world combined.

The Commission ignores armed attacks against Israel and condemn Israeli responses. For instance, in 2002, the Commission passed a resolution (which Canada, to its credit, opposed) that had as a preamble:

> Gravely concerned at reports of gross, widespread and flagrant violations of human rights in the occupied Palestinian territory, in particular regarding the violation of the right to life, the arrest and detention of civilians, the restrictions on freedom of movement, the disruption of the delivery of humanitarian and medical assistance, the destruction of infrastructure, the restriction on the freedom of the media, the detention of human rights defenders, as well as the disproportionate and indiscriminate use of Israeli military force against the people of Palestine and its leadership ...

The resolution had as an operative clause:

Condemns the frightening increase in the loss of life, the invasion
of Palestinian cities and villages, the arrest and detention of
Palestinians, the restrictions on the movement of residents as well
as personnel of the International Committee of the Red Cross and
the Palestinian Red Crescent Society, medical personnel, human
rights defenders and journalists, the refusal of humanitarian access
to United Nations Relief and Works Agency for Palestine Refugees
in the Near East, and the serious and systematic destruction of
homes, installations and infrastructure in the territory as reported
by the High Commissioner for Human Rights.[193]

The resolution did not have a peep of criticism for the Palestinian Authority.
The only hint of reference to the suicide bombing attacks was a preamble clause
referring to Security Council resolutions calling for "an immediate cessation of all acts
of violence, including all acts of terror, provocation, incitement and destruction."

Human rights organizations have been wringing their hands about the transformation of the Human Rights Commission into an abusers' caucus. Before the
Commission started its work in 2002, Algeria, Burundi, Kenya, Sudan, Togo,
Vietnam, China, Libya, Cuba, the Democratic Republic of Congo, Russia, Saudi
Arabia, and Syria were members. In 2002, Zimbabwe, Ukraine, and Sri Lanka
joined their ranks. Some of the world's worst human rights violators have made a
point of getting elected to the Commission, with the purpose of forestalling
criticism against themselves. In 2002, there were no resolutions on human rights
abuses in Iran, China, Equatorial Guinea, Chechnya, or Zimbabwe.

Joanna Weschler of Human Rights Watch said, "It is the solidarity of the
abusers. Now we have a situation where the countries that are either targets of the
Commission — or ones that are likely to be targets because of what they are doing
to their people — have enough votes together to escape censure."[194]

The disintegration of the human rights mandate of the Human Rights
Commission may be ending with a failure to act in Zimbabwe or Iran. But it
began with Israel. Once it became plain that the Commission could be a political
playground disrespectful of even the most basic human rights principles, violators
got the message. If Israel could be condemned for violations it did not commit,
simply because it could not muster enough votes, then violators could escape condemnation for violations they did commit if they could muster enough votes.

The obsessive fixation of the Human Rights Commission on Israel and its
silence about Chechnya, Iran, Zimbabwe, and China are two sides of the same
coin. Any institution by necessity has only so much time and energy. Time and
energy spent on Israel are time and energy not available to deal with the human
rights situations in other countries. Indeed, focus on Israel is the violators' tactic
of choice to avoid attention to their own misdoings.[195]

131

Israel is the only state at the Commission to have its own agenda item — under the tendentious title "Question of the Violation of Human Rights in the Occupied Arab Territories, including Palestine." The non-governmental organization United Nations Watch in 2004, relying on the title of the agenda item, had the temerity to object, in a statement at the Commission, to Syrian occupation of Lebanon. A representative of Syria replied that the UN Watch statement was outside the scope of the agenda item, which was directed only against Israel.

Each year the Commission passes a resolution under this agenda item which begins its operative section with a clause that "Reaffirms the legitimate right of the Palestinian people to resist the Israeli occupation."[196] The UN resolutions refer to occupation, but they are careful not to say occupation of what, refusing to reject the anti-Zionist position that all of Israel is occupied territory.

An indication of how far the Commission has drifted from its human rights mooring when it comes to Israel is the endorsement of the killing of innocents through the embrace of the code word *resistance*. Year after year, the Commission endorses resistance to Israeli occupation, without caveat. In the context where suicide bombing is rife, and the resolution says nothing against them, this reads as an affirmation of the legitimate right of the Palestinian people to use suicide bombers to kill innocents, as long as it is done in pursuit of the anti-Zionist cause.

It was the anti-Israel agenda item that was interrupted in 2004 for the special session to condemn the killing of Sheik Yassin. The Commission was tripping over itself to condemn Israel, interrupting the agenda item designed to lambaste Israel in order to have the special session with Israel in its sights. There has never been a special session to condemn the activities of any other state. The Commission has never voted for a special session on the terrorism of Hamas directed against Israel or to condemn the killing of its very own High Commissioner for Human Rights, Sergio De Mello.

At the United Nations, every effort by Israel to defend itself has become illegitimate. In 2002, the focus of UN criticism was the Israeli reoccupation of Jenin, the source and the planning centre of many of the suicide bombings that have plagued Israel; in 2003 the UN General Assembly decided to target the Israeli security fence in the West Bank; in 2004 the UN Commission spotlight was on the Israeli killing of Sheik Yassin, founder and leader of the terrorist organization Hamas.

Though the main instigators of anti-Zionism are the states at war with Israel, many states vote in favour of unbalanced resolutions endorsing fabricated charges against the world's only Jewish state. Most states and non-governmental organizations sit silently while the chamber of the Commission is turned into a hall of incitement against Jews.

The Commission needs to change its ways and stop providing a platform for the demonization of Israel with its consequent demonization of the Jewish people worldwide. Human rights standards prohibit hate propaganda and war propaganda. The Commission should prohibit them within the walls of its chamber, and the chair should rule the attempted demonization of Israel out of order.

Those states who are concerned with the effective functioning of human rights mechanisms at the United Nations should stand up to anti-Zionist bullying. All representatives and states and non-governmental organizations who come to the Commission out of concern for human rights should turn first and foremost against the human rights violations being committed at the Commission in front of them — the incitement to hatred against the Jewish people through the attempt to demonize the Jewish state.

Even the independent human rights mechanisms within the Office of the High Commissioner for Human Rights have been tainted by anti-Zionism. When the mechanisms mobilize to point out and condemn antisemitism, they are chastised.

Maurice Glèlè-Ahanhanzo, the United Nations Special Rapporteur on Contemporary Forms of Racism, Racial Discrimination, Xenophobia, and Related Intolerance, in his 1997 report, wrote, "The use of Christian and secular European antisemitism motifs in Muslim publications is on the rise, yet at the same time Muslim extremists are turning increasingly to their own religious sources, first and foremost the Qur'an, as a primary anti-Jewish source."[197]

A resolution at the 1997 meeting of the United Nations Commission on Human Rights decided, without a vote, "to express its indignation and protest at the content" of the statement and affirmed "that offensive reference should have been excluded from the report."[198] The United Nations has become so captive to the anti-Zionist lobby that when one of its own independent experts states that anti-Zionists are perverting Islam to promote hatred against Jews, all the UN can do is express indignation that someone would be so bold as to confront them with this reality.

The reports by special rapporteurs whose mandates in principle have nothing to do with Israel are filled with one-sided, malicious, fantastical accusations against Israel. One example is the report of Miloon Kothari on adequate housing as a component of the right to an adequate standard of living. His addendum on the West Bank and Gaza, gratuitously mislabelled as occupied Palestinian territories, is, in its entirety, little more than a piece of anti-Zionist propaganda.[199]

Another example is Jean Ziegler, Special Rapporteur on the Right to Food, whose primary concern has not been food, but beating up on Israel. He has attempted, in his capacity as UN rapporteur, to organize a boycott against Israel, writing to a tractor company, Caterpillar, warning them not to sell equipment to Israel. In 2003, the West Bank and Gaza were the only places in the world where he conducted a special mission, the only places for which he wrote a special report. In 2004, he asked the European Union to suspend its trade accord with

Israel. Yet the West Bank and Gaza have a lower rate of underweight children (3 percent) than any state in the Arab Middle East, East Asia, South Asia, sub-Saharan Africa, and Latin America, except Chile.[200] United Nations Watch has called on him to be removed from office for breach of his duties of impartiality, objectivity, and non-selectivity.[201]

John Dugard is another UN inveterate Israel basher. The very title of his mandate, Special Rapporteur on the Situation of Human Rights in the Palestinian Territories Occupied by Israel Since 1967, says it all. His reports glorify anti-Zionist terrorists, calling them "tough" and describing them as showing "determination, daring and success."[202] An earlier chapter criticized his attempts to show that Israeli responses to the attacks against it are disproportionate.

This trio of Miloon Kothari, Jean Ziegler, and John Dugard are glaring examples of anti-Israel bias. But at the UN, there are no innocents. Every special mechanism is tainted.

The special rapporteurs and representatives, independent experts, and chairs of the working groups of the special procedures of the Commission on Human Rights and of the advisory services program put out a joint statement in June 2004 that discussed three topics only: terrorism, migrants, and Israel. Israel was lambasted under the UN-speak rubric "violations of human rights and fundamental freedoms in the occupied Palestinian territories." Israel was the only country that all the UN special mechanisms could agree to denounce.[203]

The United Nations Human Rights Commission is far from the only UN battleground where the wars against Israel are fought. The struggle continues in the General Assembly. Just as the Human Rights Commission abandons its mandate of promotion of respect for human rights when it comes to Israel and actively promotes incitement to hatred against Israel and Jews, so too the General Assembly abandons its mandate of promotion of the peace and security of humanity and becomes a forum for war propaganda against Israel. There are now an estimated 250 Security Council resolutions and 1,000 General Assembly resolutions on Israel. United Nations Secretary General Kofi Annan said in 1999, "It sometimes seems as if the United Nations serves all the world's peoples but one: the Jews."[204]

In a democracy, majority rules. To avoid a tyranny of the majority over disadvantaged minorities, democracies entrench human rights protections in their constitutions.

In the United Nations General Assembly, the majority of states voting may or may not reflect the majority of the world's population. Micro states like Kiribati or Tuvalu have the same vote as states with massive populations like China or India.

States voting at the General Assembly may or may not be democracies reflecting the will of their people. Repressive governments at odds with the will of their people cast votes in the General Assembly that have the same numerical weight as votes of democratic states.

The General Assembly does not rule. General Assembly resolutions cannot be equated to statutes of a legislature. The Charter of the United Nations gives the General Assembly power to make recommendations only.[205]

There is no institutional mechanism, paralleling the courts in democracies, that can invalidate General Assembly votes that fail to meet international human rights standards. The only mechanism available is public disregard. If a General Assembly vote fails to respect the human rights of a minority, the vote should be ignored. That should be so even where the resolution represents the will of the majority of the globe.

When the General Assembly passes a resolution respectful of human rights by consensus, and that resolution is a statement obligating each and every state, then something has happened that has legal force. When the General Assembly passed the Universal Declaration of Human Rights by consensus, that was more than just a statement of political opinion. However, when the General Assembly passes a vote on what Israel should or should not do, that vote tells us what the political position of each and every state that votes is in relation to Israel and nothing more. Such a vote binds neither Israel nor the states voting in favour.

The United Nations General Assembly has become corrupted by an anti-Zionist lobby that has happily undermined the ideals of the United Nations in order to pursue a political agenda. The General Assembly is supposed to be a peace-seeking organization. Instead, it has become, in relation to Israel, a war-mongering organization, passing one politicized anti-Israel resolution after another.

Though there were many low points in the anti-Israel history of the United Nations, perhaps the lowest was the United Nations General Assembly resolution that Zionism is racism, passed by a vote of eighty-nine to sixty-seven in 1975. That resolution sat on the books unrepealed till 1991, when it was revoked by a vote of eighty-seven to twenty-five. There remain, from the last recorded vote, at least twenty-five states that maintain the position that Zionism is a form of racism.

United Nations Secretary General Kofi Annan has called the 1975 resolution "lamentable." He said, "Its negative resonance even today is difficult to overestimate."

The General Assembly has had only ten emergency special sessions in its history, and six have been devoted to Israel. The tenth session, convened in 1997 to lambaste Israel, has remained sitting almost continuously, having been reconvened, by August 2004, thirteen times. Not content with this unending special session, the General Assembly obsesses over Israel in its regular sessions. In 2003, the General Assembly passed eighteen anti-Israel resolutions.

Though Israel was admitted into the United Nations in 1949, it was denied admission to any of the regional groupings. It is the regional groupings that nominate and then vote for state members of United Nations committees. The rejection of Israel from all regional groupings meant that Israel could be elected to none of these committees. Israel could never become a member of, say, the Human Rights Commission or the Security Council because there was no regional bloc to nominate and vote for it. Many of the United Nations institutions that were condemning Israel with abandon Israel could not even join.

The arbitrariness of the exclusion of Israel was highlighted by the election of Syria to the Security Council in the summer of 2001 and its assumption of the rotating chair of the Council. Syria has had a long history of serious human rights violations, including the massacre in the town of Hama in February of 1982. Estimates of the number killed range from ten thousand to thirty thousand.

The obvious regional grouping for Israel to join would be that of the region in which it is found, the Asian grouping. However, Arab states have opposed membership in that grouping. Since the groupings operate by consensus, Israeli membership in the Asian grouping became impossible. Arab states in the Asian grouping continue to this day to let their political animus rule over the dictates of geography. Finally, in the year 2000, Israel was given a form of membership in the Western European and Others Group (WEOG). The "Others" in WEOG include the United States, Canada, Australia, and New Zealand.

The present solution is partial only. Israel is eligible on rotation to sit on United Nations committees in New York but not on United Nations committees elsewhere around the world. So, for instance, Israel is still not eligible for membership in the bureau, the leadership of the Human Rights Commission, which meets in Geneva. Israel was also barred from nominating candidates to UN posts for the first two years, from 2000 to 2002. As well, Israel's regional grouping membership was temporary, till 2004. At that time, the membership had to be renewed.[206]

The use of international institutions to whip up hatred against the Jews reached its apogee in the NGO Forum and World Conference Against Racism. These meetings were supposed to be against racism. Yet, as discussed in the first chapter, they turned out to be for racism against Jews and the Jewish state.

The United Nations General Assembly, on several occasions, called the states parties to the Geneva Convention Relative to the Protection of Civilian Persons in Time of War to convene a conference about what it labelled as "the Occupied Palestinian Territory, including Jerusalem."[207] Canada voted for the resolution in 1999. Only two nations voted against the resolution: Australia and the United States. Israel would have nothing to do with the vote. In July 1999, the states parties did convene such a conference, but adjourned the conference as soon as it began. This was the first time that such a meeting had been called since the Geneva Conventions were adopted in 1949.

By the time the planned date for the conference rolled around in July 1999, the Middle East peace process had picked up again. So the conference was postponed, but not cancelled. Canada, after voting for the conference, worked for its postponement, citing "the highly politicized nature of the conference."[208] The postponement resolution at the conference could not resist getting in a dig at Israel, declaring the settlements illegal. The conference reconvened in December 2001 and this time concluded with a declaration. In the declaration, Israel is called "the Occupying Power." The declaration is similar to the question "When did you stop beating your wife?" The question of whether Israel is committing grave human rights violations is not squarely addressed. It is just assumed that Israel is perpetrating these violations. For example, one paragraph of the concluding declaration states:

> The participating High Contracting Parties call upon the Occupying Power to immediately refrain from committing grave breaches involving any of the acts mentioned in art. 147 of the Fourth Geneva Convention, such as wilful killing, torture, unlawful deportation, wilful depriving of the rights of fair and regular trial, extensive destruction and appropriation of property not justified by military necessity and carried out unlawfully and wantonly.[209]

The paragraph assumes that Israel is committing a number of violations. The statement that Israel is "to immediately refrain" from those acts means that they were then being committed and should be stopped.

There are several other paragraphs that call upon Israel to stop doing heinous acts that the declaration just assumes that Israel is perpetrating. The declaration states that the parties "reaffirm the illegality of the settlements."[210] Four separate paragraphs call on Israel to refrain from committing one awful violation after another.

These calls to refrain are addressed to Israel only. Although some of the language of the declaration is addressed to "parties to the conflict," none is addressed to the Palestinian Authority. The absence of reference to the Palestinian Authority shows that the attempt to apply the Geneva Conventions to Israel is a charade, without any real intention to ensure compliance with the laws of war. The only purpose is to attack Israel.

The concluding declaration deplored the indiscriminate or disproportionate use of force in the Palestinian occupied territory, including East Jerusalem. The phrase "indiscriminate or disproportionate use of force" implies that discriminating or proportionate use of force would be justifiable. What has happened that would justify this? The concluding declaration of the meeting does not give even a hint.

This was the only conference of the states parties in its history. The killing fields of Cambodia did not spur the convening of such a conference. Nor did the genocide in Rwanda, the ethnic cleansing in the former Yugoslavia, the disintegration of

Somalia, or the rise of the Taliban in Afghanistan. If one were looking at the history of human rights violations from the Second World War only through the eyes of the United Nations and the states parties to the Geneva Conventions, Israel would appear to be the worst human rights violator by far. The fact that the World Conference Against Racism became a conference about Israel and the fact that parties to the Geneva Conventions on the Laws of War have met only once in their history has nothing to do with what Israel does and everything to do with the fact that Israel is.

Worst of all in the UN parade of dishonour is the United Nations Relief and Works Agency for Palestine Refugees (UNRWA). Anti-Zionists store ammunition in schools operated by UNWRA. They smuggle arms and terrorists in UNRWA ambulances. They use UNWRA social clubs to host terrorist meetings.[211] The schools financed by UNWRA are anti-Zionist indoctrination units, glorifying suicide bombers. UNWRA officials turn a blind eye to the theft of food and medicine destined for refugees for sale on the black market. The textbooks they pay for are anti-Zionist propaganda pulp. They have Hamas members on their payroll.

Paul McCann, a spokesman for UNRWA, has said, "We don't administer the camps. Our schoolteachers and doctors aren't the ones to root out Hamas. It's like saying the nurses at Bethesda Naval Hospital aren't doing enough to root out crime in southeast Washington." Yet UNRWA officials both ignore and justify the terrorism around them.

Right under the noses of UNRWA, the West Bank town of Jenin had become a centre of bomb factories and operations for anti-Zionist terrorism. Israeli soldiers entered the town in April 2002 to put an end to the operations. UNRWA Commissioner General Peter Hansen, rather than welcoming the effort to combat terrorism, called the incursion, which killed fifty-two Palestinians, of whom an estimated thirty-five were armed combatants, "a human catastrophe that had few parallels in recent history."[212] He said in defence of hiring Hamas members to work for UNRWA, "We do not do political vetting."[213]

UNRWA receives about $10 million a year from the government of Canada, through the Canadian International Development Agency (CIDA). CIDA has expressed concern about the funds it grants to humanitarian agencies being diverted to financing terrorist organizations but has decided to continue financing these agencies all the same. The rationale is that the financing reduces poverty and that poverty is a root cause of terrorism.[214] Aid officials have been instructed to control spending more tightly to prevent diversion of funding to terrorist causes. But CIDA does not control the way UNRWA spends its money.

The abuse of international institutions in the anti-Zionist cause has undermined these institutions, weakening them to the point of ineffectiveness. When they are really needed, they are ignored, because they have so discredited themselves over Israel. When the United Nations cries wolf over Israel again and again for political reasons, then when there is a wolf somewhere else, the UN is just disregarded.

The anti-Israel bias of the General Assembly, the Commission on Human Rights, the general assembly of states parties to the Geneva Conventions on the Laws of War, the non-governmental Forum Against Racism and the World Conference Against Racism are examples of a pervasive problem. Virtually every United Nations conference or assembly, whether it be on aging or housing or the environment, chews up time and resources, no matter what its mandate, on biased, venomous condemnation of Israel. All United Nations venues have become platforms for incitement to hatred against Israel and the Jewish people.

As at the United Nations Human Rights Commission, the General Assembly, and the conference of state parties to the Geneva Conventions on the Laws of War, what mattered most to the anti-Zionist global rabble at the NGO Forum Against Racism and World Conference Against Racism was condemnation of Israel. If the fight against racism and the UN system had to suffer to reach this goal, so much the worse for them. The Durban meetings came out with concluding documents that attempted to shame Israel and its supporters, but in reality shamed the institutions that produced them.

The attack on the credibility of multilateral institutions has a particular effect on the United States, which looks at the UN without a tint of the rose in its glasses that many other states have. The cooperation of the United States, as the world's only superpower and its richest nation, is as important for the United Nations as it is for the United States. The League of Nations foundered largely because the United States never joined.

The United States, in recent years, has been a notoriously poor member of the multilateral community, more often than not going its own way. In May 2002, the United States, which had signed the treaty establishing the International Criminal Court, indicated it did not intend to ratify the treaty, in effect withdrawing its signature.

While this unilateralism is in part explained by the global reach and ambitions of the United States, it is also explained by the failure of the United Nations to get its act together. The behaviour of the UN towards Israel shows the UN to be so dysfunctional that any state viewing the UN objectively would hesitate to resort to the UN for anything.

Ultimately, it is not just the Jewish people who suffer from the UN obsession with Israel. It is the whole UN system. Abstentions, calls for peace in the Middle East, absence from voting, and statements criticizing both sides are not enough. Only when states friendly to human rights are prepared not to tolerate the incessant harping on Israel will the UN human rights system be able to salvage its credibility.

The struggle against anti-Zionism has to be taken to the United Nations itself. At the United Nations, the prototype for combatting anti-Zionism is the repeal in 1991 of the 1975 resolution that Zionism is racism. That sort of repeal should be comprehensive and systematic. The human rights system, like Christianity before it, has to purge itself of its antisemitism. It can do so by only by confronting its anti-Zionism and expunging it from its records. The states parties to the Fourth Geneva Convention on the Protection of Civilian Persons in Time of War need to withdraw the conclusions of their previous meeting. The Human Rights Commission, the General Assembly, and the rest of the UN system need to express their regret for the unending stream of anti-Israel resolutions the system has generated. The next World Conference Against Racism, if there is one, has to have condemnation of the anti-Zionism that leads to antisemitism as the first order of business on its agenda.

Rejection by the UN of the "Zionism is racism" resolution took sixteen years. It will probably take as long, or longer, for the UN system to accept the wrong-headedness of all its other various forms of condemnation of Israel. Right now, matters are getting worse, rather than better. Defamation of Israel and the Jewish community in support of Israel is increasing rather than decreasing, both in vehemence and scope.

Even the biggest reversal can begin with the smallest of steps. To reverse anti-Zionism at the United Nations, that means one of two things: either walking out of meetings, thus refusing to participate in what are nothing more than anti-Israel tirades and denying them the legitimacy that the anti-Zionist lobby seeks, or using those meetings to fight the human rights cause.

When human rights violators like Iran or Libya or Syria fulminate against Israel at UN meetings, one reply should be to remind them of their own human rights records. The fact that the record of Israel is on the table but the record of the countries condemning Israel is not should be all the more reason to use the occasion to remind the world of the human rights records of the most rabid anti-Zionist countries.

The reply should also be that anti-Zionists are abusing the privilege and platform of the United Nations to promote hatred. When people promote hatred, it is wrong to take their slurs seriously as statements of fact. However, promotion of hatred should itself be taken seriously. Hate promotion should be exposed for what it is, whether it occurs inside or outside the United Nations — indeed, especially when it occurs within the walls of the United Nations.

It is hard to believe, but a conference on antisemitism held in June 2003 in Vienna was the first ever of its kind, the first time in history that governments got together to discuss antisemitism. There was no such conference before, during, or immediately after the Holocaust.

The Vienna conference was held under the auspices of the Organization of Security and Cooperation in Europe (OSCE), an organization joining together fifty-five countries of Western, Eastern and Central Europe, Central Asia, and North America. The organization is the offspring of the 1975 Final Act of the Conference on Security and Cooperation in Europe, an agreement that took the place of a Second World War peace treaty between the Eastern and Western blocs.

The Vienna conference was everything that the World Conference Against Racism held in Durban in August and September 2001 was not. Speakers were uninterrupted. Interventions were not shouted down. Meetings were not raided by hostile crowds. Antisemitic chants and slogans were nowhere. There were no marches denouncing the Jews and Israel. There were no booths set up purveying anti-Zionist and antisemitic literature. There were no posters or pamphlets to be seen propagandizing against Israel and Jewish support for Israel. There was no concluding document labelling Israel an international pariah and calling for its destruction.

Jewish voices, voices speaking against antisemitism, including its anti-Zionist component, were heard respectfully. Delegates from countries that are members of the organization listened attentively. The Jewish global leadership was present in full force.

Though the Vienna meeting was an intergovernmental conference, non-governmental organizations were allowed to address the meeting. Many Jewish organizations did so. As well, several countries had non-governmental members of their delegations. These non-governmental members were themselves active in Jewish organizations. I was part of the Canadian delegation at both the Vienna meeting and the Berlin follow-up meeting as a nominee of B'nai Brith Canada.

The global Jewish community, jaded by the treatment of Israel at the UN, has come to think of multilateral organizations and intergovernmental meetings as platforms for denunciation of the Jewish state and hostile venues for the Jewish people. The Vienna meeting was an antidote to that skepticism, a demonstration that multilateralism does not always have to be anti-Zionist and anti-Jewish.

The Vienna meeting needed to be followed up. Combatting antisemitism has to be part of the institutional structure of the OSCE and not just a one-off meeting. But the meeting in Vienna was a good start.

The Berlin conference on antisemitism that took place in April 2004 was part of that follow-up. The conference was historic, productive, and strange. It was historic because it was held in the city that had been the headquarters of the Holocaust, the place where the Holocaust was planned and ordered. It was productive because it precipitated a decision of states to do something practical to combat antisemitism: to collect and report publicly reliable information and statistics about antisemitic crimes. The decision on reporting, made by the Permanent Council of the OSCE in Vienna a week before the Berlin meeting would not have happened but for the looming Berlin meeting. And it was strange because of its silence on the cause of contemporary antisemitism: anti-Zionism. A European Union report on antisemitism that came out shortly before the Berlin meeting noted, "There is a link between the number of reported antisemitic incidents and the political situation in the Middle East" and quoted victims as identifying the perpetrators as "young Muslims," "immigrants," and "people of North African descent." This attribution begs questions because it appears to suggest that the source of the problem is foreigners, a specific community, or a religion, rather than an ideology. That anti-Zionist ideology, though prevalent in North African immigrant Muslim circles, is not confined to them.

The antisemitism that is anti-Zionism is all too often shared by polite European society. Antisemitism has again become respectable in Europe. It is pervasive, permeating political parties and mainstream journalism. The antisemitism that is anti-Zionism is as common in European society today as Aryanism was before the Second World War.

Yet in Berlin, virtually none of the state representatives wanted to talk about this form of antisemitism. The concluding statement of the chair of the Berlin meeting made an oblique reference to Israel, stating, "International developments or political issues including those in Israel or elsewhere in the Middle East never justify antisemitism." But that was it. The link between the existence of Israel and contemporary antisemitism was never drawn.

In Berlin, one state representative after another uttered ringing condemnations of antisemitism. But these were more expiations of guilt for the Holocaust than attempts to address a contemporary problem. Decrying the Holocaust today, while welcome, does not get us very far in addressing the antisemitism around us.

At the non-governmental meeting held the day before the governmental meeting, Brian Klug of the University of Oxford argued that attacks on Jews based on overheated Middle East opinions are not antisemitism. He said of attacks on Jews in Europe, "Some of it is antisemitic hatred. The other is hostility between two groups ... Ethno-religious solidarity is not antisemitic bigotry. Jews are at risk today because of the overspill of Middle East tension."

The overwhelming majority of attacks on Jews in Europe are of exactly this nature, motivated by anti-Zionism, or what Klug calls "Middle East tension." Did the silence of states at the Berlin forum about the anti-Zionist cause of contemporary antisemitism hide the perverse view that Klug expressed, that many of the attacks on Jews in Europe today are not really antisemitic? Was that silence a cover for sympathy with the anti-Zionism that pervades European society? If so, all the state denunciations of antisemitism at Berlin were hollow rhetoric. At Berlin everyone was prepared to condemn antisemitism, but almost no one was prepared to confront it in the main form in which it now exists.

Natan Sharansky, then Minister for the Diaspora in the Israeli government, came closest. He explained why and how some criticism of Israel is antisemitic, and he observed that some of this antisemitism is state sponsored, a phenomenon member states of the OSCE must address. But Israel is not a member of the OSCE, and Sharansky addressed the meeting only as a guest.

In the end, the decision of the Permanent Council that there be statistical collecting and reporting on antisemitism may be the best way to get the OSCE to face the real world of antisemitism. Right now, condemning the source of contemporary antisemitism is too politically touchy. But when the reporting makes it plain as day what is happening, one can hope that the reality of anti-Zionism as antisemitism can no longer be denied.

By 2004, international meetings on antisemitism had become a fad. In addition to the Organization for Security and Cooperation in Europe, the European Union and the Council of Europe had also hosted initiatives on antisemitism. Finally the United Nations itself joined in. The UN conducted a seminar in New York in June 2004 titled "Confronting Anti-Semitism."

The UN meeting was both the most and least significant of the lot. The most, because the UN gathers together almost every single country on the globe. The least, because the meeting was a public information session only, not an intergovernmental meeting.

The rise in antisemitism can be traced to the UN itself, because of the platform, legitimacy, and amplification the UN gives to anti-Zionism. Anne Bayefsky said at the seminar, "The UN has become the leading global purveyor of antisemitism."

The rise in antisemitism has a number of causes and sources, one of which is the United Nations. The use of the United Nations for demonization of the Jewish state and the Jewish people has given these attacks a credibility that they would not otherwise have. The United Nations is not just a venue of hate. It reinforces hate by its seeming authentication of the worst prejudices of the global anti-Zionist mob.

There was at least some comfort from the fact that these concerns could finally be raised inside the United Nations instead of just shouted from the outside. But, in itself, that is not much progress.

The nominal topic of the seminar was, "What can the United Nations do to combat antisemitism?" That was rich. If the UN just ceased purveying antisemitism and did nothing more, that alone would be a major contribution to the struggle against antisemitism.

United Nations Secretary General Kofi Annan was instrumental in making the seminar happen. He introduced its opening session with a speech suggesting that the UN pass a resolution condemning antisemitism, which the UN has never done. But Annan failed to bring the problem of antisemitism back home to the UN. He referred only obliquely to the problem, mentioning the "new antisemitism" and stating, "We must be prepared to examine today's manifestation of antisemitism more closely."

Anne Bayefsky reminded the seminar of Kofi Annan's own contribution to the new antisemitism, citing a speech Annan gave referring to November 29 —

the anniversary of the day the United Nations General Assembly passed a resolution in 1947 calling for the partition of British-mandate Palestine into a Jewish and Arab state — as a day of mourning and grief. This reminder led a questioner to wonder how helpful it was to criticize Annan now, given the steps he had taken in bringing about the seminar.

UN Undersecretary General Shashi Tharoor, who heads the Department of Public Information, which hosted the seminar, prompted a similar ambivalence. His department had been responsible for anti-Zionist seminars and displays. At the anti-semitism seminar itself, Tharoor said all the right things. A UN public informa-tion seminar has no obvious institutional follow-through. Tharoor nonetheless indicated that he would collect the suggestions made at the seminar, as well as other suggestions, and present them to his bosses. Before doing so, he would meet with representatives of non-governmental organizations to get their reactions.

As a stand-alone event, the day was an exercise in hypocrisy, bemoaning anti-semitism within the very institution that was fomenting it.

Establishing UN credibility in the fight against antisemitism has two compo-nents. The first is a change in the position of governments. Felice Gaer of the Jacob Blaustein Institute said at the seminar, "States do not need to wait for consensus to make their positions known." That is certainly true of Canada, which has all too often searched for consensus or refused to block a consensus on anti-Israel resolutions rather than take a position of principle. The second is a change in the behaviour of the UN Secretariat. The arrival from Canada of a new High Commissioner for Human Rights, Louise Arbour, holds out hope of rescuing the UN human rights bureaucracy from the anti-Zionist muck into which it has fallen.

For the Department of Public Information, which hosted the seminar, there is the least excuse for misbehaviour, since action is totally within its hands. Tharoor, at the end of the seminar, told a joke about Adam and Eve. Adam found Eve distant and asked, "Is there someone else?" Tharoor's point was that there is nowhere to go outside the UN, that the UN is the only global intergovernmental body.

But there is something other than the UN organization. There are the UN ideals. As long as the UN wanders from its ideals and offers a home to anti-semitism, those who wish to combat antisemitism will have to work against the UN and, if necessary, outside the UN, in order to promote those ideals.

ANTI-ZIONISM has consequences that go far beyond the immediate goal of weakening support for the existence of Israel. The most graphic are suicide bombings. Others are global attacks on Jewish communities worldwide, the undermining of international institutions, the buttressing of dictatorships in the Middle East, the rise of the extreme right in Europe, violations of Palestinian human rights, a weakening of promotion of respect for human rights in Israel, and the failure of peace negotiations. The most troubling is the threat of yet another genocide of the Jewish people.

The suicide killings in Israel are the crop from the hate sown by anti-Zionism. This is what anti-Zionism leads to, the killing of innocent Jews because they are Jewish. In the twenty-one months from the beginning of the second intifada in September 2000 to May 2002, more than 470 Israelis were killed by suicide bombers, and more than 3,800 were injured. Jan Cienski reported in April 2002 that in the West Bank and Gaza, amongst the Palestinian population, "there seems to be no one" opposed to suicide bombing.

Children treat bombers as role models. Palestinian society has a romance with death.[215] When children kill themselves to kill others, it is the work of adults. It is adults who provide the bombs, the funding, the recruiting, the training, and the indoctrination. Stewart Bell reported in May 2002 that suicide bombings were "planned well in advance by a cadre of senior militants who exploited vulnerable youths, turning them into human weapons."[216] Recruiters put potential bombers in seclusion, cut off from family and friends, and fill their minds with hate. Smuggling a bomber into Israel requires explosives, a vehicle, false documents, and often a disguise. In Nablus, Israeli forces in 2002 found eighteen bomb labs; in Jenin, twelve; in Tubbas, two. The anti-Zionist movement, in its crazed desire to kill Jews, is killing its own children. What greater testament can there be to the madness of anti-Zionism?

It is hard to believe any rational person or organization could ignore the reality of suicide bombings, but the Canadian organization Rights and Democracy managed to do so, observing that there are "victims on both sides (in quite unequal numbers, we should emphasize)."[217] In that one phrase, the organization equated the killing of innocents with the killing of combatants and suggested that Israel is worse than the anti-Zionists by creating a significantly larger number of victims. Consistent with its overall approach, Rights and Democracy gave no figures for victims and no place where figures could be found. According to the International Policy Institute for Counter Terrorism, during those twenty-one months, there were 506 Israeli casualties and 1,450 Palestinian casualties.[218] These figures lump together combatants and civilians. For Palestinians, they also include suicide bombers and Palestinians murdered by other Palestinians as Israeli collaborators.

The status of a combatant is sometimes not that easy to determine, particularly when those who attack Israel do not wear uniforms and are not subject to a command structure responsible for enforcing the laws of war. Nonetheless, Dan Radlauer of the International Policy Institute for Counter Terrorism estimates that 53 percent of the Palestinian dead and 22 percent of the Israeli dead were combatants. In other words, the majority of Palestinian dead were combatants. An overwhelming majority of the Israeli dead were innocent civilians. Age and sex are clear-cut and emphasize this disparity. During that twenty-one-month period, Israeli women suffered three times as many casualties as Palestinian women; Israeli men over forty suffered more than twice as many casualties as Palestinian men over forty.

These percentages show the imbalance that one can see every day in the headlines. Anti-Zionists target innocent civilians. Israel, in response, targets combatants, but in so doing, also kills innocent civilians. Deliberately killing civilians is never under any circumstance justifiable and cannot be equated with deliberately killing combatants, even when civilians also die.

At a seminar at the University of Toronto in June 2002, a contributor justified suicide bombings by the fact that anti-Zionists do not have planes or tanks.[219] Nizar Rayan, a Hamas leader in Gaza, said that Palestinians were at war with Israel and had no other choice. He added, "If we had weapons like the Israelis, we would kill them in a way that is acceptable to Americans."[220]

Yet violation of basic human rights is never acceptable, and certainly not justified by an inequality of arms. It is no defence to the killing of innocent Israelis that the attacker does not have the weaponry to launch an effective attack against the Israeli military. What is wrong with suicide bombs is not just the means but the targets. The use of planes and tanks to target innocent civilians would be no more justifiable than the use of suicide bombers.

Iraq under Saddam Hussein made substantial payments to the family of each suicide bomber. Before March 2002, those payments were US$10,000 for the family of each killer. In March 2002, Iraq bumped up this grisly payment to US$25,000 per killer.[221] A spate of suicide bombings in Israel in March and April followed close on the heels of this announced increase in payments.

An eloquent testimony to the priorities of Iraq was its pay scale. Iraq also paid money to the family of Palestinian gunners killed in armed combat with Israeli soldiers, but less. Families of gunners killed in combat are paid US$10,000. In other words, if you conformed to the laws of war and died fighting Israeli soldiers, Iraq was willing to pay your family substantially less than if you died killing Jewish innocents.

A second crop in the harvest of hate is an increase in global antisemitism. Jews worldwide are seen as demons because of their actual or even only perceived support for a demonized Israel. In Canada, Al-Qaeda planned a bombing of a Jewish quarter in Montreal, but they were arrested before the bombing was carried out. Despite the increase in hate crimes against Muslims after September 11, Jews remained the largest single victim group in Toronto in 2001.[222] Graffiti equating the Star of David with the swastika can be seen throughout Canada. Jews are the most frequent targets of bigots in Canada, leading hate crime statistics. They alone are victims of one-quarter of the hate crimes in Canada.[223]

In France, on March 31, 2002, synagogues across the country — in Marseilles, Lyon, Nice, and Strasbourg — came under attack. The Marseilles synagogue burned to the ground.[224] The same day a synagogue in Brussels, Belgium, was firebombed.

In January 2002, Jews and Jewish institutions were attacked in Paris suburbs of Goussainville, Creteil, and Montreuil.[225] In 2001 in France, there were more than three hundred such attacks. The anti-Jewish atmosphere in France has been compared to the intellectual climate at the time of the Second World War Vichy government.[226] The French ambassador to England in December 2001 called Israel "that shitty little country," and remained in his post.

The United Kingdom Community Security Trust reported in March 2002 that attacks against the Jewish community in the United Kingdom fluctuate with events in the Middle East.[227] The intifada led to increased attacks against the Jewish community in the United Kingdom. Inciters have included local Arab groups and leaders — Al Muhajiroun, Muslim cleric Abdullah Faisal, and the Islamic Society. Faisal had toured Britain calling for the killing of Jews.[228] The Islamic Society attempted to ban supporters of Israel from the campus of the University of Manchester.[229] Al Muhajiroun is considered to be the likely source of pamphlets stating, "The hour will not come until the Muslims kill the Jews."

American journalist Daniel Pearl, a reporter for the *Wall Street Journal*, was killed in January 2002 in Pakistan because he was Jewish. Kidnappers made a video of his killing in which they had him "confess" that he was Jewish. The video is a graphic portrayal of the view that being Jewish is sufficient justification for killing anyone.

Every Jewish community institution around the world has had to respond to this rise in global antisemitism with increased security. For instance, the Jewish Community Campus in Winnipeg now has security staff check photo identification of everyone who enters the building. Security precautions like this are common to Jewish community institutions worldwide.

Repression in the Middle East and strengthened dictatorships are poisoned fruit from the poisoned tree of anti-Zionism. The anti-Zionist form of anti-semitism today is what antisemitism was in Hitler's time, an ideological device to justify and increase repression. This anti-Zionist form of antisemitism, like earlier antisemitism, harms not just Jews, but everyone. It is no coincidence that the most virulent anti-Zionist states are the least democratic Arab states, the states with the worst human rights records, the states posing the greatest risk to peace for not just Israel, but all their neighbours. These states attempt to legitimize their own repression and aggression by hate propaganda and war propaganda against Israel. A report from the United Nations Development Programme writes that the Palestinian-Israeli conflict has bridled progress by supplying an excuse to stifle dissent.[230] Rachad Antonius writes, "When the conflict with Israel is not the real reason behind repressive policies [of Arab governments], it is used as a handy excuse by governments to justify such repressive policies."[231]

The greatest threat to peace and human rights in the region comes from neither the existence nor the behaviour of the state of Israel, but rather the ideology and practices of Israel's anti-Zionist neighbours. It is no small measure of the failure of the United Nations that the organization fails to register this reality.

The protests around the Arab world against Israel's attempts to defend itself against suicide bombers made evident the political manipulation of anti-Zionism. Civil wars with Arab and Muslim states and wars between Arab and Muslim states have killed far more people than the wars and terrorist attacks against Israel. Sudan, for instance, with a civil war that has claimed more than five times the victims of all the anti-Israel wars and terrorist attacks combined, witnessed demonstrations against Israel far exceeding any public opposition to their own civil war.[232] The disconnect between the reality of human rights violations at home and the public opposition in Arab countries to Israeli self-defence illustrates more than just political forces at play. It shows that success that the propaganda of hatred against Israel and Jews that anti-Zionists have achieved.

Yet another child of anti-Zionism is the rise of the extreme right in Europe. It is no coincidence that Jean-Marie Le Pen of the extreme right-wing National Front finished second in the French presidential runoff of April 2002, eliminating socialist candidate Lionel Jospin, immediately after a number of anti-Zionist attacks on Jewish community institutions in France. Racism cannot be contained. Once it is accepted against the Jews, it is accepted generally. The struggle against racism requires solidarity. Once one minority community attacks another minority community on racist grounds, it is the ideology and politics of racism that is the winner. For the supporters of Jean-Marie Le Pen, the anti-Zionist attacks on Jews prompted the response, "a plague on both their houses." For the National Front, there was no desire to sort out right from wrong. Minority victims and perpetrators are both equally wrong.

The rise of anti-Zionism in France has boomeranged against Arabs and Muslims. Le Pen is antisemitic, anti-Arab, and anti-Islam. Arab and Islamic minorities in France have as much to fear from a National Front government as the Jewish community does. Anti-Zionism means cutting the throats in Europe of the people that anti-Zionists argue they are supporting.

Anti-Zionism, like antisemitism, is not just one phenomenon, but rather a string of phenomena, from the polite to the extreme. At its extreme, it is the elimination of Israel and all those who support it. In its polite form, it is the notion that the existence of Israel is disreputable. It is a distaste, a refusal to defend, a willingness to believe criticism and slurs without foundation. It is this form of polite anti-Zionism that we find throughout Europe, what European capitals see as the middle ground between the anti-Zionist hatred in the Arab world and support for the existence of Israel.

This polite anti-Zionism has its own human rights consequences: the failure of Western societies to defend themselves against attacks on their own Jewish communities, minimizing the gravity of those attacks, pretending to explain, understand, and justify them. Human rights violations are not just the work of hooligans. They result from a state failure to protect.

Le Pen has been condemned both legally and politically for calling the Holocaust a detail of history in 1987. In France, Holocaust denial is a crime. Even Le Pen's circumlocution led to a conviction, in 1990, under French law. He was sentenced to a fine of 1.2 million francs plus costs.

Le Pen repeated this remark ten years later in 1997 on a visit to Munich, Germany. The Munich public prosecutor laid a charge against Le Pen under German law for denying the Holocaust. In October 1998, the European Parliament lifted Le Pen's parliamentary immunity so that the Munich prosecutor could proceed against him. The vote was against Le Pen by 420 votes to 20. Le Pen did not return to Munich so that he could be tried on the charge.

Yet Europe acts towards Israel as if the Holocaust were a detail of history. Honouring the memory of the Holocaust today means respecting the right of Israel to exist. Israel was created by Zionist Jews and not by the Holocaust; but the Holocaust was a catalyst to its creation. European condemnation of Le Pen for his trivialization of the Holocaust rings hollow as long as Europe continues to treat Israel so shabbily. Voters in France find it hard to take seriously French mainstream indignation over Le Pen when that same mainstream, in its attitudes and behaviour towards Israel, betrays many of the same attitudes as Le Pen articulates.

The most perverse consequence of anti-Zionism is violation of the human rights of Palestinians. I do not mean to suggest by this that anti-Zionists should be blamed for human rights violations that individual Israelis may inflict in over-reaction to provocation. Provocation goes to mitigation of sentencing, not to innocence or guilt. When and if Israelis inflict human rights violations, they must bear full responsibility for those violations, whether they are provoked or unprovoked.

The linkage between anti-Zionism and denial of Palestinian human rights violations is a good deal more direct than that. Anti-Zionism, by definition, is the rejection of the two-state solution to the conflict over the territory of British-mandate Palestine. This rejection of the two-state solution is a rejection of both states, not just one. It is a rejection of Israel. But it is also a rejection of a Palestinian state that sits beside Israel at peace with Israel.

All that is needed for respect of the rights of Palestinians is acceptance of the two-state solution. But the Palestinian and Arab leadership have consistently refused that solution. The only way the Palestinian people will ever have their own state is through acceptance of the existence of the State of Israel and the renunciation of use of the territory adjoining Israel for attacks on Israel. Anti-Zionism is a rejection of the right to self-determination of both the Jewish people and the Palestinian people.

Yet another perverse consequence of anti-Zionism is the weakening of the promotion of human rights in Israel. The corruption of human rights discourse and institutions when directed against Israel discredits promotion of respect for human rights in Israel. It becomes impossible for United Nations human rights discourse critical of Israel to be treated seriously, except as hate propaganda fodder.

Turning to United Nations documents for assistance in promoting respect for human rights in Israel is like turning to the records of the Spanish Inquisition for the promotion of respect for Christianity or resorting to the reports of the Star Chamber for the promotion of loyalty to the British Crown. No one hoping for credibility in promoting respect for human rights in Israel would cite United Nations documents or invoke UN institutions.

Israel was criticized for refusing to cooperate with the UN's proposed investigation into the events in Jenin in April 2002. Once Israel refused its cooperation, the planned investigation was cancelled. But after the UN Human Rights Commission had passed a resolution condemning Israeli forces for mass killings in Jenin and for setting fire to the Bethlehem Church of the Nativity, both of which had not occurred, but had said nothing about suicide bombing attacks on Israel, it is little wonder that Israel refused.

In Canada and in many other countries, United Nations criticism has resonance and impact. Canada takes pride in complying with international obligations and judgments. There are many instances to which one can point where Canada has gone to great lengths to avoid or react to an adverse UN judgment. Human rights advocates in Canada turn to the United Nations system to support their cause. No one serious about promoting respect for human rights in Israel would do the same. That is a pity, not just for the United Nations, but for those truly concerned about the promotion of human rights in Israel.

Non-governmental organizations have to worry about the same erosion of credibility. When the Canadian organization Rights and Democracy engaged in Israeli human rights work with a one-sided presentation of the facts, misrepresentation of the law, unsubstantiated allegations, and assumption of Israeli bad faith, that was too bad for Rights and Democracy. It was also too bad for the promotion of human rights in Israel. What impact can Rights and Democracy hope to have on the human rights scene in Israel when the organization goes about its work on such a wrong footing?

Something similar can be said about the more established international non-governmental human rights organizations like Amnesty International, Human Rights Watch, or Lawyers Committee for Human Rights. When those groups remain silent or evasive in the face of the human rights onslaughts against the Jewish community (as they did in Durban), when they endorse the non-existent Palestinian right of return, or when they employ biased researchers (see the earlier example of Derrick Pounder), the organizations themselves are tarnished. But so is the cause of respect for human rights in Israel. If governments and intergovernmental and non-governmental organizations are all prepared to abandon the cause of human rights in Israel for one-sided delegitimizing criticism of Israel, then where can the allies of respect for human rights in Israel turn for help?

Anti-Zionism has been the main obstacle to peace between Israel and its neighbours. The consequence of anti-Zionism has been unending war. By portraying Israel as the primary or sole human rights violator, UN institutions embitter the dispute. Anti-Zionists become more intransigent, more determined to destroy the State of Israel through military means.

UN condemnations do more than just reflect the anti-Zionism that is a facet of state policy of so many countries in the world. UN sanction for this bigotry gives it a credibility it would not otherwise have. It hardens the advocates of war with Israel; it makes peace with Israel harder to achieve. Any peace-seeking state should vote and speak without hesitation against each and every anti-Zionist UN resolution. The standard response of Canadian Foreign Affairs officials to this sort of suggestion is that Canada needs to adopt a balanced or even-handed approach at the UN and not support Israel without qualification. The claimed advantage is that Canada can act as an honest broker, mediating competing claims of Israel and the Arab world.[233]

This Foreign Affairs analysis of UN votes on anti-Zionist resolutions as a choice between balance and unqualified support for Israel is grossly misleading. The real choice is between remaining silent when basic values are being violated and protesting those violations. Standing for or against suicide bombing, the existence of Israel, the effective functioning of the UN — these are, in substance, what the anti-Zionist resolutions offer. Virtually all the UN resolutions on Israel at the Commission on Human Rights and the General Assembly have only one purpose: delegitimizing the State of Israel. But Canada accepts that Israel should exist. Canada should not be playing the game of the anti-Zionists by voting for or even abstaining on these resolutions. The notion that Canada can somehow help the peace process by doing so is farfetched. Each of these resolutions that passes, each vote they get, makes peace less likely. As long as anti-Zionists have UN votes in their pockets, they are fortified in their determination to destroy the State of Israel and avoid any negotiated peace.

Since 1948 and the creation of the State of Israel, the main obstacle to peace between Israel and its neighbours is rejection of the very existence of Israel by Arab states and the leadership of the Palestinian population. In the wars and terrorist attacks against Israel, exaggerated, one-sided United Nations resolutions have been ammunition, an extension of the fighting by other means. The United Nations has become a leading forum for war propaganda against Israel. Anti-Israel resolutions embolden the anti-Israel warmongers, increase their intransigence, and convince them of the rightness of their cause. With each United Nations anti-Israel resolution, the prospect of peace recedes.

The same can be said of criticism of Israel by human rights organizations. Promotion for respect of human rights should lead to peaceful settlement of disputes. However, misplaced, unbalanced criticism has the opposite effect.

Resort to violence ignores the obligation to seek peaceful settlement of disputes.[234] Suicide bombings, aside from being the antithesis of negotiations, have the effect of pushing both sides away from the negotiating table.

To superficial observers, the failure of peace negotiations is inexplicable, because the difference between the parties is so small. The Palestinian Authority, as a result of the Oslo Peace Accords, ended up in control of 95 percent of the Palestinian population of the West Bank and Gaza. The last Barak offer before peace negotiations broke off gave the Palestinians 97 percent of the West Bank and all of Gaza. The reason for the failure of negotiations, despite the seemingly small differences, is anti-Zionism.

Anti-Zionism impacts both Israeli and Palestinian negotiators. Israeli negotiators do not want to be seen to be rewarding violence. If Israeli negotiators make concessions immediately after a violent anti-Zionist attack, it gives the impression that the concessions are made because of the attacks. The concessions would then embolden the attackers and encourage further attacks. In order to convey the message that there will be no reward for violence, Israeli positions harden, or Israel breaks off negotiations altogether until the violence ceases.

Moreover, anti-Zionism raises doubts in Israeli minds about the good faith of Palestinian negotiators. Palestinian negotiators, even when they renounce anti-Zionism, have had a history of anti-Zionism. One question is whether that renunciation is real. Is the expressed desire of Palestinian negotiators for a Palestinian state a desire for two states living in peace side by side, or for a launching pad for attacks on the existence of the State of Israel free from the constraints imposed by the Israeli presence in the West Bank and Gaza?

The question of good faith is posed by the present behaviour of negotiators as well as their past behaviour. There is evidence that the Palestinian Authority has been complicit in suicide bombings. Documents seized by Israelis from the compound of Yasser Arafat showed that he personally authorized a payment of US$20,000 in June 2002 to the al-Aqsa Martyrs Brigade, which has orchestrated a number of suicide bombings.[235] When negotiations were ongoing, there was substantial violence directed against Israel which negotiators supported and which those associated with the negotiators helped to organize.

For Palestinian negotiators, anti-Zionism poses its own problems. The popularity of anti-Zionism in their own constituency means that any deal they reach will seem like a sellout. A substantial component of the population that the negotiators represent do not want any deal that accepts the existence of the State of Israel. This prevalent sentiment pushes Palestinian negotiators away from a deal, indeed away from the bargaining table.

As well, there is the intimidation. Anti-Zionist terrorism terrorizes Palestinians who are sympathetic to the existence of the State of Israel. The most vulnerable victims of anti-Zionist terrorism are pro-Israeli Palestinians in the West Bank and Gaza. Israelis are defended by their owned armed forces. Pro-Israeli Palestinians in the West Bank and Gaza are defended by no one.

Anti-Zionists are judge, jury, and executioners of accused collaborators. Those killed in the West Bank and Gaza as collaborators are in the hundreds.[236] The violent fervour anti-Zionists direct against anyone in the West Bank and Gaza seen as supporting Israel affects everyone, including journalists, human rights and humanitarian workers, and negotiators.

It is sometimes said that a casualty of war is truth. It can also be said that a casualty of lies is peace. The lies of anti-Zionism have sounded for over fifty-seven years a death knell to peace in the Middle East.

The most alarming consequence of anti-Zionism is the threat of another genocide against the Jewish people. As the Holocaust and the attacks on the World Trade Centre have taught us, there is no limit to the evil that those in the thralls of hatred are prepared to inflict. Mass destruction comes as easily to the hate-crazed as the killing of individual human beings.

The only difference between those who organize suicide bombers at cafés and those who organized the Holocaust is technology. Once a fanatic has committed to the enterprise of killing innocents, all that limits the number of dead is the access to weapons of mass destruction. With the Holocaust, it was not so much that antisemitism had reached new depths as that it had reached new technological possibilities. Today we are at yet another technological plateau, which gives new scope for eliminationist antisemitism.

For genocide, we have to look at remote possibilities. There is a tendency to avoid thinking of the worst. Denial sets in. Denial comes easier when genocide has not happened. Yet to ignore the possibility of genocide means whistling in our own graveyard.

We have to think backwards as well as forwards. We have to think about how to prevent genocide. But we also have to think, Suppose there is a genocide. What could we have done? What were the warning signs that we missed? Once there is a genocide, it is too late to do anything about it. If we are going to get the benefit of hindsight, it has to be imaginative hindsight. Although imagining genocide is a most unpleasant exercise, it must be conducted if genocide is to be prevented. So let us imagine a post-Holocaust genocide of the Jewish people. How would it, how could it happen?

The most likely way in which genocide would be perpetrated against the Jewish people today would be an attack on Israel using weapons of mass destruction. It is easy to imagine individuals or terrorist organizations who have the motivation to use weapons of mass destruction against Israel. They have the will but not the means. A state is more likely to have the means than individuals or terrorist organizations. So let us assume that this sort of attack has been launched by a state. Which is the likeliest state, and what would have been the warning signs? How could we have foreseen the threat?

One warning would have been the development of weapons of mass destruction through stealth. A second would have been vicious anti-Zionist and antisemitic propaganda. A third would have been the depersonalization of Jews in deed as well as word. A fourth would have been complicity in the mass killing, including mass killing of Jews. A fifth would have been threats of the most dire sort. These are the only warning signs we are likely to get.

No state determined to launch a genocidal attack against Israel is likely to announce in advance the timing of the attack and the exact means of destruction to be used. We would have to look for signs and indicators.

The state with all these signs in place is Iran. Iran has the deadliest combination of will and potential means. If Iran were to attack Israel with nuclear weapons, there will have been no other indicator, in hindsight, that we would have been able to pick up. If we are to contemplate the possibility of genocide, as we must, Iran has to be considered as a possible initiator of a genocidal attack against Israel.

Iran has extensive oil and natural gas resources. Yet it is developing nuclear reactors for which it has no apparent fuel need. Europe has offered to supply Iran with enriched uranium for fuel purposes, but Iran has declined the offer. It is processing huge amounts of raw uranium, sufficient to build several nuclear weapons.

The government has not been cooperating with the International Atomic Energy Agency, which is responsible for enforcing the Nuclear Non-Proliferation Treaty, which Iran has signed and ratified. Mohamed ElBaradei, the head of the agency, has called Iranian cooperation "less than satisfactory."[237] He criticized Iran for its "changing and, at times, contradictory" stories.[238]

The International Atomic Energy Agency, on inspection, discovered in Iran P-2 centrifuges that can be used to enrich uranium for nuclear weapons and sealed the centrifuges. After the inspectors left, Iran broke the seals.[239]

The development has been secret. Iran bought uranium enrichment centrifuges on the black market from Pakistan and then lied about owning them. United Nations inspectors have found in Iran many traces of enriched uranium. Enriched uranium has no civilian use; it has value only as a component of nuclear weapons. After the discovery, Iran announced it was suspending uranium enrichment operations, but it secretly bought black market magnets to operate centrifuges that would allow it to continue and enhance its enrichment operations. Russian sources report that Iran has attempted to buy black market deuterium gas, which can be used to boost nuclear explosions.[240]

Iranian Foreign Minister Kamal Karrazi rejected international restrictions on Iran's nuclear program and called on the international community to accept Iran as a member of the nuclear club.[241] President Mohammad Khatami, in response to a proposed resolution deploring Iranian lack of cooperation with the International Atomic Energy Agency, said, "If this resolution passes, Iran will have no moral commitment to suspend Iranian enrichment."

Iran has a plant in Natanz that was used secretly for uranium enrichment. Its existence was revealed by Alireza Jafarzadeh, now an Iranian exile. He said, "Iran is playing a cat-and-mouse game with the inspectors. Their cooperation is intended to confuse the International Atomic Energy Agency, to divert their attention, to buy time while they get closer to their goal — a weapon."[242]

Hashemi Rafsanjani, a former president of Iran, said in 2001 stated:

> The survival of Israel depends on the interest of global arrogance and colonialism, and as long as this base is beneficial to them, they will preserve it. Muslims must surround colonialism and force them [the colonialists] to see whether Israel is beneficial to them or not. If one day the world of Islam comes to possess the weapons currently in Israel's possession [meaning nuclear weapons] — on that day this method of global arrogance would come to a dead end. This is because the use of a nuclear bomb in Israel will leave nothing on the ground, whereas it will only damage the world of Islam.[243]

Rafsanjani also said, "In due time the Islamic world will have a military nuclear device and then the strategy of the West would reach a dead end, since one bomb is enough to destroy all Israel."[244]

Iran has missiles with a range to reach Israel that have a slogan visible in bold paint: "We will wipe Israel from the face of the Earth."[245] The religious leader of Iran, Ayatollah Khamenei, said, "The cancerous tumour called Israel must be uprooted."

Many people have understandably expressed concern about the Iranian undercover nuclear program. The response of Iranian Defence Minister Ali Shamkhani was to threaten a pre-emptive strike.[246] General Mohammad Baqer Zolqadr, deputy chief of Iranian Revolutionary Guards, and Yadollah Javani, head of the political bureau of the Revolutionary Guards, threatened an attack on the functioning Dimona nuclear reactor as retaliation against a hypothetical Israeli strike on the Iraqi Bushehr nuclear plant under construction.[247] Such a strike, if successful, would spew radioactive waste throughout Israel and make much of Israel unliveable.

The examples from Iran of demonization of Israel and depersonalization of Jews are legion. The religious leadership of Iran uses anti-Israel and anti-Jewish rhetoric as rabidly as the most crazed fundamentalist. One must keep in mind in assessing the threat from this rhetoric that it is the mullahs and not the energy bureaucrats that have full control over the Iranian nuclear program.[248]

United Nations High Commissioner for Human Rights Mary Robinson had promised that Israel would be allowed to attend the Asian preparatory meeting of the World Conference on Racism. But the meeting was held in Tehran, and Iran refused to allow Israeli delegates to attend.[249]

Iranian judo competitor Arah Miresmaeili refused, on instructions from his government, to compete against his Israeli opponent, Yudi Vaks, at the 2004 Athens Olympics and forfeited the match. President Khatami praised Miresmaeili as "the champion of the 2004 Games" and promised that he would be recognized "in the history of Iranian glories."[250]

Iranian officials have such a rabid hatred of Israel that they refuse to even call the country by its name. Instead it is called "the Zionist entity."

Since the Islamic Revolution in 1979, Iran has condemned seventeen Jews to death on various national security charges. Iran arrested thirteen Jews in January and March 1999. Charges were never made public nor even communicated to the accused. Prior to trial the accused were held in incommunicado detention for over a year.[251] I had asked Iran for a visa to observe the trial for B'nai Brith Canada. I never got a response. The trial was secret. There was no evidence against any of the accused other than coerced confessions. Ten of the thirteen were convicted in July 2000 and sentenced from four to thirteen years in prison. What appeared to precipitate the charges was, according to their advocates, the "increasingly fervent brand of Orthodox Judaism" practised by the accused.[252]

An Iranian nuclear attack on Israel would kill many who are not Jewish. Yet Iran has shown itself more than willing to kill non-Jews. Indeed, its leaders have justified the killing of Muslims whether the victims pass the mullahs' test of piety or not. If the victims are not pious, the killing is justified as punishment. If the victims are pious, the killing is justified as martyrdom.

Iran massacred an estimated thirty thousand people, including women and teenage children, in 1988.[253] They were massacred because they were actual or perceived supporters of an opposition group (the People's Mojahedin Organization); because they were leftists, intellectuals, or students; or because they belonged to ethnic minority groups. Ayatollah Khomeini ordered the executions of the Mojahedin because they were "fighters against God." He ordered the execution of leftists, intellectuals and students because they were "apostates from Islam." Those executed were already in prison, as political prisoners, and were no threat to anyone at the time of their deaths.

A suicide bomber drove a car bomb into the Israeli embassy in Buenos Aires, Argentina, in March 1992. The attack killed twenty-nine people and injured one hundred. Ibrahim Hussein Berro, a second suicide car bomber, attacked the Jewish community centre (called the Israeli-Argentine Mutual Association) in Buenos Aires in July 1994, killing eighty-five and wounding more than two hundred. The Argentinean intelligence service investigated this second attack and concluded, in a detailed report, that the attack was planned and organized by the government of Iran. The decision to mount the attack was made in August 1993 by Iran's National Security Council. Participating in the decision were then and current leader Ayatollah Khamenei and then president Hashemi Rafsanjani. Iran used Hezbollah to perpetrate the attack.[254]

Hezbollah was established by Iran in 1982. In 1983, a Hezbollah suicide bomber killed 241 American soldiers sleeping at a Marine barracks in Beirut. Family members of the deceased sued the government of Iran in the United States courts for damages. Federal Court judge Rocye Lamberth, in a May 2003 judgment wrote, "It is clear that the formation and emergence of Hezbollah as a major terrorist organization is due to the government of Iran. Hezbollah presently receives extensive financial and military technical support from Iran, which funds and supports terrorist activities."

He awarded damages against Iran for the bombing.[255]

Though on some issues there is a division between the religious leader of Iran, Ayatollah Khamenei, and the secular leader, President Khatami, on anti-Zionism, the two factions are of one mind. There is no moderate government voice in Iran when it comes Israel and the Jews. Khatami has said that he wanted peaceful relations with all states in the world but Israel.[256]

Nuclear weapons are not the only weapons of mass destruction. Iran could cease its nuclear weapons development program tomorrow and the threat of genocide from Iran would remain. More importantly, Iran must renounce its anti-Zionism. Those who want to prevent Iran from inflicting genocide must make the combat against Iranian anti-Zionism the first priority.

CHAPTER ELEVEN
Jews from Arab Countries

ANTI-ZIONISTS have fostered, sustained, and underlined the plight of Palestinian refugees in order to attack Israel. This distorted focus on Palestinian refugees is highlighted by the silence about Jewish refugees from Arab countries. Those who are truly concerned about justice for refugees would not harp on just Palestinian refugees and say nothing about Jews displaced from Arab countries.

Statistics alone tell a striking story.[257] In 1948, the year Israel began, the Jewish population of Arab countries was 856,000; in 2001 the figure was 7,800. During that same period, another 57,000 Jews were displaced from Iran. About 600,000 of the over 900,000 Jews who had previously lived in Arab countries and Iran settled in Israel.

According to United Nations estimates, the Arab-Israeli war of 1948 created 726,000 Palestinian refugees. So there were more Jewish refugees uprooted from Arab countries and Iran than there were Palestinians who became refugees as a result of the 1948 war.

Each country has its own drama. In 1948, the Jewish population of Aden was 8,000. In 2001 there were none. For Algeria, the figures for 1948 and 2001 were 140,000 and none. For Egypt, the numbers for those years were 75,000 and 100. For Iraq, the numbers were 135,000 and 100. For Lebanon, they were 5,000 and 100. For Libya, they were 38,000 and none. For Morocco, they were 265,000 and 5,700. For Syria, they were 30,000 and 100. For Tunisia, they were 105,000 and 100. For Yemen, they were 55,000 and 200.

These people were not, for the most part, voluntary migrants seeking to leave their home countries for economic reasons or wanting to immigrate to Israel for religious or ethnic reasons. They were mainly refugees forced to flee to save themselves. Before they were displaced, they were threatened, harassed, and persecuted. Their property was forfeited or confiscated, either before or after they fled. The Jews who fled Arab countries and Iran are a victim population, people who suffered human rights violations at the hands of the governments and populations in the countries in which they lived.

Listen to the voices of the anti-Zionists. During the Palestine Partition debate at the United Nations, the Palestinian delegate to the UN, Jamal al-Hussayni (representing the Arab Higher Committee of Palestine to the UN General Assembly), said, "It must be remembered that there are as many Jews in the Arab world as there are in Palestine whose positions ... will become very precarious. Governments in general have always been unable to prevent mob excitement and violence."[258]

In address to the Political Committee of the UN General Assembly on November 14, 1947, just five days before that body voted on the partition plan for Palestine, Heykal Pasha of Egypt said:

> The United Nations ... should not lose sight of the fact that the proposed solution might endanger a million Jews living in the Moslem countries. Partition of Palestine might create in those countries an antisemitism even more difficult to root out than the antisemitism which the Allies were trying to eradicate in Germany ... If the United Nations decides to partition Palestine, it might be responsible for the massacre of a large number of Jews.
>
> A million Jews live in peace in Egypt [and other Muslim countries] and enjoy all rights of citizenship. They have no desire to emigrate to Palestine. However, if a Jewish State were established, nobody could prevent disorders. Riots would break out in Palestine, would spread through all the Arab states and might lead to a war between two races.[259]

Shortly after, Iraq's Foreign Minister, Fadil Jamali, at that same United Nations meeting, said, "The masses in the Arab world cannot be restrained. The Arab-Jewish relationship in the Arab world will greatly deteriorate ... Harmony prevails among Muslims, Christians and Jews [in Iraq]. But any injustice imposed upon the Arabs of Palestine will disturb the harmony among Jews and non-Jews in Iraq; it will breed inter-religious prejudice and hatred."[260]

The *New York Times* article of May 1948 reported on a law drafted by the Political Committee of the Arab League intended to govern the legal status of Jewish residents of Arab League countries. The article stated: "It [the law] provides that beginning on an unspecified date all Jews except citizens of non-Arab states, would be considered 'members of the Jewish minority state of Palestine.' Their bank accounts would be frozen and used to finance resistance to 'Zionist ambitions in Palestine.' Jews believed to be active Zionists would be interned and their assets confiscated."[261]

According to a Syrian newspaper, participants at a Beirut meeting of senior diplomats from all the Arab states in late March 1949 concluded, "If Israel should oppose the return of the Arab refugees to their homes, the Arab governments will expel the Jews living in their countries."[262]

As one can read, there were three reasons articulated for victimizing Jews in Arab countries. One was that Jews were seen as enemy aliens. The antisemitic dual loyalty card that the Jewish community has seen for generations was played against the Jewish population of Arab countries. Expropriation and denationalization laws as well as laws restricting employment to nationals referred to Zionists or Israelis. The terms *Zionist* or *Israeli* were undefined, but in practice, they meant Jewish. This rationalization echoed the rhetoric of the Holocaust. Jews were rounded up and shipped off to Auschwitz, Treblinka, and the other death and concentration camps on the grounds that they were enemies of the Nazis. It did not matter that they shared the same nationality as their perpetrators. Their very Jewishness made them enemies.

A second reason was state-sponsored terrorism. Arab states terrorized their Jewish populations as a way of attempting to intimidate and threaten Israel. The enemies of Israel decided to attack the Jewish people in their midst as a way of attacking Israel. This victimization was a form of blackmail or extortion. But what was sought in return was not money so much as Israeli self-destruction.

A third reason was a simple tit for tat. Because, according to the anti-Zionist view of the world, Israel has created a Palestinian refugee population, anti-Zionists would in turn create a Jewish refugee population.

For each country in the region, there are specific incidents and laws to recount. Overall, there is a pattern — antisemitic mob violence that the authorities did nothing to prevent, control, or punish, as well as strikingly similar discriminatory legislation, expropriating the property of Jews, denying them employment, and refusing them citizenship status. Jews were subjected to arbitrary arrest, torture, and even public execution.

Egypt, Iraq, and Libya each illustrate this pattern. In Egypt in 1948, after the establishment of the State of Israel, bombs in the Jewish Quarter of Cairo killed more than seventy and wounded nearly two hundred. Rioting resulted in many more deaths. Two thousand Jews were arrested, and many had their property confiscated.

Many Jews lost their jobs through the enforcement of a 1947 amendment to the Egyptian Companies Law. The amendment required that at least 75 percent of the administrative employees and 90 percent of all employees of a company be Egyptian nationals. The Egyptian Nationality Code of 1926 provided that only those who "belonged racially to the majority of the population of a country whose language is Arabic or whose religion is Islam" were entitled to Egyptian nationality.[263] Thus, 85 percent of the Jews of Egypt were never citizens.[264]

In 1956, the Egyptian government, coincident with the Sinai war against Israel, ordered almost twenty-five thousand Jews to leave the country and confiscated their property. They were allowed to take only one suitcase and a small amount of cash, and were forced to sign declarations giving their property over to the Egyptian government.

In that same year, the property of the economic backbone of Egyptian Jewry, the main supporters of Egyptian Jewish institutions, was seized through the use of sequestration orders.[265] A directive authorized the sequestering agency to deduct from the assets 10 percent of the value of the sequestered property each year.[266] Over time, this charge consumed the total value of the property.

Jews leaving Egypt were allowed, by regulation, to take with them travellers' checks or other international exchange documents only up to a value of £100 sterling a person. Even this allowance was, in practice, denied those fleeing. The Bank of Egypt provided Jews leaving the country with instruments drawn on Egyptian bank accounts in Britain and France that the British and French had blocked in response to the Egyptian blocking of British and French assets in Egypt.

Approximately one thousand Egyptian Jews were sent in 1956 to prisons and detention camps. In November 1956, a government proclamation declared that "all Jews are Zionists and enemies of the state," and promised that they would soon be expelled.[267] A 1956 amendment to the Egyptian Nationality Law provided that Zionists were barred from being Egyptian nationals.[268] The amendment asserted, "Egyptian nationality may be declared forfeited by order of the Ministry of Interior in the case of persons classified as Zionists."[269] The term *Zionist* was undefined.

By 1957, there were only fifteen thousand Jews in Egypt. In 1967, after the Six-Day War, increased persecution led to more flight; Jewish population numbers dropped to twenty-five hundred. Most of those who remained were not allowed to leave. By the 1970s, after the remaining Jews were given permission to leave, only a few families stayed behind.

In Iraq, anti-Jewish rioting broke out after the establishment of Israel in 1948.[270] The propagation of Zionism became a crime punishable by seven years' imprisonment.[271] No foreign Jew was allowed to enter Iraq even in transit.[272]

In 1950, Iraqi Jews were permitted to leave the country within a year provided they forfeited their citizenship. The property of Jews who emigrated was frozen.[273] From 1949 to 1951, 124,000 Jews were evacuated or smuggled out through Iran.

In 1952, the permission to leave was cancelled and Jews were barred from emigrating. In 1963, Jews were forbidden to sell their property and forced to carry yellow identity cards. After the 1967 Six-Day War, many of the remaining three thousand Jews were arrested and dismissed from their jobs. Jewish property was expropriated and bank accounts were frozen. Jews were dismissed from public posts. Jewish businesses were shut, and trading permits that had been granted to Jews were cancelled. Even telephones of Jewish customers were disconnected. Jews were placed under house arrest or required to remain within the cities.

In 1968, dozens of Jews were jailed for alleged involvement with a spy ring and tortured. Some died of the torture. Fourteen accused, including eleven Jews, were sentenced to death in show trials and were hanged in public in January 1969.[274]

By the early 1970s most of the remaining Jews had fled with tacit Baghdad acquiescence. In 1973, the government pressured those few elderly Jews who remained to turn over title, without compensation, to more than $200 million worth of Jewish community property the fleeing Jews had left behind.[275]

Libya was under British rule at the time of the creation of the State of Israel. Rioters murdered 12 Jews and destroyed 280 Jewish homes in June 1948 to protest the founding of the Jewish state. Although emigration was illegal, more than three thousand Jews fled. The British legalized emigration in 1949. Hostile demonstrations and riots against Jews continued unabated. From 1949 to 1951, when Libya gained independence, thirty thousand more Jews fled.[276]

Libyan independence meant a sequence of anti-Zionist, anti-Jewish laws. A 1957 law provided that prohibited anyone in Libya from entering into contracts with anyone in Israel.[277] A law of 1958 ordered the dissolution of the Jewish Community Council.[278] A 1961 law provided that only Libyan citizens could own and transfer real property. Only six Jews have been identified has having been granted the necessary permit evidencing Libyan citizenship.[279]

A 1962 decree provided that a Libyan forfeited nationality if the person had had any contact with Zionism. Any person who had visited Israel after the proclamation of Libyan independence, and any person deemed to have acted in favour of Israel's interests, lost his or her Libyan nationality under this law. The law was retroactive, applying to those who had visited Israel or done anything else the authorities deemed supportive of Israel before the law was enacted. Libyan Jews were the primary victims of this law.[280]

A 1970 law provided that all property belonging to Israelis who had left Libyan territory "in order to establish themselves definitely abroad" would pass to the state.[281] The Libyan government used this law to take possession of property belonging to Libyan Jews without bothering about the fact that these Jews were not Israelis and had not "established themselves abroad."[282] Another law of 1970 decreed that the state would administer liquid funds of Jews as well as the companies and the company shares belonging to Jews.[283]

Decrees and practices discriminating against Jews in Arab countries echo the Nazi Nuremberg Laws on Citizenship and Race. And the victims, the Jews, are the same. The Nuremberg laws violated basic human rights: the right to a nationality; the right to vote; the right to equality. They were damaging in themselves and a signal of the disasters to come. They depersonalized Jews by saying that they were not legal persons in the eyes of the state.

These laws were unconscionable at the time. After the Holocaust, similar laws with the same target victims are unspeakable. Today, instead of or in addition to affiliation with the Jewish religious community, denationalization in Arab countries comes from affiliation with Zionism. *Zionist* is often just a code word for *Jewish*. Insofar as it has any separate meaning, the meaning is that Jews must denounce and reject some human rights in order to keep others. Jews must denounce and reject the right to self-determination of the Jewish people in order to keep their right to nationality.

Before the Second World War, Jews in Europe were de-nationalized because of their ties with the Jewish religion; after the Second World War, Jews in the Middle East have been de-nationalized because of their ties with the Jewish people. The violation of human rights is as basic, as repugnant, as wrong.

Despite the grotesque violations of the rights of Jewish refugees from Arab countries and Iran, the global community has been silent. The contrast with the clamour over Palestinian refugees is stark.

Since 1947, there have been more than 681 UN General Assembly resolutions dealing with virtually every aspect of the Middle East and the Arab Israeli conflict. Fully 101 of these UN resolutions refer to the plight of Palestinian refugees. In none of these 681 resolutions is there a reference to the fate of Jews living in Arab countries or to Jewish refugees.

UN agencies and organizations have been systematically mandated or specifically created to provide protection, relief, and assistance to Palestinian refugees. None were created or even mandated to assist Jewish refugees from Arab countries. Since 1947, the international community has spent billions of dollars to assist Palestinian refugees. International financial support for Jewish refugees from Arab countries has been negligible.

Only one UN organization — the Office of the United Nations High Commissioner for Refugees — responded to the needs of Jewish refugees from Arab countries. The statute of the Office of the United Nations High Commissioner for Refugees obligates the High Commissioner to provide for the protection of refugees falling under the competence of his office by, amongst other duties, "endeavouring to obtain permission for refugees to transfer their assets and especially those necessary for resettlement."[284]

In order for a refugee population to fall within the mandate of the High Commissioner, the Office of the High Commissioner or some other UN body has to determine that the population has or had a well-founded fear of persecution.[285] The High Commissioner has made such a determination for Jews from Arab countries.

In his first statement as newly elected High Commissioner, Auguste Lindt, at the January 29, 1957, meeting of the United Nations Refugee Fund Executive Committee (UNREF) in Geneva, stated: "Another emergency problem is now arising: that of refugees from Egypt. There is no doubt in my mind that those refugees from Egypt who are not able, or not willing to avail themselves of the protection of the Government of their nationality fall under the mandate of my office."[286]

Dr. E. Jahn, for the Office of the High Commissioner, wrote to Daniel Lack, legal adviser to the American Joint Distribution Committee, on July 6, 1967: "I refer to our recent discussion concerning Jews from Middle Eastern and

North African countries in consequence of recent events. I am now able to inform you that such persons may be considered prima facie within the mandate of this Office."[287]

The High Commissioner tried to get permission from Arab governments for Jewish refugees to transfer their assets from the Arab countries they fled.[288] Mostly, those efforts did not succeed. However, the efforts themselves are noteworthy. The determination by the High Commissioner that these refugees fell within his mandate was a determination that they had a well-founded fear of persecution.

Persecution is any serious violation of human rights.[289] The Office of the United Nations High Commissioner for Refugees has made an independent determination, and has confirmed publicly on at least two occasions, that Jews from Arab countries were victims of serious human rights violations that caused their flight. That determination remains valid and has consequences beyond triggering efforts of the High Commissioner to obtain permission from persecuting governments to transfer refugee assets.

Aside from the effort of the Office of the United Nations High Commissioner for Refugees to assist in the transfer of Jewish refugee assets, the international community has done nothing for Jewish refugees. Yet there are a number of differences between the two refugee populations that make the case for Jewish refugees from Arab countries and Iran even more compelling than the case for Palestinian refugees.

There is the difference between the United Nations High Commissioner for Refugees and the United Nations Relief and Works Agency for Palestine Refugees. As noted, Jewish refugees from Arab countries are under the mandate of the Office of the High Commissioner for Refugees. Palestinian refugees are not. The Statute of the Office of the High Commissioner states that the competence of the High Commissioner shall not extend to a person "who continues to receive from other organs or agencies of the United Nations protection or assistance."[290] Palestinian refugees, because they receive assistance from the United Nations Relief and Works Agency, fall within this exemption. The Office of the High Commissioner for Refugees has made a specific determination to this effect. A memorandum of February 22, 1968, from A. Rorholt, Director of the Legal Division to all Office of the United Nations High Commissioner for Refugees representatives, correspondents, and officers, stated, "Persons enjoying the assistance or protection extended by UNRWA (United Nations Relief and Works Agency) are excluded from the UNHCR (United Nations High Commissioner for Refugees) mandate."[291]

The same difference exists for the Refugee Convention. The Refugee Convention provides: "This Convention shall not apply to persons who are at present receiving from organs or agencies of the United Nations other than the United Nations High Commissioner for Refugees protection or assistance."[292] Again this difference has been confirmed by the Office of the United Nations

High Commissioner for Refugees itself. The Office of the United Nations High Commissioner for Refugees wrote, in a note on the applicability of the Convention of October 2002:

> UNHCR considers that two groups of Palestinian refugees fall within the scope of Article 1 D of the 1951 Convention:
>
> **i)** Palestinians who are "Palestine refugees" within the sense of UN General Assembly Resolution 194 (III) of 11 December 1948 and other UN General Assembly Resolutions, who were displaced from that part of Palestine which became Israel, and who have been unable to return there'
>
> **ii)** Palestinians who are "displaced persons" within the sense of UN General Assembly Resolution 2252 (ES-V) of 4 July 1967 and subsequent UN General Assembly Resolutions, and who have been unable to return to the Palestinian territories occupied by Israel since 1967.
>
> For the purposes of the application of the 1951 Convention, both of these groups include persons who were displaced at the time of hostilities, plus the descendants of such persons.[293]

A difference that flows from the difference in legal status of the two refugee populations is that Palestinian refugees have already received from the international community extensive relief through the United Nations Relief and Works Agency, relief that Jewish refugees have not received. This relief has totalled in the billions.

An interconnected difference is that Israel has already paid substantial sums to Palestinian refugees through contributions to the United Nations Relief and Works Agency. Arab states and Iran have made not comparable contributions to Jewish refugees. In fact, Israel has donated more to UNRWA than most Arab states. Until 1973, Israel was contributing more each year to UNRWA than Saudi Arabia. Until 1980, Israel was contributing more than Libya and Kuwait.[294]

Yet another difference is the manner in which the refugee populations were created. Palestinian refugees are war refugees. Many, indeed most, fled scenes of actual or impending armed combat rather than existing or feared human rights violations. Jewish refugees from Arab countries are peacetime refugees. They were not fleeing war but only actual or feared persecution. Human rights violations create a right to redress. War does not. Violations of the laws of war, humanitarian law violations, create a right to redress as much as human rights violations do. But not every war refugee flees humanitarian law violations. Some are just fleeing the war itself.

A further difference is the legal status of the refugees before they fled. Jewish refugees were nationals of the states from which they fled. Those states had a duty to protect the refugees and failed in that duty. Many Palestinian refugees fled British-mandate Palestine before the creation of the State of Israel. Other Palestinian refugees, who fled after the creation of the State of Israel, never had Israeli nationality. Israel did not breach a duty of protection it owed to its nationals, since these refugees were not nationals of Israel.

Another difference lies in the attribution of fault. The fault for the creation of both the Jewish and Palestinian refugee population lies with the Arab states. The Palestinian refugee population was created by the wars for Israel's existence. Without the attacks by Arab states against Israel from its very beginning, there would have been no Palestinian refugees. Arab governments and leaders called on Palestinians to get out of the way while Arab armies expelled the Jewish population from British-mandate Palestine. Some Palestinians fled because they heeded those calls. Others fled simply to avoid the crossfire of war.[295]

Still another difference is in mitigation and aggravation. Jews who fled from Arab countries and Iran have done everything in their power to mitigate their losses. For those who fled to Israel, the State of Israel engaged in heroic efforts to assist that mitigation. With Palestinian refugees who fled to Arab states and Iran, the effort has been in the opposite direction: to aggravate the loss for political reasons in order to magnify the Palestinian refugee problem and discredit Israel.

The Jewish community is used to seeing its victimization ignored, downplayed, and trivialized. The global amnesia about Jewish refugees from Arab countries joins a long history of denial and revisionism of Jewish victimization.

All the same, it remains worthwhile to ask, Why is this so? Why has the obvious injustice inflicted on Jewish refugees from Arab countries been so little recognized? How is it that so much public attention has been devoted to the Palestinian refugee population and so little to the Jewish refugee population?

There have been a number of attempts to draw the attention of the world community to the fate of Jews from Arab lands, without avail. Golda Meir, at the time Israeli Minister of Foreign Affairs, wrote two letters to the UN Secretary General in November 1956 "regarding the action taken by the Egyptian Government against the Jewish Community in Egypt."[296] Henry Cabot Lodge, Jr., the U.S. Representative to the UN, stated at the UN General Assembly in December 1956 that he shares "concern about reports of the plight of Jews in Egypt" and put the United States on record as "abhorring such practices as have been alleged." Philip Klutznick, on behalf of the Coordinating Board of Jewish Organizations, wrote to Secretary General Dag Hammarskjöld in January 1957 urging him to use his "good offices to induce the Government of Egypt to desist from the prosecution of a policy to bring total ruin to the old-established Jewish community of Egypt." Israeli Minister of Foreign Affairs Moshe Dayan, at the

UN General Assembly in October 1977, spoke out against the discriminatory treatment of Jews in Arab countries. UN Israeli Ambassador Yehuda Blum delivered a speech to the UN on December 3, 1979, describing the "dramatic worsening in the attitude of (and treatment by) Syrian authorities towards its Jewish community." UN Israeli Ambassador Johanan Bein, at the Session UN General Assembly in November 1987, spoke of "the war of aggression unleashed by Arab countries against Israel in 1948," which "brought about an exodus of Jews from Arab lands." And there were many more such interventions. Yet the overall result in the UN, outside the Office of the United Nations High Commissioner for Refugees, was nothing.

One explanation for the difference in response to the Jewish and Palestinian refugee populations can be traced to the difference in their treatment once they became refugees. The Jewish refugee population was absorbed and resettled, mostly in Israel, but in other countries as well. Anti-Zionists have made a point of keeping the Palestinian refugee population as a refugee population.

Anti-Zionism has created two victim populations: Jewish refugees and Palestinian refugees. Resettlement meant that the first population slipped from view. Anti-Zionism meant that the second population remained front and centre. Anti-Zionists need Palestinian misery as propaganda fodder. If the Palestinian refugee population were to resettle, the demographic weapon anti-Zionists aim at Israel and the discontent that feeds the anti-Zionist cause would disappear. The Palestinian refugee population has become both a spur to anti-Zionism and a justification for it.

The commitment of anti-Zionists to maintaining Palestinians as refugees was highlighted when Prime Minister Jean Chrétien in April 2000 and Foreign Affairs Minister John Manley in January 2001 offered to resettle Palestinian refugees in Canada. PLO spokesman Ahmed Abdel Rahman rejected the prime minister's offer. He said, "We reject any kind of settlement of refugees in Arab countries, or in Canada."[297] John Manley, in response to his offer, was burned in effigy near the West Bank city of Nablus.[298] Hussum Khader, head of the largest Palestinian Fatah militia in Nablus, said, "If Canada is serious about resettlement you could expect military attacks in Ottawa or Montreal."[299]

Israeli peace negotiation strategy has had a part to play. The government of Israel announced in February 2003 a budgetary grant of 3 million new Israel shekels to register property claims by immigrants from Arab countries. The announcement noted that nothing was done as the result of a similar 1969 decision to register property. The announcement further observed, "For years successive Israeli governments preferred to ignore the issue of property claims by immigrant from Arab countries, mostly due to the mistaken assumption that this would prevent claims by Palestinians."

That assumption was obviously mistaken in a factual sense, because Palestinians have made claims even though the Israeli government, on behalf of displaced Jews, has not.

The Israeli negotiating position over the years has been to ignore or downplay the Jewish refugee issue. The strategy was motivated by both the forlorn hope that the Palestinian refugee issue could also be bypassed and the fear that raising the Jewish refugee issue would complicate the peace process.

Zionist mythology has reinforced Israeli strategic considerations. The Zionist myth is that Jews come to Israel because they want to come. Of course, for some Jews from Arab countries that was the only reason they came. But not for all. For many, they came because they had no choice; they were effectively evicted from the countries of their ancestors and had nowhere else to go. But to say so contradicted Zionist mythology.

This combination of strategic peace considerations and Zionist mythology has created an Israeli web of silence. A consensus developed across the Israeli political spectrum not to raise the issue of Jewish refugees from Arab countries. The left were silent in their pursuit of peace; the right were silent in their pursuit of Zionism. There was no voice to speak out.

After almost sixty years of war, it is time to conclude that this silence has not worked. Rather, it has had a perverse effect. Arab and Palestinian leaders have put the Palestinian refugee issue front and centre. Israeli and Jewish leaders have minimized the Jewish refugee issue. So the Jewish component of the refugee issue has just gotten lost. The claim of Jewish refugees from Arab countries for redress is as strong as, if not stronger than, the claim of Palestinian refugees for redress. It would be an injustice to recognize the weaker case and ignore the stronger case.

Yet that is exactly what has happened in the Middle East peace process. Occasionally, the two sets of claims have been put on equal footing. A United Nations Security Council Resolution adopted in 1967 calls for "a just settlement of the refugee problem" without distinguishing between Palestinian and Jewish refugees.[300] The Camp David Accords and the Egyptian-Israeli Peace Treaty provide that "the parties agree to establish a Claims Committee for the mutual settlement of all final claims," again without distinguishing between Palestinian and Jewish claims. President Carter stated in a press conference in 1977, "Palestinians have rights ... obviously there are Jewish refugees ... they have the same rights as others do."[301]

Past Arab-Israeli agreements do not extinguish or limit the private claims of Jewish refugees against Jordan and Egypt. These agreements allow the case to be made that a comprehensive solution to the Middle East conflict will require a just solution to the plight of Jewish refugees from Arab countries.

But in practice that is not how things are working out. In 1991, the Madrid Peace Conference established a Multilateral Working Group on refugees. Its mandate was to ensure the status and rights of "all persons displaced as a result of the 1948 Arab-Israeli conflict." But those involved in the Working Group, "save perhaps the Israelis," as Kara Stein writes,[302] view their efforts as relating to Palestinian refugees only.

If one thought of Israel, the West Bank, and Gaza as on the moon rather than in the Middle East, this blinkered approach, looking at Palestinian refugees in isolation from Jewish refugees, might have a certain logic to it. Redress to Jewish refugees is not due from the Palestinian leadership. Jewish refugees did not, for the most part, flee the West Bank and Gaza.

However, if one looks at the peace process in context, if one accepts that peace in the Middle East means peace with Israel's Arab neighbours and with Iran as much as with the Palestinians, then it is impossible to overlook the issue of Jewish refugees. A settlement of outstanding disputes between Israel and its neighbours must resolve this. A 1987 tribunal relating to the claims of Jews from Arab countries chaired by former Justice Arthur Goldberg of the United States Supreme Court concluded that silence about the claims and rights of Jews from Arab countries is simply not tolerable.[303]

The contrast between the incessant, omnipresent blare about Palestinian refugees from the territory that became Israel and the virtual silence on Jewish refugees from Arab countries, whose numbers were larger and whose treatment was worse, shows in yet one more way that advocacy focused on Palestinian refugees is mostly not about a humane solution to a refugee problem, and almost entirely about anti-Zionism. Only when the silence about Jewish refugees from Arab countries ends can the expression of concerns about Palestinian refugees be credible. Only when both groups are considered as populations victimized by the wars for Israel's existence can the plight of the Palestinian refugee population hope to be resolved.

CHAPTER TWELVE
Singling Out the Holocaust

BECAUSE of the historical link between the Holocaust and the creation of Israel, anti-Zionists argue against paying special attention to the Holocaust. It is said that there is a wealth of tragedies, an array of massive violation of human rights. Why focus on the Holocaust in particular?

This anti-Zionist criticism is both an attack on Israel and an attack on the memory of the Holocaust. The response has to be both a defence of Israel and a defence of the significance of the Holocaust. The Holocaust trivialization of anti-Zionists must be answered.

One reason the Holocaust remains significant today is its centrality to human rights standards and mechanisms and to the current human rights consciousness. It is impossible to understand human rights today without understanding how and why the standards, and the mechanisms to promote those standards, developed. The Universal Declaration of Human Rights of 1948, the International Military Tribunal at Nuremberg, the Genocide Convention of 1951, and the Convention on the Status of Refugees of 1951 were all negotiated, drafted, and endorsed in direct response to the Holocaust.

The more modern instruments, in turn, built on these earlier instruments. The International Covenant on Civil and Political Rights and the International Covenant on Economic, Social and Cultural Rights were instruments meant to give treaty force to the standards in the Universal Declaration of Human Rights. Instruments after the covenants elaborated the obligations to respect specific standards in the covenants. Examples are the Convention against Torture, the Convention on the Rights of the Child, the Convention on the Elimination of All Forms of Discrimination against Women, and the Convention on the Elimination of All Forms of Racial Discrimination. The whole United Nations human rights superstructure has its foundations in the Holocaust.

The same is true of the international tribunals. The Security Council, in May 1993, created the International Tribunal for the former Yugoslavia,[304] and in November 1994, they created the International Tribunal for Rwanda.[305] A global criminal court has come into existence. A treaty establishing an International Criminal Court was negotiated in Rome in July 1998. The treaty came into force on July 1, 2002. Each of these tribunals builds on the Nuremberg precedent.

The United Nations Convention on the Status of Refugees was a direct response to the failure to protect Jewish refugees before and during the Second World War. Following an intergovernmental conference at Evian, France, in 1938, governments of thirty-two nations formed an inter-governmental committee to assist refugees leaving Nazi Germany and Austria. The Evian system was unsuccessful: everyone favoured resettlement, but no one was prepared to offer it. Without legal recourse available to refugee claimants, antisemitic or anti-alien immigration officials could prevent Evian's good intentions from having concrete results. The Canadian Immigration Department, headed by Fred Blair, was motivated by antisemitism to prevent every single Jewish refugee from entering Canada. The U.S. State Department under Breckenridge Long, Assistant Secretary for Special Problems, was compelled by an anti-alien attitude to block entry of Jewish refugees to the United States, and even suppressed news of the Holocaust to further this goal. In order to appease Arab leaders, Britain was determined to keep quotas for Jews entering British-mandate Palestine at a minuscule level. British-mandate officials turned away ship after ship of Jews from Palestine.[306] The conclusion the international community drew from this history was that voluntary commitments to resettle refugees were worthless. A binding international treaty was needed. The United Nations Convention on the Status of Refugees was the result.

There is a direct link between Canadian human rights standards and institutions and international human rights. The Canadian criminal law of war crimes and crimes against humanity is drawn from the statute of the International Criminal Court. The Immigration and Refugee Protection Act replicates the refugee protection standards found in the United Nations Convention on the Status of Refugees. Provincial and federal human rights codes, as well as the Canadian Charter of Rights and Freedoms, restate the language found in the Universal Declaration of Human Rights, the International Covenant on Civil and Political Rights, and other international human rights instruments.

Canada has made its own the human rights culture that grew out of revulsion to the Holocaust. Indeed, attachment to human rights is now part of the Canadian identity. Human rights discourse is so much part of the woodwork now in Canada that many are unaware of the importance of abhorrence to the crimes of the Holocaust in the development of this discourse. The Holocaust not only reminds us of the significance of this source, it also re-validates and re-energizes the commitment to human rights that grew out of reaction to the Holocaust.

A second reason for a focus on the Holocaust is its global sweep. The Holocaust was a crime in which virtually every country in the globe was complicit — by participating in the killings, by denying refuge to those attempting to escape, or by granting safe haven to Nazi mass murderers. The Jews were in danger everywhere the Nazis went. During the Second World War, the Third Reich ending up occupying all or part of almost thirty countries. The countries that resisted Nazi attempts to kill Jews, the countries that opened their arms to Jewish refugees, were few and far between.

The planet-wide nature of the genocide, the hatred of a people that seeped into every nook and cranny of the globe, was unprecedented before the Holocaust and has not been replicated since. Even after the war and before the creation of the state of Israel, lingering antisemitism meant that Jewish survivors sat in refugee camps in Europe with no relocation in sight.

The record of Canada was particularly dismal. Harold Troper and Irving Abella in their book *None Is Too Many* write, "Of all the nations in the Western world, of all the states that could have received refugees, theirs [Canada's] has, arguably, the worst record for providing sanctuary to European Jewry."[307]

The title of the book is the answer an anonymous senior Canadian official, in an off-the-record discussion with journalists in early 1945, gave in response to the question "How many Jews will be let in to Canada after the war?"

After the war, it was easier for Nazi war criminals than Jewish refugees to get out of the displaced persons camps and be resettled. Nazi mass murderers found immunity and safe havens around the world, including Canada. In Canada, Nazis lied their way in with ease. By a conservative estimate,[308] approximately two thousand Nazi war criminals entered after the Second World War. Once they arrived, they were home free. The Royal Canadian Mounted Police had a policy that "investigations into allegations of this nature [that there were war criminals in Canada] are not to be conducted by the Force."[309]

The Holocaust was not just a crime against humanity. It was a crime of humanity. When a genocide occurs in only one country, it is all too easy to relativize the claim, to say that it was they who did it, not us. It is impossible to say that about the Holocaust. The Holocaust shows the evil of which humanity is capable; it gives us a horrifying glimpse into the darkness of the human soul.

The planetary sweep of the Holocaust gave us examples worldwide of good as well as evil. For Canada, we can read with abhorrence of the antisemitism, the cruelty, the hypocrisy, and the indifference of Fred Blair, Director of Immigration, or Vincent Massey, High Commissioner to the United Kingdom, or William Lyon Mackenzie King, Prime Minister of Canada. We can also read with admiration of the principle, the humanity, and the commitment of George Vanier, Ambassador to France, or Mark Sorenson, Canadian Pacific Railway agent in Denmark.

Canada has only two honourary citizens, Raoul Wallenberg and Nelson Mandela. Raoul Wallenberg was a Swedish diplomat stationed in Hungary in the last months of the Second World War who is credited with saving up to one hundred thousand Jews from the Holocaust. Because Wallenberg is an honourary Canadian citizen, he is now a Canadian hero as well as a Swedish hero. Roland de Corneille, then a Liberal Member of Parliament for Eglinton-Lawrence, and Guy Ricard, then a Progressive Conservative Member of Parliament for Laval, in 1985 presented a private member's bill proclaiming Raoul Wallenberg to be an honourary citizen of Canada. The bill passed unanimously the House of Commons on December 9, 1985, and the Senate on December 10, 1985. Nelson Mandela received his honourary citizenship in June 2001.

The fact that one of Canada's two honourary citizens is a hero of the Holocaust is a Parliamentary tribute to the uniqueness of the Holocaust. It is a recognition that the good done in the Holocaust represented the best of humanity, a model for Canadians.

Eight of the ten provinces have also passed legislation recognizing the unique nature of the Holocaust by declaring as a provincial day of remembrance Yom Hashoah, the day on the Jewish calendar that commemorates the Holocaust. The Alberta legislation, the most recent, is titled the "Holocaust Memorial Day and Genocide Remembrance Act." The designated memorial day, as in all other provincial legislation, is Yom Hashoah. The body of the text of the law refers to that day as "Holocaust Memorial Day."

It is misleading to think of the Holocaust as a tale of devils and angels, of monsters and heroes. It is above all a tale of ordinary people. It was ordinary Germans who were primarily responsible for the Holocaust.[310] However, they were far from solely responsible.

Of the 6 million Jews killed in the Holocaust, only 210,000 were Germans and Austrians.[311] In the other places the Nazis went, they did not know the languages, the places, or the people. Wherever they went, they relied heavily on local police, administrative personnel, and home-grown fascists organized into militias to round up Jews for the death camps. Without the active collaboration of thousands, and the passive indifference of millions, the Nazis could not have accomplished their mission of death.

In Canada, if the government denied refuge to Jews fleeing Europe, it was in response to popular antisemitic sentiment. If governments for decades did nothing to bring Nazi war criminals in Canada to justice, it was a reflection of public indifference to justice for the Holocaust.

Human beings are moral agents who act on the basis of decisions they have made. When millions of Jews died during the Holocaust, when the nations of the world participated in the killings, denied refuge to the victims, and offered safe havens to the perpetrators, they did so because people around the world had decided that the Jews ought to die, that the Jewish people ought to be extinguished; the vast majority of humanity was indifferent to the death of the Jews. The Holocaust was an act of insanity in which the whole world went mad.

If we are to prevent other acts of global insanity, we must stare the Holocaust in the face and ask ourselves how it happened, why it happened. Although the Holocaust was the killing of millions in months, the consciousness that led to its execution was decades in the making. What was that consciousness? How did it develop? The consciousness was one of extreme antisemitism, the culmination of racist thinking that began with prejudices and stereotypes, but not with plans of murder.[312] The Holocaust is the ultimate lesson in the dangers of racism. It tells us as no other example can where racism leads, why racism must be avoided.

The Holocaust was a cauldron where hate was the fuel. One legacy of the Holocaust, one human rights standard that was articulated in response to it, was the right to be free from incitement to hatred. This right, with variations in wording, is in the Universal Declaration of Human Rights,[313] the International Covenant on Civil and Political Rights,[314] and the United Nations Convention on the Elimination of All Forms of Racial Discrimination.[315] It is difficult, if not impossible, to understand why this right is important, why it needs to be respected, without regard to the Holocaust.

The Holocaust happened not just because there were racists in power in Germany, but because ordinary people around the world shared the views of Nazis and were eager to cooperate with them in carrying out their plan to extinguish all Jewish life. The Nazis did not come to power on antisemitism alone. There was a whole set of historical circumstances that explained their rise to power. Circumstances may put Nazi-like figures in power not because of their irrational hatred of a victim group, but for totally unconnected reasons.

Whoever is in power, we need a large group of people who have the courage to resist the racism of the state. That means learning the lessons of the Holocaust. If the lessons of the Holocaust are put to one side, it becomes all that much easier to succumb to racism, should the unfortunate vagaries of history bring a racist government to power either at home or abroad.[316] Asking why we should have regard for the Holocaust when considering human rights is like asking why we should have regard for the Second World War when considering war. There have been only two world wars. The world wars deserve consideration in the history of war if for no other reason than that they were planet-wide. The same can be said for the Holocaust, that it deserves consideration if for no other reason than that it was planet-wide. This global context means that every country has a personal historical link to the Holocaust. Every single person everywhere can ask of their own country, "What did we do about the Holocaust?"

The Holocaust deserves consideration, not only like the Second World War, but because of the Second World War. There is a direct link between the two. In general, it is true that there is a link between human rights violations and war. It is unrealistic to expect those violent at home to be peaceful abroad.

For the Nazis, their antisemitism did not just embolden them to invade their neighbours. It was a primary motivation. Nazi Germany did not just kill Jews in countries it occupied. It occupied countries so that it could kill their Jews.[317] The Nazis killed innocents everywhere they went. The death camps and death squads the Nazis organized for Jews killed Romas, homosexuals, the mentally and physically disabled, trade unionists, communists, and other political opponents as well. The killing of the disabled in Germany preceded the killing of Jews.

The Holocaust tells us, more eloquently than any other human rights tragedy can, that human rights violations are a spreading, uncontainable stain. Once human rights violations are the norm, no one is safe.

Other mass killings both before and after the war were local, territorial, national. The Holocaust was unprecedented not only in its global scope, but also in its global reach. Never before or since has a group of people attempted to conquer the world so that they could kill every member of another group.[318] Jews were victims as far away from Germany and Austria as Crete, Rhodes, and Ukraine. Moreover, the Nazis were there because the Jews were there, so that the Jews there could be killed.

The Universal Declaration of Human Rights acknowledged the linkage between war and human rights violations in its first preamble. That preamble states, "Whereas recognition of the inherent dignity and of the equal and inalienable rights of all members of the human family is the foundation of freedom, justice and peace in the world."

Canada was an active participant in the Second World War. The country fought to oppose Nazism and to defeat Hitler, not just to prevent German territorial expansion in Europe. The war effort was a struggle against the racism and totalitarianism for which Nazi Germany stood. Canadian soldiers gave their lives so that Nazi values would not triumph. Putting the Holocaust to one side means ignoring the reason for the sacrifices that Canadian soldiers made. By ignoring why we fought the war, in a sense, we give Hitler a posthumous victory.

The modern civilization of Austria and Germany in the first half of the twentieth century also speaks to the universality and contemporary relevance of the Holocaust. Austria and Germany, at the time that they led the world to slaughter its Jews, were the countries of Beethoven, Bach, Mozart, Brahms, and Schubert, of Goethe, Schiller, Schopenhauer, Hegel, and Kant. It may be tempting to say of other killers in other genocides that they were nothing but uncivilized barbarians. It cannot be said of the perpetrators of the Holocaust. Even during the midst of the Holocaust, many of the most highly educated of the day were among its most enthusiastic supporters, including German philosopher Martin Heidigger, American poet Ezra Pound, and French novelist Céline. The Holocaust tells us in a way that no other tragedy can that education, culture, and intellect cannot immunize us from evil.

Cultural relativism is a convenient shield for human rights violators. Repressive regimes say that promotion of respect for human rights is an attempt to impose Western values on them. There are many different answers to this defence, but perhaps the best is the Holocaust.

In light of the Holocaust, the suggestion that human rights values are Western values being imposed on others has to make our heads spin. The West has led the way to the greatest human rights violations of this century. The Holocaust, though global in scope, was initiated by the West. If it were legitimate to argue from respect today for human rights and their promotion in the West that human rights are Western values, it would also be legitimate to argue from denial of human rights and incitement to hatred at the time of the Holocaust that violations of human rights are Western values.[319]

The progress of European civilization made the Holocaust easier rather than harder to perpetrate. The elaborate organization and systematic execution of the plan to extinguish the Jews — the identification, ghettoization, and trans-shipment; the death camps, ovens, and gas chambers — were products of an advanced technological and industrial society. The Holocaust teaches us that industrial, technological development, while increasing our material well-being, also increases our capacity for evil. In a primitive civilization, technology allows murderers to kill only those in front of them. In an advanced civilization, murderers can kill an entire world.

The advances of German civilization were not just economic and cultural. They were also legal. Antisemitism wherever the Nazis went was not just an attitude, policy, and behaviour. It was a legal structure, legislated by local parliaments and enforced by the local courts. Nazi laws stripped Jews of citizenship, forbade marriages and sexual relationships between Jews and non-Jews, stripped Jews of property, denied Jews access to the professions and the civil service. Many mass crimes are spasms of violence outside of any legal framework. The Holocaust was cosseted within an antisemitic legal framework that teaches us the difference between the tyranny of law and the rule of law — the difference between law and justice.

The Nazis dehumanized the Jews through slave labour as a form of murder. Many Jews were worked to death, rather than shot on the spot or shipped off to be gassed. Because the war ended before the Nazis had extinguished all Jewish life, many of the slave labourers survived. The modernity of the Holocaust meant that many of the employers of slave labour were corporations that continue today as thriving multinationals. The effort to compensate the surviving slave labourers, Jewish and non-Jewish alike, is a contemporary struggle against major players in today's global economy, which consideration of the Holocaust explains.

Mass murder in an advanced, literate, organized civilization meant that the killings were exceptionally well documented. There are a wealth of museums, photographs, memoirs, transcripts, exhibits, records, and monuments that serve as reminders and as educational tools. In Winnipeg, there is a monument to victims of the Holocaust on the grounds of the legislature, with the names of those killed in the Holocaust who had family members in Manitoba. There are museums in Los Angeles, New York City, and Washington, D.C., all filled with historical and reconstructed materials.

Racial looting often accompanies other race-based human rights violations. The sophistication of European society at the time of the Holocaust and the extent of the destruction gave theft a dimension it had never seen before. Major art treasures, properties, businesses, and bank accounts were stolen from victims of the Holocaust with gusto and impunity. Insurance policies with Holocaust victim beneficiaries, as well as other contracts and commitments, were nullified or ignored. We are still trying to make right these wrongs. These efforts are today's headlines. Confronting the Holocaust means coming to grips with this restitution effort.

The art treasures stolen in the Holocaust are to be found in galleries around the world. There are questions being raised today about the provenance of paintings in places as far removed from the Holocaust as Winnipeg. These stolen art treasures, found everywhere, echo the global cry of the Holocaust.

The Holocaust was not only the death of 6 million people. It was the loss of the Yiddish shtetl culture in Europe. Though the Jewish people and the Jewish religion survived, the Yiddish shtetl culture in Europe did not. What the Holocaust demonstrates is not just death in the past but loss of the future. By killing off the cultural heritage that one generation transmits to the next, the generation that participated in the Holocaust committed a crime against the future.

Facing the obliteration of the Holocaust allows us to come to grips with the ultimate obliteration: a nuclear Holocaust that would destroy all humanity. Jonathan Schell, in his book *The Fate of the Earth*, wrote, "Genocide, including, above all, Hitler's attempt to extinguish the Jewish people, is the closest thing to a precursor of the extinction of the species that history contains."[320]

Human extinction will be without precedent. Learning about the Holocaust teaches us that the extinction of humanity is not preventable simply because it is unthinkable. On the contrary, it may be all the more possible for that very reason. Only by recalling the gaping, unmendable holes in the fabric of the world left by the Holocaust can we hope to respond to the threat of nuclear Holocaust before it is realized. Overlooking the Nazi Holocaust is much like pretending that nuclear extinction is an impossibility. If we do that, we court disaster. This world cannot face squarely the dangers that threaten it by putting to one side the Holocaust it has inflicted.

We can prevent what was once unthinkable only if we think about it. Supreme Court Justice Felix Frankfurter, who was Jewish and familiar with antisemitism, when presented in 1942 with news of the Holocaust said to his informant, "I am unable to believe you." When confronted with the reliability of the information, he replied, "I did not say this young man is lying. I said I am unable to believe him. There is a difference."[321]

The Holocaust was such an incredible event that, to a cursory observer, even in retrospect it is almost impossible to fathom. It is one thing to hear about the Holocaust as a fact. It is quite another to accept and understand it as part of human experience. It is not enough simply to be told that the Holocaust happened. If we want to prevent future genocides, humanity needs to understand how the Holocaust could have happened, how massive human rights violations can still happen. Otherwise, the response will be what Frankfurter's was: incredulity and inactivity.

The Holocaust is more than the past, more than the loss of the future. It is also the present. Contemporary right-wing extremist organizations, which splinter in a thousand different ways, have this one belief in common. They have learned well from the initial success of the Nazis. The incitement of hatred against Jews is a political tool for right-wing extremists that goes far beyond attacking Jews. That the road to power for these groups is whipping up hatred against Jews is illustrated by the phenomenon of virulent antisemitism in countries with no (or virtually no) Jewish population. The incitement to hatred against Jews was and is a threat not just to Jews but also to peace, to democracy, and to all humanity.

The Holocaust, however, discredits right-wing extremists everywhere. Endorsement of the Holocaust, the belief that the Holocaust was right, truly belongs to the lunatic fringe. Neo-Nazis well realize that they have no hope of building a mass movement or even significant support based on defence of the Holocaust.

For contemporary right-wing extremists, Holocaust denial becomes a political necessity. Holocaust denial, for these extremists, serves a dual agenda. Denial co-opts the gullible into the extremists' ideology of Jewish fraud, Jewish world control, Jewish greed. As well, it legitimizes the very ideology that the Holocaust has delegitimized.[322] Learning about the Holocaust becomes one of the most effective means of combatting contemporary right-wing extremism. By learning about the Holocaust, we also learn of the fraud and the dangers of the right-wing extremists in our midst.

The same can be said about anti-Zionism. Anti-Zionists are Holocaust deniers because they see rejection of the Holocaust as paving their way to the destruction of the State of Israel. Learning about the Holocaust becomes a means of combatting anti-Zionism.

One way of assessing the importance of Holocaust awareness is looking at the countries that have avoided promoting it. In the countries of Central and Eastern Europe, under communist rule, the Nazis were much criticized. But the criticism was of their anti-communism, not their antisemitism. With the lifting of the Iron Curtain and collapse of the Soviet Union, the old ideology of communism has been replaced by a new ideology of ethnic hatred of minorities. Racially motivated crimes spurred on by untrammelled hate speech are almost everywhere in Central and Eastern Europe, as well as in the former German Democratic Republic, East Germany. The racist violence of the former communist states is the bitter fruit of Holocaust ignorance.

In considering the Holocaust, we must avoid both false symmetries and false dichotomies. The Holocaust was unique in its dimensions, its techniques, its global sweep and penetration. It is a mistake too often made to compare the Holocaust to other tragedies. Indeed, at their extreme, these analogies become trivializations of the Holocaust, forms of Holocaust denial themselves.

In Canada, Yves Michaud, a candidate for the Parti Québecois nomination in Montreal's Mercier riding, said sarcastically in December 2000 on a Montreal radio station that Jews "are the only people in the history of the world to suffer. It's never the same for them. The Armenians didn't suffer. The Palestinians aren't suffering. The Rwandans did not suffer." Michaud said he told Jewish Senator Leo Kolber, "It's always you people. You are the only people in the history of the world to suffer."

Lucien Bouchard, premier of Quebec and leader of the Parti Québecois, said that he could not stand as party leader and defend such remarks, that the party must decide if it wants to be accused of trivializing the suffering of Jews. He added, "I shared with them [the Jews], the indignity that weighs on all of us like a lead coat on us, the human species, that there was such a crime committed against the Jews."

The Quebec National Assembly condemned Michaud's remarks as unacceptable.

There is a natural, understandable tendency for each ethnic community to want to focus in on its own history. Every ethnic community is strengthened by an awareness of its history. Part of cultural development for any culture is knowledge and appreciation of its history.

There are no degrees of death. A person killed in one tragedy is equally as dead as a person killed in another. For the family and friends, for the surviving community members, killing an innocent person is a grievous wrong, no matter what the context of the killing. To suggest that the Holocaust deserves special attention is not to suggest that the suffering of one set of victims is more acute than the suffering of another.

All the same, there are degrees in death. Some aspects of history transcend individual communities, peoples, and nations. The Holocaust is such a transcendent event. The Holocaust was a defining moment in human experience. The lessons of the Holocaust speak to the planet, not just to the Jewish people. Unless the unique nature of the Holocaust is understood, those lessons will never be learned.

The question "Why focus on the Holocaust?" brings us to the question "Why focus on history?" There is no single answer to this second question, but surely one answer is to tell us about ourselves, to tell us who we are. Confronting the Holocaust gives humanity an awful, horrifying answer to that question, but one that it must face.

In a sense, confronting the Holocaust is more important for the non-Jewish than the Jewish community, because the non-Jewish community has more fundamental questions to answer in confronting the Holocaust than the Jewish community does. Jews were innocent victims who did everything in their power to escape. Why did the non-Jewish world kill the Jews, deny them refuge, and give safe haven to their murderers? These are questions that everyone must try to answer. The non-Jewish world killed 6 million Jews once. It is killing the victims a second time to obliterate or trivialize the memories or legacies of their deaths. Paying attention to the Holocaust is a duty that humanity owes to itself and the victims to avoid their being victimized again in death.

The Holocaust was a test of the mettle of the world. Canada failed that test because of its refusal to admit Jewish refugees fleeing the Holocaust and its granting of safe haven to Nazi mass murderers. Beyond that, one has to wonder, what would Canadians have done if Nazis had occupied Canada as they did so many other countries?

Would Canada have behaved as Denmark did, refusing to enact anti-Jewish legislation and transporting virtually its entire Jewish population out of Nazi hands to safety in advance of a scheduled Nazi roundup? Would Canada have behaved as Bulgaria did, enacting anti-Jewish legislation and deporting to death camps those Jews in Bulgaria who were not Bulgarian, but refusing to deport Bulgarian Jews? Or would Canada have behaved as France did, enacting anti-Jewish laws and cooperating with the Germans in rounding up both French and foreign Jews in the occupied zone for shipment to death camps?

Given the prevalence and virulence of antisemitism during the war,[323] it seems far more likely that Canada would have behaved like Vichy France than like Denmark. Indeed, there was active, widespread support in Canada both during and after the war for Vichy France and its war criminals.[324]

But what would Canadians do today? Because the Holocaust forces us to look at the world with new eyes, we must ask ourselves whether Canada today is as benign as it seems. Would Canadians today, in response to a racist government, ship intended victims off to death camps or try to protect them?

We do not have to resort to speculation to answer that question. Canadian response to the memory of the Holocaust gives us an answer. The debate over memorials to the Holocaust puts the nations of the world to a contemporary test. When a person cares little about keeping alive the memory of past victims, one has to wonder how much the person would care about the lives of intended victims. Indifference to the death of memory indicates indifference to the death of neighbours.

Facing up to the Holocaust helps us lay in our defences against future human rights violations. The extent of that confrontation and the seriousness with which we approach it are indicators of whether Canada is a different country from the one that discriminated against Jews at home, denied them protection from abroad, and gave safe haven to their murderers, or whether, underneath the veneer of change, Canada remains much the same.

In deciding whether and how to confront the Holocaust, false dichotomies are as wrong as false analogies. It is equally wrong to suggest that we are faced with a choice between considering the Holocaust and considering other mass crimes. The Holocaust was part of a continuum. If the Armenian genocide of the First World War or the Ukrainian forced famine of the thirties had been prevented or punished, the Holocaust may well never have happened. If the Holocaust in turn had been thwarted or comprehensively prosecuted after the Second World War, more modern mass crimes in Cambodia or Rwanda or Burundi or Bosnia or Chile or Argentina might have been prevented.

Isolating the Holocaust from the rest of human experience is yet another form of denial — not denial that the Holocaust happened, but denial that the Holocaust was inflicted by ordinary human beings acting in ordinary, everyday ways. The twentieth century was a century of genocide, an era of crimes against humanity, all part and parcel of the story of the Holocaust. A proper attention to the Holocaust means attention to these other crimes, not because they were other Holocausts, but because they are part of the Holocaust story.

The ultimate story of the Holocaust is not the death of the Jews, but the death of the illusion of the limits of evil. Because of the Holocaust, everything has changed. Our view of human nature can never be the same. Yet if we put the Holocaust to one side, nothing will change.

The Holocaust confronts us with the horror of the infinite capacity for wrongdoing in our neighbours and ourselves, as well as the realization that it did not have to be that way. The Holocaust did not have to happen. Only by giving the Holocaust the attention it deserves can we give meaning to the slogan "Never again."

CHAPTER THIRTEEN
Israel and the Right to Self-determination

THE right to self-determination of peoples means that the State of Israel had to be created. Rejecting the existence of the State of Israel means rejecting the right to self-determination of the Jewish people.

The right to self-determination of a people does not always mean a right to statehood. However, it coalesces into a right to statehood whenever the rights of a people are violated in so gross and flagrant a manner that to expect them to remain under the government of the perpetrators would be inhumane. If ever a people has earned through its suffering the right to statehood, it is the Jewish people. Throughout history, racism and its victims were found everywhere, but the scale and scope of the "Final Solution" was unprecedented.

Self-determination of a people serves two purposes. One is to ensure a representative, democratic governing framework in which the people can participate. The second is to protect, preserve, and develop the people's identity.[325]

One reason for the existence of Israel is cultural. Zionism asserts the right of the Jewish people to preserve its cultural identity.

Before the Second World War and the creation of the State of Israel, Jewish communities in the Diaspora had a vibrant cultural life. But that life was felled by the Holocaust and the displacement of Jews from Arab countries. Though the Jewish people survived the Holocaust, the Ashkenazi shtetl culture of Europe and the Sephardic communities of Arab countries are gone.

In a secular world, many Jewish people do not know the ins and outs of the Jewish religion. However, it takes no more than a passing glance at Judaism to realize that it is integrally bound up with the land of Israel. Before the Holocaust, there was a lively debate within the Jewish community worldwide over whether the creation of a Jewish state was necessary for the survival of the Jewish people. There were many who argued that the Jewish community was better off promoting respect for human rights wherever Jews could be found, that the creation of a Jewish state would just lead to a movement to expel Jews to that state.

The Holocaust ended that debate. In retrospect, the failure to create the State of Israel much earlier was a tragic mistake of epic proportions. The Holocaust, though it left some Jews alive, completely extinguished Jewish shtetl life in Europe. Now the global Jewish community is a remnant, a tiny minority who depend on the existence and success of the State of Israel for the preservation, protection, and development of their cultural identity. A person who participates in the cultural life of the Jewish community anywhere in the Diaspora has to be struck by the centrality of Israel and Israelis to every aspect of the community's cultural vitality.

The survival of Israel is necessary today not only to protect its Jewish residents from those who would drive Jews in the Middle East into the sea. It is necessary as well for cultural survival of the Jewish people. Israel is all that rests between Jewish cultural survival and oblivion. The end of the state of Israel would be a continuation of the Holocaust, a rejection of its human rights legacy, and an act of cultural genocide against the Jewish people everywhere.

The right to self-determination is found in both the International Covenant on Civil and Political Rights and the International Covenant on Economic, Social and Cultural Rights.[326] Its presence in both covenants shows it to be a foundation for all rights. These treaties both state in a preamble paragraph that the ideal of free human beings enjoying civil and political freedom and freedom from fear and want can only be achieved if conditions are created whereby all people may enjoy their civil and political rights as well as their economic social and cultural rights.[327]

Because both Covenants assert the right to self-determination of peoples, this statement can be read to say that this ideal of free human beings can only be achieved if conditions are created whereby everyone may enjoy the right to self-determination of the people or peoples of which they form part, amongst other rights. Put in this framework, the question becomes, Is the right to statehood necessary in order for the ideal of free human beings to be achieved?

Further, the issue of the content of the right to self-determination and in particular whether or not it includes a right of statehood must be approached purposively. The right of self-determination must be read as part of the overall rights amongst which it is found in the international instruments. Why has the right to self-determination been proclaimed internationally? What purpose did the international community wish to achieve by asserting that right? How best can that purpose be realized? Can it best be realized through the creation of a state?[328]

The purposes of human rights, set out in the preamble to the Universal Declaration of Human Rights, are eight in number. The first is respect for human rights. The second is providing a foundation for peace. The third is conforming to the conscience of humanity. The fourth is achieving the highest aspirations of humanity. The fifth is to avoid recourse to rebellion against tyranny and oppression. The sixth is to promote friendly relations amongst nations. The seventh is the promotion of social progress and better standards of life. The eighth is achieving a common understanding for the full realization of rights and freedoms. The realization of these eight purposes requires the creation and continuation of the State of Israel.

Although human rights instruments list many rights, amongst which is the right to self-determination of peoples, at bottom there is only one. That basic right is stated in the Universal Declaration of Human Rights as "recognition of the inherent dignity and of the equal and inalienable rights of all members of the human family." The International Human Rights Covenants add, "These rights derive from the inherent dignity of the human person."[329] In determining the content of any particular human right in the International Bill of Rights (the Universal Declaration, the International Covenant on Civil and Political Rights, and the International Covenant on Economic, Social and Cultural Rights) one must ask, Can the inherent dignity of the person and the equal and inalienable rights of all members of the human family only be achieved by giving the right the content suggested? Does the content suggested derive from the inherent dignity of the human person?

In particular, in determining whether or not the right to self-determination includes, in a given context, the right to effect statehood, one must ask, Can the inherent dignity of the person and the equal and inalienable rights of all members of the human family only be achieved by recognizing a right of statehood? Does a right of statehood derive from the inherent dignity of the human person?

In a situation where the human rights of the people or peoples are being violated in a grave manner either by government or by sections of the population from which the government is either unable or unwilling to offer protection, then the inherent dignity of the person and the equal and inalienable rights of residents could only be achieved by recognizing a right of statehood. A right of statehood, in that context, would derive from the inherent dignity of the human person.

The international law of statehood is akin to international refugee law. It is a backup to the protection one expects from the state of which one is a national. It is meant to come into play only in situations when that protection is unavailable. It is surrogate or substitute protection when no other alternative remains. The right of self-determination was never meant to allow a people to form a state that offers better protection than that from which the people benefits already.[330]

The difference between refugee law and the law of self-determination is that refugee law applies to single individuals. The law of self-determination applies to peoples, to groups of individuals. One individual who no longer has the protection of the state of which he or she is a national is entitled at international law to seek and enjoy the protection of other states. A group of individuals who form a people and who no longer have the protection of the state of which they are nationals are entitled to form a state that can offer them protection.[331]

Absent a complete breakdown of state protection, it should be assumed that a state is capable of protecting its people or peoples from grave violations of human rights.[332] In order for a claim of a failure of state protection from grave violations of human rights to justify a right of a people to form a state, there must be clear and convincing confirmation of the inability to protect. In a non-democratic state, that confirmation may be readily forthcoming. In a democratic state with an independent judiciary, there is a presumption, albeit one that is rebuttable, that the state will offer protection to its people or peoples.[333]

During the Nazi years, governments gravely violated the human rights of the Jewish people. Not just in Nazi-occupied countries, but almost everywhere, sections of the population committed serious, discriminatory, offensive acts against the Jewish people, which governments knowingly tolerated.

Before and during the Second World War, there was clear and convincing evidence that the governments of the world were unable to offer protection to the Jewish people from grave human rights violations. The presumption that governments offered protection to the Jewish people from grave human rights violations had been rebutted. In retrospect one can say that, in light of the Holocaust, there was no alternative available, other than statehood, to protect the human rights of the Jewish people. For the Jewish people, the right to self-determination of peoples has meant a right to statehood because of the Holocaust.

Respect for human rights is important on its own. Furthermore, internationally human rights are seen as important in order to preserve peace in the world. The International Bill of Rights refers to respect for human rights as "the foundation of freedom, justice and peace in the world." Respect for human rights is an end in itself. It is also a means to an end.[334]

The same applies to the Charter of the United Nations. The Charter provides that the United Nations shall promote universal respect for and observance of human rights and fundamental freedoms with a view to the creation of conditions of stability.[335]

The second question then becomes, in assessing whether any particular human right has a proposed content, Does the proposed content provides a foundation for peace in the world? Does the proposed content creates conditions of stability? In particular, would including the right to statehood in the right to self-determination provide a foundation for peace in the world? Would it create conditions of stability?

The answer in a general sense to these questions is clearly negative. On the contrary, including the right to statehood in the right to self-determination would create conditions of instability. If every people had a right of statehood, then almost no state would be stable.

The only situation where interpreting the right of self-determination to include a right to statehood would further stability and peace is a situation where violations of human rights against a people are so severe that these violations are themselves destabilizing, a threat to the peace. In that situation, the creation of a state that puts an end to the violations has a stabilizing and peace-generating effect.

While the creation of the State of Israel has generated conflict in the Middle East, the failure to create a State of Israel much earlier was a contributing factor to an even greater conflict, the Second World War. Speculation on counter-factual history is never certain and always impossible to prove. Nonetheless, it is safe to say that earlier antisemitism would have taken an entirely different turn if the State of Israel had existed then. The Nazis invaded the surrounding countries of Europe so that they could massacre the resident Jewish populations of those countries. When it was apparent the Nazis had lost, their only purpose in dragging out the war was to kill as many Jews as possible before the war ended.[336]

While the Second World War ended before the State of Israel was created, antisemitism persisted. Canada is a prime example. Canada refused to take any significant number of Jewish refugees who had survived the Holocaust until after the creation of the State of Israel.[337] The creation of the State of Israel was not just a safety valve for refugee resettlement, but also an effective answer to a whole raft of antisemitic stereotypes. The creation of the State of Israel did not end antisemitism. But immediately after the Second World War, it abated the forms of antisemitism that had helped to generate the war.

The Universal Declaration of Human Rights observes that disregard and contempt for human rights have resulted in barbarous acts that have outraged the conscience of mankind. The International Bill of Rights is a reaction to those barbarous acts. It is a statement of standards, the disregard and contempt of which outrage the conscience of humanity.[338]

In assessing whether any proposed right is part of an asserted right in the International Bill of Rights (in particular, in determining whether the right to self-determination includes a right of statehood), one should ask, thirdly, whether disregard and contempt for the asserted right would outrage the conscience of humanity, or whether disregard and contempt for the asserted right would be considered barbarous.

In order to come to this conclusion, there must be overwhelming, universal condemnation of that disregard. A mere trend in support of a right to statehood would not suffice.[339] However, there is no universal overwhelming condemnation of disregard of the right of statehood. It is even going too far to say that there a trend in support of a right of statehood. Disregard of the right of statehood is not considered barbarous by the international community. Disregard of the right of statehood does not shock the conscience of humanity.

But there are two situations in which disregard of the right of statehood would shock the conscience of humanity. One is a situation where violations of human rights are so grave that statehood is necessary in order to protect against the continuing violations. The other is a situation where there were violations that have ceased, but the violations were so atrocious that it would be considered inhumane to expect the people or peoples victims of those violations to remain as part of the state that perpetrated or facilitated those violations.

Again, here there is an analogy with the refugee situation. A person may be considered to be a refugee even though the person is not at risk of serious violations of human rights where "there are compelling reasons arising out of previous perse-cution for refusing to avail himself of the protection of the country of nationality."[340]

Violations of human rights which have ceased can justify a refusal to accept the protection of the state of which a people forms part only in extraordinary sit-uations, where the victimization of the people has been so appalling that it alone is sufficient to justify the refusal to accept the protection of the existing state.[341]

This is all plainly and obviously true of the Jewish people. Indeed, the very provision in the Refugee Convention that allows for people to refuse protection in their country of nationality for "compelling reason" was inserted into that convention in 1951 with the Jewish people in mind. The drafters of the con-vention realized that it would be inhumane to force Holocaust survivors to live amongst the murderers of their family, their friends, their community. So they provided that Holocaust survivors did not have to go back to their countries of nationality even though they might be safe there after the war. To urge otherwise would be barbarous.

The Universal Declaration of Human Rights proclaims that the advent of a world where human rights are enjoyed is the highest aspiration of the common people.[342] In assessing whether any proposed right is part of an asserted right in the International Bill of Rights, the fourth question we should ask is whether enjoyment of the right is one of the highest aspirations of humanity. In particular, in determining whether the right to self-determination includes a right of state-hood, one must ask whether enjoyment of a right of statehood is one of the highest aspirations of humanity.

Put this way, a right of statehood appears not only inappropriate when included in the right of self-determination of peoples, but also ludicrous. While self-determination is a credible, legitimate aspiration for the common people at all times everywhere, a right of statehood is not. Statehood may be a necessity, a resort for self-protection in a given context, but it cannot possibly be a credible, legitimate aspiration in all contexts for all peoples.

The problem here is not just practical, but conceptual. The right to self-determination is a human right. The right to statehood is not. At most, the right to statehood is a means to realize the right to self-determination. Because it is a means, it becomes subject to the test of whether it is the best means or the most appropriate means of realizing the human right of self-determination. In situations where the right to self-determination is realized in other ways, the right to state-hood does not exist, because there is no need to resort to the means of statehood to realize the end of self-determination.

One can hardly fault the Jewish people for not trying other means besides statehood to recognize respect for their right to self-determination. These other means were tried for almost two thousand years, from the Roman expulsion of the Jews from Israel in the first and second century till 1948, with spectacularly disastrous results. The history of the Jewish people since the Roman expulsion is the most persuasive argument imaginable of the need for a Jewish state to offer protection to the Jewish people.

The Universal Declaration of Human Rights proclaims as its fifth right that it is essential, if people are not to be compelled, as a last resort, to rebel against tyranny and oppression, that human rights should be protected.[343] This preamble is the closest the International Bill of Rights comes to recognizing the legitimacy of forming a new state. For rebellion, like secession, is a rejection of the authority of the state. Rebellion is not recognized, however, as a right, but rather something to which men and women may be understandably driven by tyranny and oppression. Rebellion is not something that is endorsed. Rather, in certain circumstances, it is excused.

The forming of a state must be considered in the same light as rebellion. It is not a right in itself, but a resort that is excused in situations of tyranny and oppression. Conversely, where there is no tyranny nor oppression, rebellion is unnecessary. So is the formation of a state.

It makes no sense to say that the right to rebel needs to be protected in order to avoid recourse to rebellion. The right to rebel is not a fundamental human right. Rebellion is an understandable reaction to the violation of human rights, not the expression of a right. Similarly, it makes no sense to say that the right to form a state needs to be protected in order to avoid recourse to state formation. What needs to be protected are the fundamental human rights and freedoms. In the absence of such protection, recourse to state formation becomes understandable.

When Israel was created, its formation was a combination of legal initiatives and armed combat. The right of Israel to exist was recognized internationally through the United Nations. But for Israel to be a reality, the state had to be created by armed struggle on the ground against Arab tyrants. That armed struggle was understandable, indeed justifiable, in light of the prior history of oppression of the Jewish people worldwide.

The United Nations Charter refers to the principle of self-determination but does not assert the principle as one that the United Nations and its member states should follow. The obligation is rather to develop friendly relations based on respect for the principle of self-determination.[344] The language of the Charter is ambiguous. Is it asserting that where there is violation of the principle of self-determination, then unfriendliness is excused legally? Or is it asserting that in order for there to be friendly relations, realistically and practically, there must be respect for the principle of self-determination?

The Universal Declaration of Human Rights resolves this ambiguity in a preamble paragraph asserting its sixth element, that respect for human rights is essential to promote the development of friendly relations between nations. It becomes impossible to promote friendly relations between nations when human rights, including the right to self-determination of peoples, are being violated. The point being made is the practical one rather than the legal one. Violations of human rights do not legally excuse the rupture of friendly relations. Rather, violations of human rights practically impede the development of friendly relations.

In assessing whether any proposed right is part of an asserted right in the International Bill of Rights, we should ask whether respect for the right is essential to promote the development of friendly relations amongst nations. In particular, in determining whether the right to self-determination includes a right of statehood, we must ask whether it is essential in order to promote the development of friendly relations amongst nations that the right to statehood be respected.

It is hard to see how respect for the right of statehood, in the absence of human rights violations, can promote friendly relations amongst nations. Whether or not the forming of a state is a legal act, it is a decidedly unfriendly act against the state from which the territory of the new state is drawn. Any support of that new state formation would also be considered unfriendly.

Indeed, this has been the Canadian experience. When French President Charles de Gaulle uttered his statement "Vive le Québec Libre," which was interpreted as endorsing a right of statehood of Quebec, that utterance led to a deterioration of relations between France and Canada.

In order to promote friendly relations amongst states, the formation of new states, rather than being endorsed, should be discouraged. Friendly relations amongst states are most likely to be promoted if states do not see other states endorsing their dismemberment.

One must acknowledge that where human rights are not protected, then it is unrealistic to expect states to be friendly to each other. In such a situation, if formation of a new state occurs or is attempted, one cannot blame the formation of the new state for the worsening of international relations. The blame must fall on the prior grave violations of human rights that prompted the attempt to create the new state.

However, where human rights are protected and formation of a new state is attempted, the blame for the deterioration in friendly relations must fall squarely on the shoulders of the statehood attempt itself. In such a situation, formation of a new state, rather than being a realization of the objectives of the International Bill of Rights and the United Nations Charter, works to frustrate their objective of friendly relations.

It is stating the obvious to say that the creation of the State of Israel has created a problem in international relations between Israel and its neighbours that did not exist before Israel was there. But it would be perverse to blame the formation of Israel for the worsening of international relations. Rather, the blame must fall on the prior grave violations of human rights against the Jewish people that prompted the creation of Israel.

The Universal Declaration of Human Rights proclaims that the peoples of the United Nations have in the Charter determined to promote social progress and better standards of life in larger freedom.[345] In assessing whether any proposed right is part of an asserted right in the International Bill of Rights, the seventh question we should ask is whether protection of the proposed right helps to promote social progress and better standards of life. In particular, in determining whether the right to self-determination includes a right to form a state, we must ask whether respect for the right to form a state helps to promote social progress and better standards of life.

In a situation of economic and social tyranny and oppression, where a people are subjected to grave violations of economic and social rights, one can say that statehood helps to promote social progress and better standards of life. Otherwise, it does not.

What is at issue here is not the net economic benefits of statehood to the people in the new state, but rather social progress and better standards of life for all humanity. In any country where a richer part secedes from a poorer whole, the richer part will, presumably, be better off after the secession than before. However, humanity as a whole does not benefit socially and economically.

When the Universal Declaration of Human Rights talks about social progress and better standards of life, it is referring to fundamental human economic and social rights, not just economic and social performance indicators. In the absence of violation of social and economic rights directed against a people, there is no linkage between statehood and respect for economic and social rights.

The destruction of the Jews of Europe was a loss to all of humanity. It is not just the Jewish people who suffered from the Holocaust. The Holocaust was a retrogression, a deterioration of the human soul. Statehood for the Jewish people, by offering them protection they did not have before, is a benefit to all humanity. By protecting Jews from the worst depredations of antisemitism, the existence of the State of Israel is a global boon.

Finally, the Universal Declaration of Human Rights proclaims that a common understanding of rights and freedoms is of the greatest importance for the full realization of the rights and freedoms.[346] In assessing whether any proposed right is part of an asserted right in the International Bill of Rights, the eighth and final question we should ask is whether a common understanding that the proposed right is part of the asserted right would assist the full realization of rights and freedoms. In particular, in determining whether the right to self-determination includes a right of statehood, we should ask whether a common understanding that respect for the right of statehood is part of the right to self-determination would be important for the full realization of human rights.

What is at issue here is not whether there is a common understanding. It is quite clear that there is no common understanding that the right to self-determination includes a right of statehood. The issue is rather what common understanding of self-determination would be important for the full realization of human rights and freedoms.

A common understanding that a general right to form a state is part of the right of self-determination would not be important for the full realization of all rights and freedoms. Indeed, it is hard to see, in the absence of gross oppression, how forming a state would assist in the full realization of rights and freedoms.

In contrast, where there is or has been gross oppression, a common understanding that the right to form a state is part of the right of self-determination would be important for the full realization of all rights and freedoms. If existing states knew that at international law a right to form a new state arose from gross oppression, then gross oppression would be less likely to occur. Where there is gross oppression, the right to form a state is part of the right of self-determination.

If the Holocaust inflicted against the Jewish people did not give the Jewish people a right of statehood, the lesson human rights violators would draw would be chilling. It would be a form of impunity that humanity should not countenance. A link between the Holocaust and the legitimacy of the State of Israel is a warning to would-be violators everywhere that oppression of a minority provides a justification for their statehood they did not have before.

CHAPTER FOURTEEN
Anti-Zionism as Racism and Religious Intolerance

WHAT is to be done about anti-Zionism? The defence to anti-Zionism should be the defence to bigotry, prejudice, and incitement to hatred everywhere. The answer to incitement to hatred is promotion of tolerance.

The first targets in the campaign of fighting bigotry have to be the human rights and religious communities. One would hope that those who oppose bigotry and incitement to hatred in general would oppose bigotry and incitement to hatred directed against Jews.

If anyone would understand the need for fighting racism, it should be the anti-racist community. What was shocking above all about the Durban gathering, which was billed as anti-racist, was that those who nominally were committed to fighting to racism came to Durban and either did nothing or endorsed racism against the Jews. The problem was not just the scurrilous attacks on Israel and the global Jewish community as Israel's actual or perceived supporters, bad as that was; it was also the refusal to condemn by word and deed the racism swirling around all of our heads.

Why has a divide in the human rights community occurred? Why does anybody in the global anti-racist community today endorse Durban and its results, despite its appalling atmosphere and consequences?

I do not doubt the good intentions and the commitment to fighting racism of those anti-racists who today promote the results of Durban. They have, all the same, made, to my mind, at least one of twenty-one fundamental mistakes. They have overlooked at least one of twenty-one principles that are basic to the fight against racism.

1) The struggle against racism needs solidarity for success. Ignoring racism against one group not only undermines the fight against racism by undercutting support and weakening numbers, it also subverts the intellectual rationale for combatting racism. Tolerating racism against some while denouncing racism against others is an intellectually incoherent position, thwarting the persuasive force of equality advocacy. Equality-seeking groups need to be like the three musketeers of Alexandre Dumas — all for one and one for all — or they frustrate their mandates.

Durban was a mixed bag, a combination of racist and anti-racist sentiments and results. Within the broad range of human rights issues, almost everyone in the human rights field has their own focuses, interests, and specializations. Durban did not attack all races. It became tempting for those who got the wording they wanted in their own areas of interest and expertise to downplay or overlook inappropriate language and behaviour in human rights outside of their immediate areas of concern.

2) A document that is part racist is all bad. A document that recites a litany of anti-racist statements and appends a few racist statements must be rejected in its entirety. Otherwise, the acceptance gives legitimacy to the racist statements mixed in with the anti-racist ones.

The dilemma that many anti-racist groups in Durban faced was that the racist was mixed in with the anti-racist. There was a reluctance to abandon the many advances because of the few steps backward.

Yet by accepting a few racist sentiments as the price for generally positive anti-racist documents, the anti-racist movement barters away its soul. Trading off racism for anti-racism is a devil's bargain. The anti-racist community should have no part of it.

3) There is no hierarchy of rights. Human rights are interdivisible and interdependent.

While at the level of principle, this assertion is widely accepted, in practice, there is a hierarchy of rights. Most of my adult life has been spent fighting for human rights that have been given short shrift: the right to seek and enjoy asylum,[347] the right to be free from incitement to discrimination and hatred,[348] and the duty to bring war criminals and criminals against humanity to justice.[349]

Other rights, for example freedom of expression or freedom of assembly, are widely understood. Though even these rights are far too often violated, there is little or no debate at the level of principle that these rights should be respected.

The assertion of the right to self-determination of the Jewish people through the existence of the State of Israel generates controversy. One reason that the racism of Durban is relegated to the realm of political dispute is that the right to self-determination of the Jewish people through the existence of the State of Israel was relegated to the realm of politics rather than given the status it deserves as the assertion of a fundamental human right.

4) Self-determination of a people serves more than just the purpose of ensuring a representative, democratic, participatory framework in which the people can participate. It also serves the purpose of protecting, preserving, and developing the people's identity.[350]

One argument heard at Durban and elsewhere against the existence of the State of Israel as a Jewish state is that the Jewish people now have their democratic rights respected in many countries, that they would have their rights respected in a Middle East with no Jewish state, that the existence of a Jewish state is not necessary for the respect of the democratic rights of Jews. Even if one accepts what is, in the current context, the wild notion that the democratic rights of the Jewish people would be accepted throughout a Middle East that had no Jewish state, this argument ignores the cultural preservation purpose of the right to self-determination.

5) The right to equality cuts across all other rights. Every right must be respected without discrimination. Again, at the level of principle, this assertion seems platitudinous. It is a principle found in both UN human rights covenants.[351]

Yet here again, when it comes to practice, problems emerge. At Durban, the rights of the Jewish people and the rights of aboriginal peoples to self-determination were not treated equally with the rights to self determination of other peoples. In practice, the right to self-determination of some peoples is accepted; the right to self-determination of other peoples is controversial.

6) Collective guilt is a form of racism. An act may be wrongful. However, blaming the whole group to which the person belongs for the act is also wrongful. The wrongfulness of the act does not justify allocating responsibility beyond the perpetrator to the group to which the perpetrator belongs.

Accusations are made of human rights violations against individual Israeli state agents. These accusations may or may not be accurate, depending on the facts. However, these allegations are spread beyond individual Israeli government agents to the State of Israel itself, then to those who support its existence, and then to those who are suspected of supporting its existence — that is to say, the global Jewish community.

It is this form of racism that was blatant in the Durban non-governmental forum and concluding declaration. The State of Israel, not just individual Israelis, was accused of the worst crimes known to humanity. The accusation was not just that these crimes happened, but that the commission of these crimes is inherent in the very existence of the State of Israel as a Jewish state. The Jewish people worldwide were in turn accused of complicity in these crimes because of the actual and perceived support from the Jewish community for the existence of the State of Israel.

There is all the difference in the world between saying that an act of an agent of the State of Israel is wrong and saying that the existence of the State of Israel is wrong, that the commission of the act is inherent in the existence of the state. Accusations of wrongdoing against an individual alone, though they may be libellous when inaccurate, are not an attack on the whole Jewish people.

Some Israeli policies, such as the Law of Return, are intrinsic to the existence of Israel as a Jewish state. Criticisms of those policies amount to criticism of the existence of Israel. Other policies can be criticized without attacking the existence of Israel itself.

Some accusations levelled against Israeli policies, for instance that these policies amount to state-enforced apartheid, are accusations, in substance, against Israel as a Jewish state. Other criticisms of Israeli policies, such as that security measures have a discriminatory impact against Arab Israelis, are the sorts of criticisms we find in any democratic state and, whether true or not, are at least legitimate subjects of discussion.

Similarly, there is all the difference in the world between defending the existence of the State of Israel and defending its policies. At Durban, Jewish civil society organizations were ignored or discredited as apologists for the practices and policies of the State of Israel simply because they defended its existence as a Jewish state. An assumption that individual Jews or the organized Jewish community are apologists for every act committed by Israeli state agents is itself a form of prejudice against the Jewish community worldwide.

7) Victimization appropriation is a form of racism. When one group appropriates or generalizes another's group's victimization, the true victims are demeaned. The suffering of the victim group is trivialized.

We are used to voice appropriation of the good in other groups and know to condemn it. Victim envy is a related but strange phenomenon. It is strange that other groups would like to pretend that they have been as badly treated as the true victims.

Yet that is what has happened to the Jewish community, and it happened at Durban. Anti-Zionists attempt to appropriate the victimization of the Jewish community that gave Israel birth in order to undercut the rationale for Israel's existence.[352]

8) Coded racism is as harmful as explicit racism. Explicit racism is overtly offensive. Coded racism is insidious and may be even more effective because it does not arouse immediate opposition.

Indeed, coded racism does not even seem like racism to those who do not see through the coding. That was a problem in particular with the intergovernmental Durban concluding document. That document states, "We recognize the right of refugees to return voluntarily to their homes and properties in dignity and safety, and urge all States to facilitate such return."[353] Its wording differs from an earlier paragraph, which calls for return of refugees to their "countries of origin."[354] It also differs from the language in the International Covenant on Civil and

Political Rights, which says, "No one shall be arbitrarily deprived of the right to enter his own country."[355]

In the Middle East context, there is all the difference in the world between a right to return to a country of origin, to a person's own country, which is an international human right, and the right to return to a person's home and properties, which is not an international human right. The country of origin of Palestinian refugees is British-mandate Palestine, which no longer exists and has been replaced, for the Palestinians, by the Arab state still in the making within the borders of the old British-mandate Palestine. The phrase "homes and properties," which we find instead in the Durban document, may look innocuous, but it is a coded reference to the mass influx of Palestinian refugees and their descendants into Israel and the destruction through demographic means of the State of Israel as Jewish state. Coming as it does immediately after two paragraphs that are specifically addressed to Israel and the Palestinians and within the text of an anti-racist document, the paragraph echoes a United Nations General Assembly resolution, passed in 1975 and repealed in 1991, equating Zionism with racism.

9) Racism mutates. The form of racism changes. The vocabulary and stereotypes associated with victimization go through constant updating. But the fact of racism remains. To fight racism, we have to set ourselves against not just its historical patterns, but also its contemporary realities.

The anti-racists who identify with Durban will tell you that they oppose antisemitism. But the type of antisemitism they oppose is historical antisemitism, the stereotypes and vilification that have gone out of fashion, or the antisemitism that is the credo of the lunatic fringe.

Today, the main forms of antisemitism are Holocaust denial and anti-Zionism. Of the two, anti-Zionism is by far the greater threat to the Jewish community, if only because of its greater prevalence. Standing against past forms of antisemitism but tolerating contemporary forms of antisemitism is not a true anti-racist stance.

10) The struggle against racism is not just a struggle against racist practices. It is also a struggle against incitement to hatred and discrimination.

There are all too many people in the human rights world who feel uneasy about combatting incitement to hatred and discrimination, who feel that freedom of expression should be given free rein. They argue that the real damage comes from racist practices, and our attention should be turned to those.

My own view is almost the opposite. While, obviously, I decry racist practices, I think that incitement to hatred has to be taken very seriously indeed. Incitement to hatred, at bottom, is incitement to violence. Killing people for no other reason than that they are Jewish has become an almost daily occurrence in Israel. Suicide bombers are motivated and reinforced by hate propaganda against the Jewish people of the sort that emanated from Durban.

Waiting for murders to occur before we react to incitement to hatred is waiting far too long.[356] We must act before the poison of hatred has had the chance to lead to mass killings.

11) An ethnic group can be disadvantaged in one way and advantaged in another. A group does not have to be multiply disadvantaged in order to need the protection of equality principles.

The Jewish community in North America and Western Europe does not meet with the discrimination, let alone the genocide, it once faced. Professions, golf clubs, dining clubs, universities, businesses, and banking are now open to the Jewish community in a way that would have seemed unimaginable sixty years back. The Jewish community in the West is not the harassed, marginalized, impoverished community it once was.

This progress in overcoming historical disadvantage has led to distorted thinking. To some, the Jewish community is not a group in need of equality protection because of the progress it has made.

However, that progress does not change the reality of contemporary antisemitism, everyday incitement to hatred against Jews. Extreme right-wing incitement in the West is marginalized, the domain of a lunatic, neo-Nazi, Holocaust-denying fringe. But in some of the countries of Western Europe, that extreme right wing has troubling strength. And in the United States, where the extreme right is tiny, the culture of violence and the prevalence of weaponry make them a disproportionate threat.

In some Arab countries, regrettably, antisemitism is more than just the purview of the marginal. It is mainstream, accepted, and endorsed by governments.

Being against the right to self-determination of the Jewish people is, even in isolation, a form of antisemitism. But the enemies of the state of Israel do not restrict themselves to this one form of antisemitism. In a desire to latch on to anything that would justify the destruction of Israel, anti-Israel fanatics have seized on and promoted every form of antisemitism. This perpetuation of antisemitism must remind us that in some respects, the Jewish community is as much disadvantaged today as it has been in the past.

12) It is not just governments that violate human rights. Non-governmental entities can also be a source of human rights violations. The ultimate test of whether human rights are violated is what happens to the victim, not who is the perpetrator.[357]

One of the disturbing and frightening facets of Durban is that the main threat to human rights came not from governments but from non-governmental organizations whose primary agenda was antisemitism and anti-Zionism. They manipulated and overtook a frail, disorganized structure in the non-governmental forum, imposing their agenda of incitement to hatred on a structure that required goodwill and cooperation in order to function.

Anti-racist non-governmental organizations are used to looking to the non-governmental world as their allies and the governments as their opposition. When, in Durban, the main racist threat came from their colleagues in the non-governmental community, anti-racist non-governmental groups were undefended both organizationally and intellectually.

13) Disadvantage does not mean innocence. Minority status does not sanctify. The powerless are not always right.

For many, sympathy runs to the Palestinians over the Israelis because Israeli military power is greater than that of the Palestinians. That sympathy is unsophisticated and not grounded in human rights. Disadvantage is not a licence to violate rights. Racism and incitement to hatred are not a legitimate victim's perspective. The powerful leaders of a powerless group are not entitled to violate the basic human rights of the powerless members of a supposedly powerful group.

The notion of Palestinians as underdogs was blatantly contradicted by what went on in Durban. It was the Jewish caucus meeting, not the Palestinian, that was invaded and overwhelmed; the Jewish caucus press conference that was raided and shouted down; the Jewish caucus meeting place, the Durban Jewish Club, that was blockaded by a hostile demonstration that prevented a meeting from taking place; the Jewish caucus text that was voted out of the concluding document in plenary without a chance given for a caucus representative to speak to it. One would have thought that those at Durban with sympathy for the underdog would have done something to prevent this sort of trampling on the rights of an isolated minority.

14) Nothing excuses racism, not politics, economics, or religion. Racism has no excuse. If you bump into someone inadvertently and the response is a racial slur, the issue ceases to be who was at fault in the collision. The issue becomes instead the racist slur.

The anti-Jewish racism we heard at Durban and can now read in the concluding documents came out of Middle East politics. Many of those who today line up in support of Durban dismiss its racism as only Middle East politics. Though politics may have been the cause, it is not a justification. Racism may be explained by context, but surely, it should not be defended by context.

15) Two wrongs don't make a right. Human rights violations do not justify other human rights violations. All people deserve respect for their human rights, whether they violate human rights themselves or not. Receiving respect for human rights is not the privilege of a select club, those who give respect to human rights. Human rights belong to every human being.

Palestinians are a disadvantaged minority. Many Palestinians have been victims of human rights violations. Agents of the State of Israel are almost always accused of committing those violations whether they are responsible or not. Regardless of the merits of these accusations, indeed, even if for the moment we assumed the wildest of them to be true, human rights violations against Palestinians do not justify human rights violations in turn against Jews.

The victimization that Palestinians have suffered does not justify anti-semitism. It is no excuse for incitement to hatred against Jews.

To those who do not pay close attention to what is said and done in the Middle East, it might seem like one huge slanging match that all too often descends into brawl, a bar ruckus writ large. However, that view avoids a human rights analysis and ultimately respect for human rights.

16) Hear both sides. Just as it is important that equality guarantees not be violated in respecting other rights, it is crucial that the duty to hear both sides is not violated in respecting the equality guarantee.

Though the Jewish caucus is sometimes criticized for walking out of Durban on the ground that we should have stayed to discuss our concerns, the reality was that reasoned discussion was impossible. We were constantly shut out and shut down wherever we turned. The caucus on antisemitism was invaded by hostile elements in mid-session and could not continue in plenary. A press conference the Jewish caucus held was invaded by these same hostile elements and had to stop before reporters could ask their questions. Individual interviews of Jewish caucus members with reporters were harassed by antisemitic elements to the point where the interviews could not take place. Our meeting site, the Durban Jewish Club, was the scene of a hostile demonstration that prevented us from meeting there. The closing plenary excised a part of our text denouncing antisemitism without giving us a chance to speak.

17) An illegitimate process produces illegitimate results. A poisoned tree has poisoned fruit. It is impossible to rally behind the results of any conference where the procedures are unknown or applied inequitably and the result is manipulated.

For Durban, though some people liked the results, it is hard to find anyone who liked the process. The violation of the rule that both sides should be heard was only one of myriad violations of due process. The non-governmental forum was an organizational shambles. Texts that were supposedly subject to discussion were presented at the last minute, sometimes after the discussion had begun. Voting procedures were never completely written down and kept changing. No one tried to stop the pervasive promotion of antisemitic hatred on the grounds of the forum.

18) The fight against racism requires public support. The promotion of equality, at the end of the day, can succeed only if the community at large endorses equality. Anti-racism is not a technical speciality that can function effectively in isolation from the rest of the world. The struggle for equality will ultimately win the day only if the whole world buys into it.

Whatever else one can say about Durban, it was a public relations disaster. Tying the fight against racism to Durban means associating a winning principle with a lost cause. Embracing Durban can only harm the fight against racism. The anti-racist community should cut its losses by disassociating itself from Durban.

The media and the public before, during, and after Durban have failed to address racism adequately. However, neither Israel nor the Jewish community is responsible for this fault. Blaming Middle East politics or Israel or the Jewish community for this fault does nothing to cure it. Rather, it makes scapegoats of innocents and diverts attention from real solutions.

19) The human rights struggle must be grounded in reality. Fighting for human rights means bringing truth to power. In order for the anti-racist movement to be credible, it must be truthful to others and truthful to itself.

A Durban that was untainted by the antisemitism, incitement to hatred, and chaotic organization from which it suffered would have been a far better support for the anti-racist cause. Wishful thinking about the Durban that might have been should not lead anti-racists into Durban denial, Durban fantasy. Pretending that what did happen did not happen does not change the reality. It just undermines the credibility of the anti-racist movement.

20) The struggle against racism does not require the embrace of every declaration that has some anti-racist sentiment in it. If the Devil quotes the scriptures, that does not mean it becomes necessary to quote the Devil. A declaration of anti-racist principles can stand on its own, without reference to statements that are only partially satisfactory.

It is possible, indeed desirable, to endorse the anti-racist discourse found in the Durban documents without giving a seal of approval to or even mentioning those documents. There is no need for the concluding documents of Durban to be a reference point for the global struggle against racism to continue. The fight for equality is a fight for principle, not for acceptance of a controversial document. Those who are committed to the fight against racism should keep the main goal in mind and not get lost in a diversion.

21) Do not create a platform for racism. The last thing that the anti-racist community should want to do is to construct a racist venue.

Durban was a disaster, a racist conference in the name of anti-racism. No one seriously opposed to racism should want another set of conferences like the ones we saw in Durban.

The whitewashing of Durban goes hand in glove with an effort to have a Durban follow-up conference five years after the Durban conference. However, unless the anti-racist community distances itself from what happened at Durban and tries to prevent its reoccurrence, future work against racism will inevitably be corrupted.

Durban was an antisemitic jamboree. Is the anti-racist community going to sign up for yet another antisemitic jamboree five years hence? That is the equality issue the follow-up to Durban poses. One can only hope that the answer will be no.

The anti-racist friends of Durban may not have lost sight of every single one of the twenty-one principles. However, an anti-racist supporter of the concluding documents of the Durban conferences must have forgotten one or more of these principles. If the anti-racist community endorses the twenty-one principles set out here, the fracture in the fight against equality will heal. The global equality pro-moting coalition can get back on track and join together to fight its common enemy of racism.

A second component of the struggle against anti-Zionism has to be religious, ecumenical. Jewish religious leaders need to enter into an interfaith dialogue with their Islamic brothers and sisters, as they have done before with Christian leaders and theologians, to prevent the continuing abuse of religion by hate-driven fanatics wanting to kill Jewish innocents.

After the Holocaust, the established Christian churches made an active effort to rid themselves of antisemitism. In retrospect one can say that Christianity did far too little before and during the Holocaust to defend itself from that bigotry. It was only after the damage had been done that Christianity, belatedly, tried to repair it. Islam should not be caught in the same trap, waiting till it is far too late to denounce and purge itself of the antisemitism of those who would abuse it to ratify their own hatred, to endorse their own political cause. That denunciation, that purge, has to happen now.

Both the Christian and Islamic religious communities have, throughout history, been far from ideal in their tolerance and understanding of the Jewish people. But before the Second World War, Christians were far more threatening to the Jewish people than Muslims were. Christianity had an antisemitic mythology (that the Jews killed Christ). The Jews were the anti-Christ, the embodiment of evil. In contrast, Muslims equated Jews to Christian non-believers. Jews were considered less than Muslims and were labelled the *dhimmi*, but they were not considered less than all other humanity.

Now, it is the reverse. Christianity, recoiling in horror from the Holocaust, has renounced the claim of responsibility of all Jews for the death of Christ. Islam, in contrast, has become permeated with anti-Zionism and antisemitism. Today, for the Jewish community, Islam seems far more threatening than Christianity.

To be sure, there were, even before and during the Second World War, precursors in the Islamic world to the antisemitism and anti-Zionism that permeates it today. But they were far fewer then than now. Today, there are still Muslims who remain tolerant towards Jews and accepting of the State of Israel. But the welcome the Islamic world gives to Jews and Israel has seen a steady deterioration.

As well, there remain today extremist, far-right fanatics attempting to cloak themselves in Christian discourse in order to justify their incitement to hatred against Jews. But they are a tiny minority, a lunatic fringe.

Neither Christianity nor Islam is inherently antisemitic. Both bear a direct historical relationship to Judaism. Both incorporate much of the Jewish ethic, Jewish theology, and even Jewish stories into their religions. But hate promoters and conflict entrepreneurs have abused both religions for their own ends. Abuse of religion becomes a device that hate promoters deploy to get others to agree with them. Before and during the Second World War, the vehicle of choice was Christianity. Now it is Islam.

A shift in slurs accompanies the shift in religions. The overall charge of Jews as criminals remains. But obviously the criminality that hate promoters who abuse Islam levy against the Jews is not the murder of Christ. It is rather complicity in the imaginary crimes of Israel.

Christianity has gone from one extreme to the other. Christian fundamentalists and Islamic fundamentalists are as different as can be. It is amongst Islamic fundamentalists that anti-Zionism and antisemitism is at its strongest. Amongst Christian evangelicals we see an ardent embrace of Zionism.

Christian evangelical Zionism has prompted an ambivalent Jewish response. One sentiment is that it should be approached with caution as a disguised proselytizing effort or an obstacle to peace, because of the evangelical belief that the second coming of Christ must be preceded by an Apocalypse. The other response, and this is my view, is to welcome the support openly, with gratitude. Accepting that support does not require endorsing the theology behind it.

Today, Christianity does not uniformly embrace Zionism. Some of the Protestant denominations have issued condemnations of Israel that are repugnant, feeding into the myth of Israel as a criminal state and echoing in contemporary form the old Christian slurs of Jews as a criminal population. Christianity has not totally abandoned its old bad habits of attacking the Jews. Today, for some Christian denominations, the form of attack has changed — an attack on Jews as a people through an attack on their state rather than an attack on Jews as individuals. But the gravamen of the attack, outlandish accusations of criminality, remains.

Anti-Zionism, like all forms of bigotry, comes in a continuum, from the direct to the indirect, from the plain to the euphemistic, from the crude to the sophisticated, from slurs and slang to the pretence of scholarship. We see anti-Zionism in its most basic form, calling for the killing of Jews, coming from those attempting to hide behind Islam. We see anti-Zionism in its most euphemistic and indirect forms attempting to hide behind Christianity.

One example, though many could be given, is a statement of the World Council of Churches Executive Committee adopted February 19, 2004, on the Israeli security fence. The statement is unabashed anti-Zionist propaganda.

One need go no further than the title "Statement on the Wall in the Occupied Palestinian Territories and Israel's Annexation of Palestinian Territory." Israel's security fence is called a wall, though the fence takes the shape of a wall for only a small portion of its length, and much of that wall portion has been in existence for years.

The title assumes that part of the territory in Israeli possession is Palestinian occupied territory. The body of the statement indicates that the territory that the World Council of Churches has decided to allocate to the Palestinians is the territory on the Arab side of the armistice lines of 1949.

Israel is sitting in possession of land that will eventually form the territory of an independent Palestinian state when and if the Palestinian leaders abandon their determination to destroy Israel and decide instead to embrace a Palestinian state living side by side in peace with Israel. That land may be all or some of the territory on the east side of the 1949 armistice line. But it could also potentially include some land swaps, with the parties exchanging some land on the west side of the line for other land on the east side of the line.

What exactly the future boundaries of a Palestinian state would be remains to be determined in peace negotiations that have not taken place. The territory of a future Palestinian state cannot be determined by the World Council of Churches, only by Israel and its attackers, in peace negotiations. In the meantime, it is sheer fantasy to call any territory Palestinian occupied territory.

The title of the statement further assumes that Israel is annexing the land between the armistice line and the west side of the fence. Yet Israel has not done so and has not indicated any intention of doing so. That territory will remain, as it has done since 1949, in a state of suspended legal animation, awaiting the arrival of a peace-seeking Palestinian leadership.

The World Council statement calls the security fence — a construction that is perhaps the most benign and least violent form of self-defence in which Israel has engaged in its history — a "grave breach of international humanitarian law." Grave breaches of international humanitarian law are amongst the worst offences known to humanity. These breaches lead not just to state liability, but to individual criminal liability as well. For the World Council of Churches, people building a fence to keep out suicide bombers are amongst the worst criminals in the world today. And the supporters of these fence builders, who must be everyone who wishes Israel well, are presumably complicit in this crime.

That is bad enough. But it gets worse. The statement then goes on to incite the Palestinians to violence against Israelis in pursuit of the World Council of Churches' determined borders of a prospective Palestinian state. The statement asserts, "The Palestinian people's right for resistance against the Israeli occupation inside the Occupied Palestinian Territory." By egging on violence against Israel, the World Council of Churches fortifies the Palestinians in their determination to attack Israel and makes peace less likely.

The World Council of Churches is not the voice of all Christianity. The Pentecostal Christian denominations are not members of the World Council.

The hostility of some Christian elements to the Jewish state makes the Zionism of Christian evangelicals all the more welcome. Evangelical Christianity has become an island of Jewish refuge in a global never-ending storm.

The question becomes, Where do we go from here? What can those who share the Zionist ideal do together to promote that commonality? The answer I suggest is combatting anti-Zionism. Fighting antisemitism, including the anti-semitism that is anti-Zionism, cannot be left to just the Jews. If only the Jews are left to combat antisemitism, the struggle is unlikely to succeed.

Antisemitism in any of its forms, including anti-Zionism, is not inherent in Islam. But Islam has become prone to anti-Zionism. Anti-Zionism is an ideological disease to which Islam has shown itself to be susceptible. In order to assist Islam in fighting off this disease and developing immune systems, the Jewish community needs help. It is help that the Christian evangelical community can give.

There needs to be a cross-cultural, multi-denominational, ecumenical dialogue, a dialogue amongst Christians, Muslims, and Jews, to combat anti-Zionism. Yesterday it was Christianity, through this sort of dialogue, that renounced its accusations that the Jews killed Christ. Tomorrow it must be Islam, and regret-tably still, some elements of the Christian community, that will, with the help of this sort of dialogue, renounce their accusations that the Jewish state is a criminal state.

The rhetoric against Israel and the Jewish people emanating from some Islamic quarters knows no bounds, threatening a new conflagration of the Jewish people. All religions must work together to prevent that from happening.

CHAPTER FIFTEEN
Combatting Antisemitism: Differing Perspectives

How do we combat antisemitism? Jewish community organizations and general human rights organizations answer that question in very different ways both as a matter of technique and as a matter of substance.

In the not too distant past, the Jewish community was a victim community everywhere. Today, many Jews are still victims. That victimization has generated a variety of responses. One of them is avoidance. Not every victim wants to fight his victimization. Some want only to flee. Another response of Jewish communities to the threat of antisemitism is denial. Denial gives a sense of security, albeit false. It paints a picture of the society in which Jews live that many would like to believe.

The overall effect of promotion of hatred run rampant against a victim group is to weaken self-assertion by members of the group.[358] The Jewish community has only to look at its own experience to see the effect antisemitism has on its ability to fight against it.

The fear of stirring up antisemitism is a constant concern. There is apprehension that Jewish visibility, perhaps not in every arena, but in support of some people or some causes, will create resentment against the Jewish community and play into and reinforce existing stereotypes.

In democratic societies, this sense of risk, of being guests in a host society, has vied with a quest for emancipation and equal rights. Everywhere, the fear has been challenged by Zionism, the assertion of the right to self-determination of the Jewish people. Nonetheless, when antisemitism emerges so does the sense of vulnerability.

The internalization of external repression affects the form of advocacy, as well as its existence. Historically, Jewish community advocacy has gravitated towards polite requests to high officials behind closed doors, an attempt to persuade officials privately in a non-confrontational way rather than making a public case. The advocacy has had an air of soliciting indulgence or seeking kindness, rather than asserting rights. Advocates have avoided public reports, press conferences, proposals for legislative reform, litigation, marches, and demonstrations.

Jewish opponents of antisemitism avoid public advocacy in part because of a sentiment that the fight against antisemitism would not resonate with the public. There is a belief that even in countries and times where antisemitic views are not rampant, indifference to antisemitism is. There is, as well, a fear that a public campaign against antisemitism would endanger the advocates by bringing them to the attention of violent antisemites.

Indeed, this is the case in some societies for human rights defenders generally. In countries where human rights defenders are at risk for combatting anti-semitism, members of the Jewish community who combat antisemitism in a public way are even more at risk. The repression within the victim community reinforces the incomprehension of outsiders. When victims themselves evade the harm of antisemitism, rather than confront it directly, the tendency of outsiders is to ignore it completely.

As well, this going cap in hand to governments leads to a pretence that govern-ments are not themselves responsible. Governments end up being whitewashed so that their cooperation can be invoked.

Jewish community organizations have themselves reached out to other victim communities. Jewish community organizations offer and hope for solidarity. But general human rights organizations go far beyond that, attempting to mobilize the public at large, whether that public has any personal or community experience with victimization or not.

General human rights organizations function through confrontation and thrive on public advocacy. They mobilize shame against violators, bring truth to power. Their technique for modifying human rights violating behaviour is to develop a public human rights constituency that will not tolerate those vio-lations. The difficulties these organizations must overcome within their target constituencies are not so much the fear and repression of victimization but rather the indifference and sense of helplessness of the outsider.

Jewish community organizations report on antisemitism for the purpose of security. One participant at the 2003 Jacob Blaustein Institute's seminar on anti-semitism in Vienna, Austria, said, "Monitoring is for us a security issue, for security planning." Security is undermined by openness. But secrecy is antithetical to human rights advocacy. Human rights advocates do not always function through public confrontation. They work strategically, and sometimes strategy dictates lobbying behind closed doors. However, if they did only that, their human rights vocation would wither.

Because of its security focus, Jewish community reporting on antisemitism tends to be telegraphic and decontextualized, without ranking the seriousness of incidents, explaining why they are serious, or giving the history of antisemitism in the country. Jewish community reporting is an alarm to those who know and understand in order to warn, rather than information to the public at large in order to mobilize to action.

It is possible to think of Jewish community incident reporting information being made public, at least in part. In many countries, it is public. Sources and preventive security measures would have to remain confidential. However, one has to think not just of the manner of presentation of information, but the purpose for which it is accumulated. Information accumulated for security purposes is inevitably going to be different from information accumulated for human rights advocacy purposes.

The purpose of accumulating information for security purposes is to improve safety and strengthen protection of members of the community. Antisemitic behaviour is taken as a given. While impacting that behaviour is desirable, that is not its primary purpose. Indeed, when circulation of information is restricted, the people intended not to have that information are those most likely to engage in antisemitic acts. Jewish community organizations that are focused on security will work together with the authorities. They share information and strategies.

General human rights organizations are outsiders. For them, collaboration with government authorities is the exception rather than the rule. General human rights organizations accumulate information to improve respect for human rights, to end abuses. The hope is to eradicate or undermine attitudes and practices that lead to human rights violations. The information may serve a general educational value. It is to be circulated as widely as possible so that the positions and the attitudes in the material will be adopted as widely as possible, so that either the abusers will be persuaded by the information or the information will cause enough protests to lead to change. Establishing a collaborative relationship with the authorities ranks lower than developing a public human rights constituency.

Effecting change requires both public advocacy and collaboration with the authorities. It is impossible to say that one is better or more important than the other. But they are different, and it is often difficult or impossible for the same person or organization to do both. Public advocacy sometimes undermines the trust and exchange of information that is necessary for collaboration with enforcement agencies.

Jewish organizations who are collecting information about antisemitism but not distributing it widely must realize that there is a price to be paid for this limitation on distribution. Even if restricted circulation of antisemitic information may help Jewish community organizations in their collaboration with the police, there is a loss in public knowledge and public mobilization to combat antisemitism.

While an informed police is an important defence in the struggle against antisemitism, an informed public is equally important. Jewish organizations whose focus is security need to package their information on antisemitism in a way that it can be distributed publicly, and then disseminate that information widely.

Security considerations suggest that general human rights organizations have the potential to be more effective than Jewish community organizations in combatting antisemitism. Religion and ethnicity are central to perceived identity. Membership in a general human rights organization is not. The Jewish community in a country cannot escape retaliation from persecutors by remaining quiet and having only the organized Jewish community outside the country take up their cause. As a result, the global Jewish community would almost always ask the local

Jewish community before opposing a particular violation against Jews and would quite likely do nothing if that were the wish of the local community.

General human rights organizations are not restricted in this way. Amnesty International, for instance, has asked its members, as a general rule, not to work on violations in their own countries. There are a number of reasons for this rule, and one is protection. For some countries, those outside face no risk from confronting a violator, but those inside would be at risk from the same confrontation. As a result, Amnesty International would almost never ask its group or section in a country whether AI should oppose a violation within that country and would almost certainly take up a violation that justified intervention whether the local membership opposed the AI action or not.

All this seems to suggest that the Jewish community is worse at the business of combatting antisemitism than the general human rights community, which is not afflicted by the distortions of antisemitism. But in some ways the Jewish community is far better at the business of combatting antisemitism than the general human rights community.

General human rights organizations do not take advantage of the Jewish community reporting that is publicly available. The general human rights organizations do not monitor antisemitism on their own. And they do not draw on Jewish community monitoring.

One advantage the Jewish community has is its ability to recognize antisemitism. Antisemites are often hypocritical. The non-Jewish community is not as adept at picking up that hypocrisy. Before the Holocaust, antisemitism was open, considered a legitimate point of view. People would admit to being antisemites and would advocate antisemitism. Today, even the most blatant antisemites do not call themselves antisemites. They may replicate the ideology or mouth the stereotypes. But they do not apply the word *antisemite* to themselves. It takes at least some awareness of what antisemitism is to pierce through this facade.

When visible Jewish community institutions, or people who are visibly Jewish, are attacked, members of the non-Jewish community often fail to identify the potential antisemitic cause. Unless the culprit is caught and his motivation made evident, there has been a tendency by general human rights organizations not to classify attacks against those visibly Jewish or against Jewish community institutions as antisemitic.

Even when the culprit is caught and his motivation made plain, there is often a downplaying of this motivation, unless the person is organizationally and historically identified with antisemitic groups. There is a tendency by general human rights organizations to classify lone acts of antisemites as the work of people who are troubled or mentally disturbed, rather than as human rights violations directed against Jews.

Antisemitism is frequently coded, suggestive. It communicates to those susceptible to the messages of hate. The Jewish community recognizes it. But general human rights organizations are oblivious to the message. What they hear seems benign or trivial or nonsensical rather than dangerous. Where the issue is identifying torture or killing or imprisonment, the wrong may be immediately obvious. Where the issue is identifying an antisemitic motivation or incitement, the wrong may not be so obvious. Those susceptible to antisemitism are not, one can presume, human rights activists. Indeed, their very vocation as human rights activists would make them, one would expect, impervious to antisemitism. While that, of course, is positive, it has the consequence of denying them any subjective feel for the power and danger of antisemitic incitement and motivation. Antisemitism is, to general human rights activists, akin to a foreign language they do not understand. A foreign language can be learned; it can be interpreted. But unless the language of hatred is learned by general human rights activists, they will remain blind to the reality and dangers of antisemitism.

One consequence of the Jewish community's heightened sensitivity to antisemitism is improved reporting of the reality on the ground. Antisemitic street violence is almost never reported by human rights organizations, nor, for that matter, by states. The Lawyers Committee for Human Rights wrote a report decrying the lack of governmental reporting on antisemitism.[359] But it is also a human rights organization problem.

It is not just a matter of Jewish community organizations knowing of incidents that others do not. These organizations will recognize antisemitic attacks for what they are, and they are far more likely to be troubled by an attack on a visibly Jewish person or a Jewish community organization as potentially antisemitic than general human rights organizations. Jewish organizations are far more likely to accept a stated motivation of antisemitism for what it is rather than attempt to explain it away as frustration or mental disturbance.

The Jewish community itself has reporting limitations. Not every Jewish victim comes to the Jewish community to record the victimization. The failure of reporting is particularly acute in the former Soviet Union, where Judaism was repressed after 1917; many Jews there today, though attacked because they are Jewish, have no Jewish community affiliation, no Jewish self-identity, and no contact with Jewish organizations. But even there, there is a good deal more reporting by Jewish community organizations than by others. The Union of Councils for Soviet Jews produces an excellent report for Russia.[360] But in Ukraine, for instance, where antisemitism has been as bad as or worse than in Russia, there is no comparable reporting by anyone.

This problem, though, is compounded for general human rights organizations, which rely on information from victims to collect the data they need for their work. Jewish victims do not come to general human rights organizations to report their victimization. Nor do the Jewish community organizations who have accumulated information of victimization.

Victims know that something is wrong, but they do not necessarily know that what is happening to them is a human rights violation. Being a victim, even being a victim community, does not mean that you know your rights, that you know what to do about your victimization.

Attempting to pour anything into a closed vessel just leads to a big mess. In order for communication of Jewish victimization to general human rights organizations to have any value, those organizations have to be willing to take up the fight against antisemitism. Right now there is neither the will nor the informational means.

Reporting on antisemitism is often linked to the ability to prove the existence of a crime. But the two are different. A reporting focus has to be different from a criminal focus. In some countries, the difference between a hate crime and an ordinary crime can be seen in sentencing. The motivation of hatred leads to enhanced sentencing. The elements of the crime, what has to be proved for conviction, is the same whether the offence is motivated by hatred or not. In other countries, a hate crime is a different crime from an ordinary crime. What the prosecution has to prove to establish commission of a hate crime is different from and often more difficult to prove than what has to be established in order to prove commission of an ordinary crime. Where a hate crime is a separate offence, then the motivation of hatred becomes a constituent element of the offence. Motivation becomes relevant to proving criminal intent.

In those countries where a hate crime is different from and more difficult to prove than an ordinary crime, there is a tendency for police and prosecutors to characterize offences as ordinary crimes rather than as hate crimes in order to make convictions more likely and to ease their own work burden. As well, there may be a tendency of state institutions to downplay the existence of antisemitism and to impose overly strict requirements of proof of antisemitic criminal motivation, sometimes because officials are sympathetic to antisemitism, other times because officials do not want to portray the state in a bad light. These tendencies distort government information about the prevalence of antisemitism, making them seem less than they are.

A focus on motivation and an inquiry into the existence of antisemitism, combined with a skepticism that it is there, can mean a diversion from the horror of the violence. Sometimes state institutions trying to exonerate themselves from tolerating antisemitism spend so much energy on disproving the existence of anti-semitism that the seriousness of the violent act is lost.

There needs to be an awareness of indicators of motivation and a sensitivity to patterns. A person cannot be convicted or given enhanced sentencing for a hate-motivated act without proof of the person's motivation beyond a reasonable doubt. However, where there is a pattern of attacks on Jewish community institutions and Jewish individuals, that pattern should be enough to indicate motivation even if the individual culprits are not caught, even if the motivation of each and every culprit cannot be proved beyond a reasonable doubt.

Some countries insist on the testimony of witnesses who are not victims for a crime to be proved or for the motivation of a crime to be proved. Whatever the merits of that evidentiary rule in general, in this area, it is not an excuse for governmental inaction in the face of a pattern of violent antisemitic acts. Authorities must be prepared to accept the testimony of witnesses to hate crimes even when those witnesses are victims.

One has to distinguish between establishing the motivation of an individual for the purposes of a criminal conviction or sentencing and the motivation behind a pattern of incidents for the purpose of instituting preventive and remedial measures. The standards of proof and means of proof are widely different. Insistence on a criminal standard of proof, beyond a reasonable doubt, by evidence admissible only in court in order to acknowledge that a disadvantaged minority has a problem and to do something about the problem is an evasion, a denial of responsibility.

Equality principles teach us that motivation may be hidden. Indeed, motivation, at the end of the day, may not matter. Equality must be substantive as well as formal. If, in reality, minority groups are disadvantaged, and there is no other explanation for their disadvantage than their minority status, then the fact that there is lip service to equality and no overt expressions of bias is not enough to satisfy equality principles.

A person cannot be convicted or receive an enhanced sentence for a hate crime on statistics alone. But it is possible to establish the existence of bias, racial discrimination, and violence by statistics alone. Through statistics we can establish discrimination by impact if not by intent. If there is a pattern of discrimination, harassment, and violence directed against a disadvantaged minority and all other possible explanations are ruled out, then the explanation of hatred remains.

Where is this statistical reporting? Jewish community organizations do it somewhat. General human rights organizations do not do it at all. Because they do not, they may not even be aware of the problem of discriminatory impact abuse. General human rights organizations tend to gravitate to the one big, clear, unequivocal, egregious wrong. This is more than an attempt to focus scarce resources. It is a technique for mobilizing the public at large. If the public is already outraged, the work of mobilization is that much easier. The subtle wrongs, the wrongs that need study or explanation, and the accumulation of smaller wrongs are pushed to one side. The public outrage into which general human rights organizations can tap is smaller. The work identifying the wrongs is greater.

A person can die from one vicious stab wound. And a person can die from a thousand cuts. It is easy to express concern about the one fatal stab wound. But general human rights organizations have difficulty figuring out when to start to be concerned about a thousand cuts — is it the first cut, the last, or some cut in between?

This difference in the form of violations plague the fight against anti-semitism. Often, it is the accumulation of antisemitic incidents that makes the behaviour grievous.

General human rights organizations focus on behaviour of governments. Yet antisemitism often comes from non-state agents: street thugs, neo-Nazi groups with no official status. Jewish human rights organizations commonly focus on what these groups do. If those responsible for state protection are sympathetic to the sirens of hate that lead to violence against Jews, then the victims have a problem not just with the non-state perpetrators but also from those who are supposed to protect them. The state can be blamed for inade-quacy of state protection, and that inadequacy may itself may have an antise-mitic motivation. But government officials cannot be blamed directly for the antisemitic attacks.

Amnesty International has had a difficult time adjusting to the struggle against human rights violations by non-state agents. Although Amnesty International began in 1961, it was not until 1991, thirty years later, that it decided to combat abuses by non-state agents. Amnesty began as a letter-writing organization. But neo-Nazis often have no fixed address. A letter-writing campaign by the membership in these cases becomes impossible. Amnesty International is a membership organization. In combatting street thug abuses, it becomes more difficult to get the membership involved.

There is even a vocabulary problem. General human rights organizations, as well as some governments, are reluctant to call breaches of human rights standards by non-state agents human rights violations. Instead they are called abuses, on the ground that only states can "violate" the standards in the international instru-ments that states ratify.

Human rights organizations function by calling governments to account, asking them to keep the promises they have made in human rights instruments. The typical human rights report contrasts state commitments with state behaviour and calls on states to keep their human rights promises. But street neo-Nazis have made no promises to respect human rights. It is sometimes said that responsibility for human rights violations, under international law, rests with governments. It is sometimes argued that a focus on abuses by street thugs could be used to deflect attention away from human rights violations by governments. General human rights organizations are far more sensitive to this argument than Jewish community organizations.

Human rights are rights that belong to individuals.[361] As long as a person's rights are breached, it should not matter whether the breach comes from the state or a non-state agent. Whether a person is killed by a state or non-state agent, the person is equally dead.

What distinguishes an antisemitic killing, which is a human rights violation, and a bank robbery killing, which is a simple crime, is that first is an attack on an attribute fundamental to the identity of a group, and the other is not. When someone is killed because he or she is Jewish, it is every Jewish person that is under attack.

Different labelling of breaches from states and non-state agents suggests it does matter, that the victimization a person suffers from a non-state agent is not the loss of a human right. The difference in labelling is a form of denial or dispossession of human rights. The different labelling also creates an imbalance in general human rights reporting and condemnation of breaches, giving more weight and attention to breaches by states than to breaches by non-state agents. This difference in labelling is harmful to the fight against antisemitism because it creates an imbalance in the reporting and condemnation of breaches by non-state antisemites.

The typical governmental response to an accusation of complicity in a human rights violation is denial. Whether accusations are made against state agents or non-state agents, the reaction commonly is that it did not happen.

Of course, sometimes these denials are real. Not every accusation is accurate. But all too often the denials are evasions, attempts to avoid responsibility. Forms of violations change in order to avoid accountability for violations. For instance, as general human rights organizations became effective in combatting political imprisonment, we saw an increase in disappearances. As these organizations became effective in calling attention to governmental human rights violations, we saw an increase in abuses by government-supported private militias throughout the globe, from Colombia to Indonesia.

We have seen this shift in antisemitism. Today, antisemitism often does not come from governments. It comes rather from non-state agents. Sometimes these non-state agents are off-duty police and military. Like the death squads or the private militias that governments of some states use to victimize their political opponents, neo-Nazi groups peopled by off-duty police and military are sometimes the new and disguised face of state antisemitism. At other times, violent antisemites are people from the private sector to whom state institutions turn a blind eye.

The denial by states, in this context, is more difficult to counter. When states say, "We are not responsible for torture," and human rights organizations produce the testimony of one torture victim after another, the denials are effectively disproved. When states say, "We are not responsible for antisemitic street violence," that denial is not rebutted merely by producing the testimony of a number of Jewish victims. More is needed.

General human rights organizations are sometimes flummoxed by the need for this "more." They may not even attempt to produce it. But because they cannot or will not produce it, and because they tie everything to government behaviour or inaction, the result is all too often just silence.

Even if we accept an insistence on a governmental nexus to a violation in order to mobilize a human right concern, there almost always is such a nexus. The nexus may not be direct government participation. But there is almost always either complicity or inaction. It is rare for government agencies to be so over-whelmed or stymied that it can be said that there is nothing more that they could do. It is much more common for government agencies to pretend that there is no problem, to insist on standards of proof that are impossible to meet, to ignore obvious connections in a pattern of incidents, to downplay the seriousness of incitement to hatred, or to excuse violent behaviour as common criminality or emotional instability rather than hatred.

Are governments collecting hate crime statistics? Do police have specialized hate crime units? Do the laws have enhanced sentencing for hate-motivated crimes? Do the authorities tolerate incitement to hatred in state-run or state-regulated media? Do they allow political parties with an ideology of hate to run for election? Do the police fail to investigate the hate dimensions of hate crimes? Do they look only to the seriousness of the act and not the apparent motivation in deciding on the resources to allocate to the investigation of a crime? Is there a human rights commission promoting human rights education? Do the schools discipline hate-motivated bullies? Are workers protected against hate-poisoned work atmospheres? Do political leaders and legislators speak out against hate speech and racist groups, helping to isolate them and those who support them?

There are a myriad of possible institutional responses to antisemitism. Where antisemitism is rampant and the state does not engage such responses, then the state is violating international human rights equality standards. Where these responses are missing, there is more than enough to activate general human rights organizations who insist on a governmental nexus to the wrong.

Jewish community organizations and general human rights organizations have worked together in the past, in the Soviet Jewry campaign. But in that campaign, the target was active government misbehaviour. For general human rights organizations, this was just part of their standard work. Here the situation is different.

In spite of all that, the focus on human rights standards by general human rights organizations is an asset to their reporting. Violations are contextualized within the framework of standards. Calling on governments to protect against violations reminds both us and them that by providing this protection governments are not merely granting a favour to the victim community; they are doing their duty.

Jewish community organizations are far more likely to attack the root cause of antisemitic behaviour (incitement to hatred) than are general human rights organizations. General human rights organizations are two steps removed from the combat against antisemitism. Their first step away is a focus on government behaviour, rather than non-government behaviour. Their second step away is a focus on violent behaviour rather than on speech.

Indeed, some human rights activists have made the astounding statement that antisemitism is not a human rights violation and not properly the concern of human rights organizations. They come to this amazing conclusion by arguing that anti-semitism is either a common crime committed by non-state agents or protected speech. Human rights organizations do not normally concern themselves with either.

The general human rights community has a blind spot to one component of the international human rights structure: the right to be free from incitement to hatred. Broad interpretations of the right to freedom of speech in the general human rights community have led to the obligations to prohibit incitement to hatred being downgraded or ignored.

This difference in approach of general and Jewish human rights organizations to speech has an impact on reporting. Because reporting is geared to action, and because the views of action on speech differ markedly, the reporting of speech also shows large differences. Jewish community organizations will report on verbal and written threats, graffiti, incitement, and media reporting over the edge. The general human rights community stays away from all of that.

It is rare for general human rights organizations to say that government is doing too little. The typical human rights stance is that the government is doing too much, but of the wrong sort. The more recent shift of human rights organizations to calling for prosecution of war criminals and ratification of the statute of the International Criminal Court represents a shift, not just in calling for prosecution, but more generally in calling for state action.

Human rights violations did not end with the end of the Cold War. But the form of many violations of human rights changed. No longer is the archetypal violation perpetrated by a repressive totalitarian state, motivated by a global ideology, whether it be communism, apartheid or fascism. Instead, violations are more typically by non-governmental actors, motivated by ethnic hatred. The end of Communism has led to a privatization of everything, including a privatization of repression.

These dangers teach us that there can be too little government as well as too much. Government inaction can be as much a cause of human rights violations as government action. It used to be that advocacy of law and order was read as coded urging for a police state. Today it is much more obvious that a breakdown of law and order can be as disastrous for human rights as an overemphasis on law and order. National and international armed forces are no longer seen as only a threat to human rights. They may also be necessary for the protection of human rights.

The general human rights community is coming around to the need to combat violations by non-state agents, but slowly, indirectly, and from a history of looking the other way. One sees this clinging to the past in the differences in responses to terrorism by the general human rights community and the Jewish community.

Laws against terrorism can be both too weak and too strong, both impinging civil liberties and leaving victims undefended. Amongst general human rights organizations, virtually all we read, even today, is criticism of the breadth of anti-terrorism laws. General human rights organizations seem to consider it bad form — indeed, dangerous — to call for the enactment of anti-terrorism laws or advocate for their strengthening or even their enforcement.

Jewish community organizations are not so reluctant. They are well aware that human rights violations can come as much as or more from non-state agents as from the state. Jewish organizations are much less hesitant to call on the state to combat the violations or abuses by non-state agents.

The Jewish community struggle against antisemitism often means asking state authorities to take positive action. This request for positive action provides an additional explanation for the difference in mode of advocacy of the two communities, with the Jewish community often having more private meetings with government officials and doing less public advocacy than general human rights organizations.

Jewish community organizations and general human rights organizations diverge over the antisemitism that is anti-Zionism. General human rights organizations are often not even clear on the link between two.

General human rights organizations that combat racism do not combat antisemitism, because of a perception that the Jewish minority is not marginalized the way other minorities are. The traditional discrimination that Jews suffered before the Second World War (denial of access to services) has disappeared almost entirely from many countries, though by no means from all. This acceptance of Jews at an individual level blinds general human rights organizations to the dangers individual Jews face from the denial of the existence of Jews as a people.

It is possible, indeed necessary, to focus on the relationship between anti-Zionism and antisemitism without delving into Middle East politics. There is a standard rule that permeates human rights and humanitarian and anti-terrorism law that violations of these laws are never excused by politics. That principle is as true as the right to be free from incitement to hatred. It is part of everyday reality that violations of human rights and humanitarian and anti-terrorism standards occur in one political context or another. But addressing these political contexts is the wrong way to go about addressing the violations.

Although there are chapters in this book about the charge of Israeli occupation of the West Bank and Gaza, the settlements in those territories, and the West Bank security fence, the point is not to take a position on the political issues of whether Israeli control of the West Bank and Gaza should or should not remain, whether the settlements should or should not be there, or what the route of the fence should be. Those chapters were written to show how what should be only political issues have instead been turned into vehicles for antisemitism and attacks on the Jewish community worldwide.

It is easy, even trite, to say that if there were no war, no insurrections, no dissatisfactions, and no grievances, then there would be no violations of either human rights or humanitarian or anti-terrorism laws. But neither war nor grievances, no matter how justified themselves, justify these violations.

Incitement to hatred against the Jewish people worldwide is wrong, abusive. Even if we can think of the Middle East conflict in the fanciful terms of some commentators, not as a struggle for the existence of Israel but merely as a territorial struggle over the West Bank and Gaza, and even if, piling false hypothetical upon false hypothetical, we accept the view of these commentators that Israel is in the wrong in this territorial conflict because it is suppressing the right to self-determination of the Palestinian people, that would not excuse incitement to hatred against the Jewish people worldwide.

What is wrong with stereotypes is not just the answers that are given. It the questions that are asked. Are Jews greedy? Do Jews control the world? Did Jews kill Christ? Did Jews kill Christian children yesterday to use their blood to bake matzoh? Are Jews killing Palestinian children today to harvest their organs? Surely we do not counter the vicious, defamatory stereotypes embedded in these questions by pointing out some charitable or powerless or kindly Jews. The problem with prejudice is not that it gets the facts wrong. Prejudice, by its very nature, is oblivious to the facts, a prejudgment. If we attempt to answer the questions of the prejudiced in their terms, we mistake the phenomenon and its danger.

Talking about anti-Zionism is not the same as talking about the Middle East. Antisemitism can focus on any location as an excuse for beating up on Jews, including outer space.

David Icke asserts a conspiracy to control the world led by Jews who are shape-changing lizards from outer space.[362] Discussing the antisemitism that is anti-Zionism does not mean that all we are talking about is Middle East politics any more than discussing the antisemitism which smears Jews as shape-changing lizards from outer space means that all we are talking about is zoology and astrophysics.

The failure to make the distinction between Middle East politics and anti-Zionism as a form of antisemitism has given a new respectability to antisemitism. The traditional Nazi antisemitism is marginalized. It is the purview of the fringe, adopted neither by mainstream media nor established public figures. But the antisemitism that is anti-Zionism has permeated respectable public discourse, incorporating the hoary antisemitic stereotypes of Jews as vindictive and bloodthirsty.

Sometimes anti-Zionism is opportunistic antisemitism, an attempt to bring new converts to an old hatred. Sometimes it is the other way around, anti-Zionists seizing on traditional antisemitic vitriol to expand and buttress their indoctrination. The old antisemites and the new anti-Zionists share common cause — the hatred of Jews.

Do general human rights organizations not see anti-Zionism as antisemitism, or do they not see antisemitic incidents at all? The answer is both. And one big reason that general human rights organizations do not see antisemitic incidents at all is that they do not see anti-Zionism as antisemitism.

That answer would be clear-cut if all antisemitic incidents were anti-Zionist. Then it would be obvious that those who do not see anti-Zionism as antisemitism would not see any antisemitism. That answer is pretty compelling even when only some and not all antisemitic incidents are anti-Zionist. Given the sorry state of human rights in the world, general human rights organizations must prioritize. They cannot chase down every single human rights violation. The more severe violations take priority over the less severe. The more numerous violations take priority over the less numerous.

Some antisemitic incidents are not anti-Zionist. But when we take anti-Zionism out of the antisemitic mix, both the number and severity of antisemitic incidents decrease. That leads to a lower priority for these abuses in the planning and programming of general human rights organizations. The motivation behind many incidents is cumulative. For some, anti-Zionism is the sole source of their antisemitism. For others, anti-Zionism is irrelevant. For many antisemitic attacks today, anti-Zionism is a reinforcement, joining with traditional antisemitism to form a poisonous cocktail.

We can see the impact of anti-Zionism on antisemitism by looking at the identified perpetrator population. There has been a huge increase in attacks against Jews by Arab Muslims, notably in Europe. The first victims of hate propaganda are those consumed by hatred. Antisemitism puts Jews at risk of loss of life and limb. Antisemites have already lost their grip on reality.

The purveyors of anti-Zionist propaganda attempt to cultivate an Arab Muslim constituency. A lot of anti-Zionism is in the Arabic language and couched in Islamic religious terms. Many of the leading fomenters of anti-Zionism are Arabic-speaking Muslim clerics. When we see that it is Arab Muslims who are attacking Jews, that tells us that the antisemitism which is anti-Zionism is at work.

For many incidents, the individual motivation is unexplained, since we do not know the culprit. But we can see spikes of attacks against Jewish communities worldwide whenever anti-Zionist propaganda gets particularly hot and heavy (for instance, at the time of the fabrications of a massacre at Jenin in April 2002). Unless organizations keep firmly in mind the linkage between anti-Zionism and antisemitism, the chance of their identifying incidents with Jewish victims as anti-semitic is significantly reduced.

The problem the Jewish community faces from general human rights organizations is one of too much as well as too little. All too often general human rights organizations make the connection between attacks on Jewish victims and anti-Zionism too easily, perhaps to avoid involvement. The analysis to determine impact discrimination and persecution is corrupted when anti-Zionism is differentiated from antisemitism. Anti-Zionism becomes an excuse for general human rights organization inaction. Some of those within general human rights organizations dismiss as anti-Zionism Jewish victimization where the motivation is unclear. The implication is that attacks on the Jewish community worldwide are an extension and continuation of armed conflict in the Middle East. The best answer to that implication is that the anti-Zionism that leads to the attacks on innocent Jews and antisemitism are the same.

The general human rights community, of course, accepts that the targeting of innocents, even in the context of armed conflict, is always wrong. But to view anti-Zionist–motivated attacks on the Jewish community worldwide as different from antisemitism is to misunderstand the nature of anti-Zionism. It is impossible to combat hate-motivated crimes effectively without understanding the nature of the hatred. As well, locating in the Middle East the cause of attacks against Jews worldwide suggests that the solution is in the Middle East rather than at home.

Furthermore, this approach — combatting anti-Zionist attacks on Jews only on the basis that it is the wrongful targeting of innocents in the context of armed conflict — fragments antisemitism. This has the effect of minimizing the extent of the overall problem. Each piece of the problem may seem small enough to justify not devoting time, energy, or resources it. The magnitude of the problem, if it were ever appreciated for what it truly is, may trigger active involvement. But that true magnitude is missed.

Jewish community organizations do not reach out to general human rights organizations. But why is that so? Surely one big reason is the failure of human rights organizations to recognize the linkage between anti-Zionism and anti-semitism. This failure generates suspicion and downright hostility within the Jewish community.

General human rights organizations do not focus on Europe to the same extent that they do other continents. But why is that so? Again, surely one big reason is the failure of human rights organizations to recognize as human rights violations government inaction over the abuses inflicted in Europe. A major blind spot of general human rights organizations is the linkage between anti-Zionism and antisemitism in Europe. Human rights organizations can see the violation when, in Rwanda, a Hutu attacks a Tutsi for no other reason than that the victim is Tutsi and the Rwandan government does nothing, but miss the same violation in France when an Arab attacks a Jew for no other reason than that the victim is Jewish and the French government does nothing.

There is a link between substantive and technical issues. Technical failures rarely have just technical explanations. Procedure is the handmaiden of substance.

Technical reasons are a convenient runaround, bureaucratic face-saving devices. The failure of general human rights organizations to come to grips with anti-semitism cannot be fully explained by methodological lapses. The problem is not just the way; it is also the will.

The demonization of Israel by the anti-Zionist lobby has led to wide divergences between the Jewish and general human rights communities, not just in relation to Israel but also in relation to the struggle against antisemitism and human rights violations generally. An obvious difference is the willingness to invoke United Nations standards and mechanisms.

The United Nations has become so corrupted by the anti-Zionist lobby that it has little or no credibility within the Jewish community. There is hardly a component of the United Nations system that has been immune from the disease of anti-Zionism; the human rights component of the UN has been particularly susceptible to the virus. Jewish community organizations want nothing to do with the United Nations. They see its entrenched anti-Zionism as a cause of global antisemitism. If they are involved at all, it is to combat UN efforts to delegitimize the State of Israel and undermine the right to self-determination of the Jewish people. The United Nations human rights system, with few exceptions, is not a friend to the Jewish community; it is widely seen and understood to be an enemy. The Jewish community is torn between going to the United Nations to combat its anti-Zionism and boycotting the institution. The advocates of boycott argue that even showing up provides the institution a legitimacy it does not deserve.

This temptation to boycott is, in my view, mistaken. United Nations human rights standards and mechanisms are legacies from the Holocaust. The Jewish community, of all communities, should work to prevent the distortion and misuse of this legacy. Honouring that legacy means continuing to struggle for human rights in the United Nations arena, even if, indeed I would say especially because, Israel and the Jewish people are attacked within the UN in the name of a deformed and twisted human rights. Bertrand Ramcharan, then acting United Nations High Commissioner for Human Rights said in June 2003, "You cannot give up on your own creation."[363]

General human rights organizations have a far more benign view of the United Nations than Jewish community organizations do. General human rights organizations will acknowledge that the UN is political. They pigeonhole its anti-Zionism as politicization and nothing more. They distinguish between standards and mechanisms. The mechanisms and the implementation may be weak. But the standards that the United Nations adopts are useful for calling governments to account. General human rights organizations set about trying to help the United Nations do the human rights work it should be doing. They provide the information the United Nations system lacks, the analyses United Nations institutions are too timid or discreet to do.[364]

Anti-Zionism, understandably, looms large for the Jewish community. For the general human rights community, it does not have the same significance. The general human rights community is far more willing to put anti-Zionism aside and attempt to work with the parts of the UN system that are functioning in a rational way, or with the whole of the UN system for those parts of the world where the UN as a whole is functioning rationally. On a practical level, for general human rights organizations, the United Nations represents an opportunity, a forum. It is unrealistic to them to turn down an opportunity to express their concerns on the world stage.

General human rights organizations have, as well, a sympathy for the underdog. It seems to them that Israelis are rich and Palestinians are poor, that Israelis have sophisticated weaponry and Palestinians have only stones, that Israelis are powerful and Palestinians are powerless.

Jewish community organizations do not see it that way. An overly narrow focus of human rights organizations, looking only to the West Bank and Gaza, rather than the whole of the Middle East, considering today as if yesterday never happened, creates a power inversion and diverts sympathy to the Palestinians.

The Israeli military advantage looks a good deal less significant when it is placed in the total Middle East context, rather than in the context only of the West Bank and Gaza. In the Middle East as a whole, Israel is vastly outnumbered and surrounded by enemy states.

The Israeli political disadvantage at the United Nations is overwhelming. It is almost alone at the United Nations, the only state in the United Nations whose very existence is constantly attacked by a significant number of other states.

Israel gathers together the remnants of a victim community nearly extinguished not that long ago. It is faced with an opponent prepared to stoop at nothing, including the mass killing of innocents.

The incomes of the Palestinians in the West Bank and Gaza, though less than those of Israelis, are far greater than those of people in many other parts of the world. How much greater would they be if Palestinians did not have a corrupt leadership but rather one that gave priority to the welfare of Palestinians over the destruction of the State of Israel?

All of this speaks to the suspicions and reservations that Jewish community organizations have about general human rights organizations. But those suspicions and reservations are mutual. Because general human rights organizations mostly do not see the connection between anti-Zionism and antisemitism, because they often cannot see beyond the smokescreen of the allegations of human rights violations against Israel to the reality of their exaggeration, manipulation, and sometimes straight fabrication, these organizations end up thinking of Jewish human rights organizations as defenders of human rights violations of a state, the State of Israel, rather than as defenders of a global minority victim community.

The typical response of general human rights organizations to assertions of the connection between anti-Zionism and antisemitism is that criticism of the behaviour of the government of Israel should be legitimate, that no government should be immune from criticism. They feel that Jewish criticism of their work against Israel is insensitive to the human rights vocation of these organizations.

The statement that Israel should not be immune from criticism is one of those statements, like the statement "Some of my best friends are Jewish," that, taken in isolation, seems harmless. Yet neither mantra should be an excuse for antisemitism. Antisemitism that takes the form of anti-Zionism is no more legitimate than antisemitism in any other form.

General human rights organizations almost always miss the point when they see Jewish community organizations combatting anti-Zionism. What Jewish community organizations are doing is fighting against a form of antisemitism. What general human rights organizations think they see is the Jewish community defending Israel against any and all criticism. These general human rights organizations are not close enough to the Jewish community to realize that there is as much divergence within the Jewish Diaspora as there is within Israel about the behaviour of the government of Israel, that when it comes to real, legitimate criticism of Israeli governmental behaviour, rather than fantastical accusations against the State of Israel designed for the purpose of demonization and delegitimization, the Jewish community is as divided outside Israel as inside Israel.

This combination of differences in willingness to work with the United Nations, in willingness to support resort to armed force to protect human rights, in perspectives of who is the powerful, and in appreciation of the link between anti-Zionism and antisemitism, when added to the free and easy way that general human rights organizations levy charges of war crimes and crimes against humanity against governments in general and Israel in particular, have led to major divergences between the two sets of organizations. The divergences exist both in substance and form. The two sets of organizations go about their work in different ways and are often at odds.

Ideally, both communities, the Jewish community and the general human rights community, can learn from each other. What are the lessons that the Jewish community can learn from the general human rights community and those that the general human rights community can learn from the Jewish community in the struggle against antisemitism?

The lessons to be learned by the Jewish community, I suggest, are these:

1) Make information about antisemitism publicly available.

2) Provide a context for incident reporting that would include a synopsis of the history of antisemitism in the country.

3) Rank the seriousness of incidents.

4) Explain why incidents are serious.

5) Report state failure to protect against antisemitism as a violation of international human rights standards.

6) Confront governments directly and publicly on their failure to protect against antisemitism.

7) Attempt to mobilize the public at large in the battle against antisemitism as part of the overall struggle for human rights.

8) Use multilateral institutions, including the various components of the United Nations system, as forums to combat anti semitism and anti-Zionism.

The lessons to be learned by the general human rights community, I suggest, are these:

1) Take advantage of the Jewish community reporting on anti semitism that is publicly available.

2) Take abuses by non-state agents as seriously as violations by governments.

3) As a corollary, oppose as consistently and systematically state inaction that fails to protect against violations by non-state agents as state action that perpetrates violations.

4) Report on antisemitism whether inflicted by state or non-state agents.

5) Oppose government inaction on discriminatory abuses where the discrimination is identified by impact as well as by intent.

6) Take as seriously the obligations to protect against incitement to discrimination and hatred as all other human rights obligations.

7) Report on human rights violations that take the form of government inaction on incitement to hatred.

8) Acknowledge the connection between anti-Zionism and antisemitism.

It is sometimes said that women's rights are human rights, children's rights are human rights, and so on. The point is not just to connect the rights of the group to human rights but also to connect human rights to the rights of the group. In order to promote human rights generally we have to promote the rights of the group. Failing to address women's rights is not just a loss to women, but a loss for human rights.

The indivisibility of human rights is more than an intellectual concept. It is a practical reality. Human rights violators often do not compartmentalize their violations. They attack a wide variety of victims; they endorse an ideology of human rights violations. If we ignore the attack of these violators on their most visible victims, we may miss the overall danger these violators pose for human rights.

All this is true for antisemitism. Jewish rights are human rights. Antisemitism is an indicator of an anti–human rights ideology, a forewarning of the general danger to human rights that anti-Semitic perpetrators pose. Ignoring antisemitism means ignoring an overall threat to human rights with a wide range of potential victims.

It is inevitable that the two communities, the Jewish community and the general human rights community, will diverge at least to some extent because of their differences in focus. However, the differences are now so great that Jewish community organizations and general human rights organizations view each other with suspicion, a situation that is healthy for neither. Both the struggle against antisemitism and the overall struggle against human rights violations suffer.

Jewish community organizations fighting the battle against antisemitism and general human rights organizations fighting the war against all human rights violations must converge, join forces. There needs to be a joint human rights Jewish community agenda. That convergence will happen only if each community learns from the other.

CHAPTER SIXTEEN
Strategies for Combatting Anti-Zionism

W<small>HAT</small> makes strategic sense in combatting anti-Zionism? Given the pervasiveness and accepted foolishness of anti-Zionism, the task may seem overwhelming. Where do we begin to make a difference? The answers vary in Canada, in Arab and Muslim countries, and at the United Nations.

In Canada, when anti-Zionism reaches the level of incitement to hatred against Jews, the response cannot be just verbal. It has also to be legal. Incitement to hatred should prompt the imposition of both civil and criminal penalties. The overall goal should be ending the promotion of hatred. Law enforcement should approach antisemitism as a single, integrated phenomenon. Regrettably, law enforcement agencies fragment antisemitism.

Traditional antisemitism is recognized as such. Antisemitism that takes the form of anti-Zionism — attacks on Jewish people for their actual or presumed support for Israel — is all too often not recognized as antisemitism. Instead, it is called Middle East politics.

Whether law enforcement is directed to hate crime statistics, enhanced sentencing for hate crimes, or prosecution of hate speech, there must be no distinction between forms of antisemitism. The antisemitism that is anti-Zionism must treated as seriously and confronted as directly as any other form of antisemitism. Only when that is done can law enforcement be effective in combatting antisemitism.

Anti-Zionist graffiti should be removed. Wall paintings glorifying suicide bombers should be painted over. Posters should be torn down. Literature should be confiscated. Broadcasts should be shut down. Public platforms should be denied. Funds should be seized. Organizations should be banned. The worst, most persistent hate promoters, the anti-Zionist terrorist organizations, should be convicted, sentenced, and jailed.

We should see this panorama of responses everywhere. We should certainly see them in Canada. But even in Canada the effort has been fraught with difficulties.

It should seem obvious that the Canadian funds of the anti-Zionist terrorist organizations Hamas and Hezbollah should be frozen and that the organizations should be banned. Yet the struggle to freeze the funds of these organizations and ban them was hard fought. At one time, the government of Canada split the organizations in two, listing one wing and not the other. The regulations listed the military wing of Hamas, called Hamas-Izz al-Din al-Qassem. However, Hamas has two wings, a political wing as well as a military wing. The political wing of Hamas was not listed. That meant that Hamas could raise money in Canada and transfer it out of Canada to do its "political" work in Israel, the West Bank, and

Gaza. Canada has no control over the transfer of Hamas funds from its political wing to its military wing once the funds leave Canada. The government of Canada has no right or opportunity to see the books of the Hamas operations in the West Bank and Gaza. Money could leave Canada under the name of the Hamas political wing and be transferred abroad to the Hamas military wing, and Canada would be none the wiser.

Furthermore, it is Hamas as a whole that is an anti-Zionist terrorist organization, not just its military wing. The political wing preaches anti-Zionist terrorism; the military wing practises it. The political wing indoctrinates and incites hatred against the Jewish state and the Jewish people; the military wing channels that hatred into suicide bombings. A Security Council resolution called on states to freeze the funds of terrorist organizations.[365] By freezing the funds of only the military wing of Hamas, Canada was violating that resolution. A suicide bombing operation requires more than weapons and targets. It requires a steady stream of willing suicide bombers. It is the political arm of Hamas, through the incitement to hatred in the schools, youth clubs, and mosques it finances in the West Bank and Gaza, that provides these suicide bombers.

Hamas is an Arabic acronym for Islamic Resistance Movement. It is also an Arabic word meaning "zeal." The organization was founded in 1987 as an overtly antisemitic organization. Its founding covenant charges Jews with an international conspiracy to gain control of the world. Its covenant says that "Islam will obliterate" Israel. Hamas has been engaged in suicide bombings in Israel since 1994. The Anti-Defamation League of B'nai Brith reports, "Through systematic indoctrination, social pressure and the promise of paradise, Hamas religious and military leaders recruit young, poor men for suicide missions and other attacks."

Hamas is a social service organization in the West Bank and Gaza. In addition to schools, mosques, and youth groups, it funds daycare centres, athletic clubs, and medical clinics. But it is a social service organization with a twist. The Anti-Defamation League further reports, "The boundaries between Hamas' political/social and its military activities are blurred, particularly since Hamas leaders use mosques, kindergartens, and youth clubs as forums for spewing anti-Israel propaganda and mobilizing support for violence against Israel."

It is no comfort and no answer that it is only the military wing of Hamas that sends the suicide bombers to their deadly tasks. Hamas supporters should not be allowed to get away with saying that once the money goes to schools, mosques, and youth clubs, what they teach and preach in those places is their own business. Nor does the good that Hamas does in the West Bank and Gaza cancel out or justify the gross violations of human rights it incites against Jews.

It was the political wing of Hamas, not its military wing, that sent an appeal to the Organization of Islamic Conference meeting in Qatar on December 9, asking for support for its suicide operations. Their appeal said, "The suicide operations come as part of the war of attrition waged by our people …" Hamas urged the conference to differentiate between suicide attacks on Israelis and those carrying out terrorist acts. It is the political wing of Hamas, not its military wing, that gives money to surviving families of suicide bombers. This money provides an incentive for new suicidal killers to volunteer.

It is naive to think that we can separate incitement to terrorism and terrorism itself. Without the hate propaganda of the sort that the political wing of Hamas foments against Israel, Israelis, and Jews, the suicide bombings would never occur.

By allowing any money at all to go from Canada to Hamas, Canada was complicit in terrorism. The freezing of the Canadian assets of Hamas should not have been limited to its military wing. All the Canadian assets of Hamas should have been frozen.

Eventually that did happen. An order in council of December 14, 2001, listed Hamas as a whole.[366] The accompanying regulatory impact analysis statement said, "The change has been made on the basis of the deterioration of the situation in the Middle East. There are reasonable grounds to believe the Hamas organization as a whole is involved in or associated with terrorist activities."

The shift for Hezbollah took a lot longer. Like Hamas, originally the regulations listed only the military wing of Hezbollah, called the Hizballah External Security Organization.

Everything said about the split in Hamas could also be said about the split in Hezbollah. Nizar Hamzeh, professor of political science at the American University of Beirut and author of a book about Hezbollah,[367] in an interview from Beirut, Lebanon, with Stewart Bell of the National Post in February of 2004, said that he had "no doubts" that money given to Hezbollah for humanitarian work is diverted for military purposes.

The split in Hezbollah ended only in December 10, 2002, one year later, and only after I launched, on behalf of B'nai Brith Canada, a lawsuit on the matter. B'nai Brith Canada wrote a letter to the Minister of Foreign Affairs asking that the government of Canada include Hezbollah in its entirety in the United Nations Suppression of Terrorism Regulations list.[368] Minister Bill Graham wrote back to B'nai Brith Canada refusing that request.[369] B'nai Brith then went to court to ask that that decision be·set aside and to order the government of Canada to list Hezbollah in its entirety.[370] Shortly before the government had to deposit its file on the decision in court, the cabinet reversed the decision to split Hezbollah and listed it in its entirety.[371] Once that was done, B'nai Brith discontinued its lawsuit. If the matter had gone to court, the position that B'nai Brith would have taken is that Hezbollah is legally indivisible. In the organization's view, a determination that a part of Hezbollah is terrorist is a determination that all of Hezbollah is terrorist.

This time the Canada Gazette regulatory impact analysis statement said:

The change has been made on the basis of the close connection between the organization as a whole and the Hizballah External Security Organization, and the recent statement by Sheikh Hassan Nasrallah, the Secretary-General of Hezbollah, encouraging suicide bombings. There are reasonable grounds to believe the Hizballah organization as a whole is involved in or associated with terrorist activities.

The strategy for combatting anti-Zionism in Arab and Muslim countries has to be different from the strategy in Canada, because the appreciation of the harm of anti-Zionism is less. When it comes to countries like Iran or Syria, any suggestion that they ban anti-Zionist hate propaganda or that they criminalize Hezbollah or Hamas is, in the short run, a pipe dream. That does not mean, however, that there is no remedy.

Practically, the leaders of anti-Zionism in the Arab and Muslim countries are Palestinian organizations from the West Bank and Gaza. Often, when the Organization of Islamic Conferences takes anti-Zionist positions, it acts on the suggestion of its Palestinian organization membership. Strategically, the most effective way to combat anti-Zionism in the Arab and Muslim world would be to confront it in the West Bank and Gaza.

The 1995 Israeli-Palestinian agreement on the West Bank and Gaza provided that both Israel and the Palestinian Authority would "abstain from incitement, including hostile propaganda, against each other and, without derogating from the principle of freedom of expression, shall take legal measures to prevent such incitement by any organizations, groups or individuals within their jurisdiction."[372] The agreement further committed the parties to "refrain from the introduction of any motifs (in their respective educational systems) that could adversely affect the process of reconciliation."

Anti-Zionist propaganda is hostile propaganda against Israel. The obligation to abstain from hostile propaganda against Israel is an obligation to abstain from anti-Zionist propaganda. Anti-Zionist propaganda is incitement against Israel, Israelis, and Jews. The obligation to take legal measures to prevent this incitement is an obligation to take legal measures to prevent anti-Zionist propaganda.

Anti-Zionism adversely affects the process of reconciliation between Palestinians and Israelis. The obligation on the Palestinian Authority to refrain from the introduction of any motifs in the Palestinian educational systems that could adversely affects the process of reconciliation between Palestinians and Israelis is an obligation to refrain from the motif of anti-Zionism.

Obviously, since the 1995 agreement, none of that has happened. The Palestinian Authority has breached that agreement. There has been no real effort at compliance. The breach has been blatant, systematic, and unrepentant. One response from Israelis to the systematic breach by the Palestinian Authority of this and other agreements is to consider these agreements null and void. The argument is that Israel should not consider itself bound by agreements and attempt to respect them when the Palestinian Authority ignores them and makes no effort to comply.

My own view is that promotion of compliance remains a worthy effort. Israelis and Palestinians should abstain from incitement, including hostile propaganda, against each other, whether there is any peace agreement requiring this abstention or not. Once there is such an agreement to abstain, that agreement should be used as a tool to promote abstention, to combat anti-Zionism. The agreement should not just be put to one side because of the regrettable Palestinian Authority non-compliance to date.

Relying on the obligation of the Palestinian Authority to prevent incitement of hatred against Israel and the Jewish community, abstain from anti-Zionist propaganda, and refrain from the use of anti-Zionist motifs in West Bank and Gaza educational systems would have been appropriate, for instance, at the time of brouhaha about the Israeli incursion into Jenin in April 2002. It was predictable that Israel's attempts to defend itself against suicide bombers by seeking them out in their lairs in the West Bank would lead to accusations of atrocities against Israel. It was also predictable that the United Nations' reaction to those accusations would be to investigate the Israel defence efforts alone and to pay no heed to the complicity of the Palestinian Authority in the suicide bombing attacks. Launching a war crimes investigation into an Israeli effort of self-defence reeked of an attempt to intimidate Israel into refraining from that defence.

A true investigation into wrongdoing in the West Bank would have examined the organization of suicide bombings and the inculcation of hatred that led to their perverse behaviour. Any assessment of compliance with international standards should assess compliance of both Israel and the Palestinian Authority. Assessment of compliance with the obligations of the Palestinian Authority should have been front and centre in the investigation.

Many of those today who pile criticism of the most extravagant sort on Israel do not see themselves as antisemitic, but rather just sympathizing with the underdog. But even if one takes the perception at face value, to go from that perception to blaming Israel for the underdog status of the Palestinians is a wild, irrational leap. It is inevitable that the suicidal are going to be worse off than others. Palestinians who seek death are always going to be worse off than Jews who embrace life.

Though not every Palestinian is a suicide bomber, the suicide bomber is a metaphor for the Palestinian plight. Individual Palestinians would rather kill Jews than live. The leadership of the Palestinian people would rather destroy Israel than have a state living side by side at peace with Israel.

The Palestinian people, ever since the creation of the State of Israel, have had sitting in plain view for the taking the realization of their right to self-determination and the creation of a Palestinian state. For more than fifty-seven years the Palestinian leadership has spurned that opportunity; for decades they have inflicted on their people a continuing national suicide in order to pursue the nightmare of destruction of the Jewish state.

Abba Eban, former Israeli ambassador to the United Nations, used to make fun of Yasser Arafat by saying that he never missed an opportunity to miss an opportunity. That remark made Arafat seem clumsy. It glossed over the reality of a decided strategy. The Palestinian leadership has missed opportunity after opportunity for peace by design rather than by accident. Peace with Israel and destruction of Israel are incompatible. If there is an opportunity for peace, anti-Zionists must miss it in so that the policy of destruction of Israel can be pursued.

Israel defends itself, and Palestinians suffer from this self-defence. But to blame Israel, Israelis, or the Jews is surely perverse.

Those who sympathize with the plight of the Palestinians must turn their minds to resolving it. Destruction of the Jewish state and denial of the right to self-determination of the Jewish people is not an option. It is the modern equivalent of resolving antisemitism through the Holocaust. Before the Second World War, there was no Jewish problem, only a problem of antisemitism. Today, there is no Israeli problem, only a problem of anti-Zionism.

The myths and stereotypes that have created and sustained anti-Zionism must be confronted. The suicidal fervour of the Palestinian people is buttressed by such fantasies as a non-existent right of return. It is kept at fever pitch by the claimed illegality of every effort of Israeli self-defence — including the reoccupation of Jenin in 2002, the building of the security fence, and the killing of the founder and leader of the terrorist organization Hamas, Sheik Yassin. It is stoked by rejection of the settlements, a rejection that is another variation on the same old theme: "We do not want Jews in our neighbourhood." It is reinforced by the harping on the fantasized leadership of Ariel Sharon in the massacre of Sabra and Chatilla.

If we really want to help the Palestinians end their disadvantage, we must wean them from their self-destructive beliefs. Yet the anti-Zionists endorse those beliefs. By doing so, they fan and inflame the ardour of the Palestinians; they push Palestinians on their course towards self-destruction.

A true friend of a would-be suicide tries to lead the unfortunate away from the suicidal idea. A true friend of a would-be suicide does not shout, "Jump."

But when it comes to polite anti-Zionist circles in politics and journalism, that is exactly what is happening. When Palestinian anti-Zionists proclaim a right of return, discuss the illegality of the Israeli security fence, blame Ariel Sharon for the Sabra and Chatilla massacre, or label Israel as an imperialist, colonial state, there are all too many voices who proclaim, "Right on."

Fighting antisemitism means more than collecting statistics, adding to sentences for hate-motivated crimes, and teaching human rights. A meaningful program of action for combatting antisemitism has to include confronting and rejecting the myths and stereotypes that are fuelling anti-Zionism. If that is done, both anti-semitism and the underdog status of Palestinians will be countered. If that is done, both Palestinians and Jews will benefit.

Combatting anti-Zionism at the United Nations is even more of a dilemma than combatting anti-Zionism in the Arab and Muslim world. When and if anti-Zionism disappears from the Arab and Muslim world, it will disappear at the United Nations. But can it disappear or even recede before? One strategy may be focusing at the United Nations on the harm to children.

I am not referring here to the fantastical claims spewed out by anti-Zionist propagandists of Israeli victimization of Palestinian children, which the United Nations has no trouble endorsing. I do not even refer to the victimization of Israeli children by suicide bombers, which the United Nations cannot bring itself to condemn.[373] I refer rather to the victimization of Palestinian children by anti-Zionism.

Just perhaps, the UN may be persuaded to express concern about child suicide bombers. Here are some examples of the problem. In February, Israel announced the arrest of three boys, aged thirteen, fourteen, and fifteen, who were planning to carry out a shooting attack in the northern Israeli town of Afula.

A child of sixteen from Nablus killed himself and others in a suicide attack.

Israeli soldiers at Hawara checkpoint on the West Bank, on March 16, 2004, stopped an eleven-year-old with a bomb hidden in his bag. This child did not even know about the presence of the bomb, which was wired to be exploded by remote from a cellphone. A week later at the same checkpoint, Israeli security stopped a fourteen-year-old child stopped wearing a grey vest packed with explosives.[374]

Amnesty International, in a press release dated March 24, 2004, titled "Israel: Children must not be used by armed groups" gave as background information that in January 2004 a seventeen-year-old Palestinian detonated an explosive belt he was wearing as he was being tracked down by Israeli soldiers, killing himself. Palestinian armed groups have pressured families of dead suicide bombers, including children, to endorse their relatives' actions.

The phenomenon of child soldiers is all too widespread. It has been found in the Balkans, North Korea, Uganda, Sierra Leone, Liberia, Iran, and elsewhere. The abuse of children in armed conflict is horrifying enough. The Palestinian twist of sending these children to kill innocent civilians, as a weapon of terror, plunges abuse of the human rights of children to new, disgusting depths.

So, this is the problem. The victims these children kill are innocents. But so are the children themselves. The human rights of the victims are violated. But so are the human rights of the children. The people who recruit these children, indoctrinate them, train them, equip them with weapons or bombs, send them off on their missions, and then claim credit afterwards, and all those who fail to prevent this child abuse from happening — these are the true human rights violators. The United Nations Commission on Human Rights should say and do something about this form of human rights violation of children, but so far there is nothing.

The obvious place for condemnation of this form of child abuse is the United Nations Commission on Human Rights resolution on children. There needs to be language in this resolution condemning incitement of children to hatred, deploring the use of children to kill and harm others. Inserting such language in the resolution about children is simple common sense. It is also basic human rights.

The Convention on the Rights of the Child is now signed and ratified by every country in the world, except the United States and Somalia (even the United States and Somalia have signed it, but not ratified it). Its widespread acceptance means that the Convention has reached the status of customary international law. And using children as suicide bombers is a violation of one provision of the Convention after another.

The Convention states an overall principle, that, in all actions concerning children, the best interests of the child shall be the primary consideration.[375] It goes without saying that sending children off on suicide missions is not in their best interests.

The Convention reminds us that the obligation to prevent child abuse falls on governmental authorities.[376] Child abuse, in the first instance, is often carried out by non-state actors. In the West Bank and Gaza context, the recruiters, trainers, weapons suppliers, and mission planners of child suicide bombings are non-state entities, terrorist organizations like Hamas or Islamic Jihad or al-Aqsa or the Popular Front for the Liberation of Palestine. However, that does not mean that the Palestinian Authority can wash its hands of the mess. It falls on the Palestinian Authority to prevent this abuse.

In particular, the Convention obligates educational authorities to take measures to protect children from mental violence and exploitation. That means using the educational system to counter incitement to hatred. When the Palestinian Authority uses its power over the educational system to foster hate propaganda and war propaganda against Israel, that is a direct violation of the Convention.

The Convention reminds us of the direct link of this treaty with other, more general human rights instruments. It states that the education of children shall be directed to the development of respect for human rights.[377] The Convention requires states parties to direct education to develop respect for the child's cultural identity. Israel is the relevant state party. The Palestinian Authority is not a state and is not party to the Convention.

Yet it would be unrealistic to expect Israel to take over the education system in the West Bank and Gaza, despite the fact that this education system is now being run in a way that violates the Convention on the Rights of the Child. Such a direct takeover, while it might solve the problem of the abuse of that system to inculcate hatred, would create difficulties in developing respect for the child's own cultural identity. Developing respect for a Palestinian child's own cultural identity is likely to be more effective in an education system run by Palestinians than by Israelis.

A belief in violation of human rights is not part of any culture. It is an aberration in every culture. The Universal Declaration of Human Rights is called "universal" for that very reason. When Palestinians use their authority over the educational system to teach their children to hate, they are not passing on their culture. They are violating universal human rights values that are part of every culture. It is intolerable that the Palestinian Authority uses its control over the education system to turn schools into breeding grounds for hatred. The price that the Palestinian Authority must pay for educational autonomy is respect for the rights of children.

The Palestinian Liberation Organization, the governing party of the Palestinian Authority, has made a declarations of accession to the Geneva Conventions on the Laws of War. A common article of the Conventions states, "It shall be open to any Power in whose name the present Convention has not been signed, to accede to the Convention."[378] There is a view amongst international legal scholars that the word *Power* in these provisions is not limited to states. It also includes national liberation movements. Once a national liberation movement accepts and applies or undertakes to be bound by the Conventions, it can be held accountable for violations of the obligations the same way as governments.

It is, of course, tendentious to call the PLO a national liberation movement. In my view, the land of Palestine was liberated by Zionists in 1948 when the State of Israel was formed. In my view, it is more appropriate the call the PLO a national oppression movement, because it denies the Palestinian people statehood and the right to self-determination in pursuit of the destruction of the State of Israel ahead of all other goals, including a Palestinian state.

However, that is my view, not their view. Their view is that the PLO is a national liberation movement. But if it is, then it must respect the Geneva Conventions on the laws of war, which commit each party to the conflict to respect basic minimum principles of human rights and humanitarian law.

It is not possible to say to the Palestinian Authority that they have violated the Convention on the Rights of the Child, which not is binding on them because they have not signed and ratified it. But one can say, "You have violated standards to which you hold Israel accountable." One can also say, "You have violated the humanitarian laws of armed conflict, which you have accepted and undertaken to apply."

The Convention on the Rights of the Child maintains responsibility of governmental authorities even when education is private. The Convention allows for private education. It asserts the right of private sector individuals and bodies to establish and direct educational institutions. But the Convention also asserts that this right is subject to the observance of the principle that the education of children shall be directed to the development of respect for human rights. So it is no excuse for the Palestinian Authority to say that education of this group of children or that is in the hands of Hamas or Hezbollah or any of the other terrorist factions operating in the West Bank or Gaza. The Palestinian Authority remains as responsible for incitement to hatred in Hamas-run schools as in its own schools.

The Convention asserts the right of the child to be protected from any work that is likely to be harmful to the child's health.[379] It is stating the obvious that sending a child off on a suicide mission is likely to be harmful to the child's health.

If, by some miracle, the incitement to hatred and induction into suicide bombing pervading the West Bank and Gaza were to stop today, that would not end the problem. There would remain a damaged child population, infected by the incitement to hatred to which they have already been exposed. That infection requires a cure, lest the children grow up into hate-filled adults, stepping into the shoes of the adult terrorists who have victimized them. The Palestinian Authority must engage in a program of detoxification and recovery, providing antidotes to the poison of hatred, to which many children in the West Bank and Gaza have already succumbed.[380]

The Universal Declaration prohibits incitement to discrimination.[381] Put that together with the Convention on the Rights of the Child, and we have an obligation to direct the education of children to the development of respect for freedom from incitement to discrimination.

The International Covenant on Civil and Political Rights prohibits war propaganda and hate propaganda.[382] Along the same line is the International Convention on the Elimination of all Forms of Racial Discrimination. That convention too prohibits incitement to hatred.[383] Asking that children not be exposed to hate propaganda or war propaganda is hardly revolutionary stuff. There are some states and individuals that hesitate to embrace the obligations to prohibit hate propaganda or war propaganda because they view these obligations as undue limitations on freedom of expression. Whatever one thinks about that argument in relation to adults, it has no place in the world of children. The human rights paradigm for children is not freedom, but rather the best interests of children. There is no place for the argument that steeping children in hate propaganda and war propaganda is in their best interests.

CONCLUSION

DOUGLAS RUSHKOFF argues that Judaism should be concerned with ethics, not survival. He writes, "How effective a retention strategy is it, really, to treat Judaism as a tribe to be measured in numbers of surviving members, rather than as an ethical proposition …?"[384]

This argument ignores the linkage between the two. If Jews pursue ethics without regard to survival, the Jewish people will die. Jewish ethics will kill the Jewish people.

Tragically, that has been the historical experience. Judaism was followed by Christianity and then Islam, both inspired by the Jewish ethic. There is a connection between the Holocaust and a perverted Christianity. Without the notion of Jews as Christ-killers, of Jews as deicides, of Jews as Satan, the Holocaust could not have happened.

The Jewish community realized all too late that an ethical dialogue with Christianity was a dialogue of survival. Christianity today has, with only fringe exceptions, purged itself of the antisemitism that generated and reinforced the Holocaust. Who now would say that the Jewish-Christian interfaith dialogue that assisted in that purging was, for Jews, a misplaced effort in survival, an unnecessary diversion from attention to ethics?

Today one can assert the same about both human rights and Islam. The Universal Declaration of Human Rights, the human rights components of the United Nations, and the massive proliferation of international human rights standards and mechanisms since the Second World War have the Jewish experience of the Holocaust as a source. The post–Second World War global human rights superstructure has two words as its foundation: "Never Again." The surviving Jewish community around the globe played keys roles in building this human rights edifice. Yet this very human rights world has turned against the Jews. Because of the Holocaust destruction of the Diaspora culture of Europe, Zionism — the existence and flourishing of Israel as the expression of the right to self-determination of the Jewish people — has become central to Jewish cultural survival worldwide. Jewish people who want to survive as a people have to want the survival of the State of Israel.

Anti-Zionists, eager to seize on any physical or verbal weapon in their goal of destroying the state of Israel, have used the votes of friendly states to corrupt the United Nations human rights system and turn it against Israel. Anti-Zionists attempt to delegitimize the State of Israel by labelling the state as a massive violator of human rights, a criminal state. By extension, the Jewish population worldwide, seen as supporters of the existence of the State of Israel, is perceived as a criminal population.

Much the same can be said of Islam. Aggressive conflict entrepreneurs, with their sights fixed firmly on the destruction of the State of Israel, have perverted Islam into an antisemitic credo as vicious as the pre–Second World War anti-semitism of a twisted Christianity. Anti-Zionists today attempt to turn Islam into an ideology of death, a religion preaching the killing of innocents world-wide, Jews first of all.

While the root cause of today's antisemitism — anti-Zionism — is different from the pre–Second World War root cause, the consequences are much the same. Jews around the world are harassed, discriminated against, and attacked. Synagogues are bombed; Jewish community centres are defaced. The fact that the reason now is the Jewish presumed support for imaginary crimes of the State of Israel rather than Jewish presumed complicity in the killing of Christ makes no difference to the result.

The debauchery of the UN human rights system and the warping of Islam instigated by the crazed hatred of anti-Zionists threaten not only the Jews. They undermine the cause of human rights and the credibility of Islam for everyone. If there are two global ethical struggles that should be given the highest priority, they are the struggles to liberate the human rights system and Islam from anti-Zionism.

Even for those who believe that the primary concern of the Jewish people should be ethics and not survival, it is a poor commentary on the ethic Jews preach if that ethic leads to Jewish destruction. Jews can hardly hope to persuade others of the value of an ethic that is self-destructive.

One can legitimately ask, if the Jewish ethic is so wonderful, why are the Jews so dead, murdered in such great numbers by people acting out crazed versions of Jewish-derived ethics? Non-Jews catch the disease of antisemitism, and Jews die from it. The Jewish community would want a cure for antisemitism in any event. But when a primary cause of antisemitism is the perversion of Jewish-inspired ethics and religions, those committed to the Jewish ethic and religion must sit up and take notice.

There is a theological dispute within Judaism about the relationship between the Holocaust and Israel. On one side of this dispute is Emil Fackenheim, who writes:

> The event [the Holocaust] therefore resists explanation — the historical kind that seeks causes, and the theological kind that seeks meaning and purpose. More precisely, the better the mind succeeds with the necessary task of explaining what can be explained, the more it is shattered by its ultimate failure. What holds true of the Holocaust holds true also of its connection with

the state of Israel. Here, too, the explaining mind suffers ultimate failure. *Yet it is necessary, not only to perceive a bond between the two events but also so to act as to make it unbreakable.* [Italics in the original][385]

On the other side is David Novak, who writes:

> So, what is the theological connection between the Holocaust and the reestablishment of the State of Israel? If by "connection" one means some sort of causal relation, then, theologically speaking, there is none and there should be none. If there were any such causal relation, then it would seem we would have to "thank" the Holocaust in one way or another for the blessing of the State of Israel. The State of Israel does not have to claim the Holocaust as its necessary precondition in any theologically significant way.[386]

In my view, from a secular perspective, giving meaning to the Holocaust gives meaning to the suffering and deaths of the victims. A failure to confront the reality and the horror of the Holocaust, to face up to the risks of anti-Zionism, is itself a condemnation of the Jewish ethic. Asserting that nothing good can come from the Holocaust renders the death of the victims meaningless.

This is not a mere historical, philosophical, or religious debate to determine what significance to give to the past. We need to combat a present danger. In doing so, we must learn the lessons of the past. To say that there are no lessons to be learned from the Holocaust is a counsel of despair.

There is obviously something amiss in an ethic that leads to the destruction of those who preach it. The antisemitism unleashed by a perverted Christianity, a warped Islam, and a corrupted human rights system — when all three have been inspired by Judaism and the Jewish experience — suggests that the Jewish ethic is incomplete. Though Judaism cannot be blamed for the antisemitism endorsed by the adherents of the ethical systems Judaism and the Jewish experience inspired, that antisemitism has to concern the Jewish community. Those who want to get the Jewish ethic right, who want the Jewish ethic to be persuasive, have to work today to purge human rights and Islam of its anti-Zionism.

The very suggestion that the Jewish people should be concerned with ethics before survival is ethereal, topsy-turvy. Once the Jewish people are gone, who will be left to pursue the Jewish ethic? The notion of Judaism without Jews is meaningless. For the Jewish people, the struggle against the anti-Zionist corruption of human rights and Islam is not just a matter of perfecting Jewish ethics. The lives of Jews, the survival of the Jewish people and ethic, depend on it.

Antisemitism has existed since biblical times. Antisemitism surfaced in the days of the Pharaohs in Egypt, before the birth of Moses. The Old Testament records:

> ... there arose a new king over Egypt who knew not Joseph. And he said to his people:
>
> Behold the people of the children of Israel are too many and too mighty for us; come let us deal craftily with them lest they multiply and it come to pass when there befalls to us any war, they also join themselves to our enemy and fight against us or get out of our land.
>
> Therefore they did set over them taskmasters to afflict them with burdens.[387]

Now antisemitism has survived the Holocaust. We have to resign ourselves to the fact that an affliction that has lasted this long and survived such an obvious refutation as the Holocaust is unlikely ever to disappear. Unlike smallpox or polio, which we can hope to eradicate, it seems that antisemitism will always be with us. We can expect that anti-Zionism, which is just antisemitism directed to Jews as a people, will continue to exist as long as Israel exists.

However, antisemitism and anti-Zionism can be contained. Their existence may be inevitable, but their extent is within our powers. Those concerned with respect for human rights must do everything possible to contain them.

Stewart Bell writes, "Hamas and Hezbollah are a problem for Israel, but they are not just Israel's problem. Israel happens to be at the front line of a global phenomenon — the spread of radical Islam, which sees the non-Muslim world, and particularly the Western world, as a threat to be vanquished by force."[388] Israel and the Jewish community worldwide are fighting on several fronts at the same time. One front is radical Islam. Another front is corrupted human rights standards and institutions.

Reverend Martin Niemoller wrote in 1945, "First they came for the Jews. And I did not speak out — because I was not a Jew. Then they came for the communists. And I did not speak out — because I was not a communist. Then they came for the trade unionists. And I did not speak out — because I was not a trade unionist. Then they came for me. And there was no-one left to speak out for me."[389]

Ultimately, the struggle against antisemitism and anti-Zionism is the struggle for respect for human rights. The degradation of United Nations organs in order to demonize and delegitimize Israel, the terrorist attacks that kill both non-Jews and Jews in order to kill as many Jews as possible — all show where anti-Zionism is heading. If those concerned with respect for human rights are not prepared to stand for the right of Israel to exist and against anti-Zionism, the time will come when there will be no one to speak for human rights at all.

SUGGESTED FURTHER READING

Phyllis Chesler. *The New Anti-Semitism*. John Wiley and Sons Ltd. (Jossey-Bass), 2003.

Alan Dershowitz. *The Case for Israel*. John Wiley and Sons Ltd., 2003.

Abraham H. Foxman. *Never Again? The Threat of the New Anti-Semitism*. Harper San Francisco, 2003.

Yaacov Lozowick. *Right to Exist: A Moral Defense of Israel's Wars*. Doubleday, 2003.

Derek Penslar, Michael Marrus, and Janice Gross Stein, editors. *Contemporary Antisemitism: Canada and the World*. University of Toronto Press, 2005.

Ron Rosenbaum, editor. *Those Who Forget the Past: The Question of Anti-Semitism*. Random House, 2004.

ENDNOTES

1   *R.V. Sandouga*, 2002 ABCA 196, August 27, 2002, Alberta Court of Appeal.

2   Toronto: Summerhill Press, 1987.

3   Toronto: Summerhill Press, 1989.

4   Toronto: Dundurn Press, 1994.

5   Winnipeg: Bain & Cox, 2000.

6   "The Durban Debacle," *2002 Fletcher Forum of World Affairs* 26.

7   She is quoted at www.wiesenthal.com.

8   Articles 26, 27, 50, and 51.

9   For another analysis of this phenomenon, see Stephen Scheinberg, "The New Antisemitism: The Transformation of Hate," *2001 Audit of Antisemitic Incidents*, section 5, B'nai Brith Canada.

10   See Irwin Cotler, "New Anti-Jewishness," Jewish People Planning Institute alert paper (November 2002).

11   "The Non-Jewish Jew," in *Prophets Outcast: A Century of Dissident Jewish Writing about Zionism and Israel*, ed. Adam Shatz (Nation Books, 2004).

12   Jewish Telegraphic Agency, "Muslim group wins Holocaust denial lawsuit," November 26, 2002. The broadcast was subject to litigation. See Aziz Hartley, "Jewish board welcomes ruling in Radio 786 hate speech case," *Cape Times*, September 7, 2004.

13   *Ce que diffuse la television palestinienne dont Israel a détruit les studios*, from the list serve responses-Israel@yahoogroupes.fr, January 19, 2002.

14   Anti-Defamation League, "Holocaust Denial in the Middle East: The latest anti-Israel, antisemitic propaganda theme," 2001.

15   Presentation to the Commission on Antisemitism, NGO Forum for the International Association of Jewish Lawyers and Jurists.

16   Irving Abella and Harold Troper, *None Is Too Many: Canada and the Jews of Europe, 1933–1948* (Toronto: Lester & Orpen Dennys, 1982), 204.

17   http://www.us-israel.org/jsource/Holocaust/Brunner.html

18   UN Commission on Human Rights Report on 53rd Session, UN Document E/1997/23, Resolution 1997/74.

19   See Lorne Shipman and Karen Mock, "It's time to end word games and combat racism," www.bnaibrith.ca.

20   Paragraphs 46 and 79 of the NGO Forum Declaration.

21   Paul Lungen, "Canada urged by speak out against international antisemitism," *Canadian Jewish News*, November 30, 2002

22   "Jewish conspiracy," *Canadian Jewish News*, January 10, 2002.

23 Paul Lungen, "Holocaust denial finds new home," *Canadian Jewish news*, February 22, 2001.

24 "Hitler's book struggles on," *The Guardian*, Editor section, March 23, 2002.

25 Rabbi Michael Melchior, "The New Antsemitism," www.mfa.gov.il, August 20, 2001. Quote from the official Egyptian newspaper, *Al-Ahram*, June 23, 2001.

26 David Shyovitz, "Camp David 2000," www.Jewish Virtual Library.org.

27 *On War* (1832).

28 Resolution 106.

29 Walter Laqueur, *A History of Zionism* (Holt Rinehart Winston, 1972), 579.

30 Resolution 181.

31 Resolution 273.

32 United Nations Charter Article 1(3).

33 NGO Forum Declaration: Working Draft, August 6, 2001, paragraph 232, bullet 4.

34 Article 7

35 Article 20

36 Article 4(b)

37 Lynne Cohen "PM's UNESCO appointment concerns Canadian Jews: B'nai Brith," *Jewish Tribune*, August 19, 2004.

38 Article 2(1)(b).

39 See, for instance, Article 6 International Convention for the Suppression of the Financing of Terrorism, adopted by the General Assembly of the United Nations in resolution 54/109, December 9, 1999.

40 Jonathan Head, "Islamic summits hits terrorism snag," news.bbc.co.uk, April 2, 2002.

41 Associated Press, "Muslim Nations Wrangle Over Terrorism," April 2, 2002.

42 See www.rense.com

43 "The Bombing of the King David Hotel," www.jewishvirtuallibrary.org/King_David.html.

44 Resolution 2002/8, paragraph 13.

45 Paragraph 9.

46 For this and other examples, see "The Israeli-Palestinian situation is confusing enough," *National Post*, April 15, 2002.

47 Protocol I, Article 57(2)(a)(iii).

48 Article 85(3).

49 See Protocol I to the Geneva Conventions, Article 57(3).

50 Protocol I to the Geneva Conventions Article 51(7).

51 Article 51(8).

52 United Nations Document E/CN/4/2004/6, 8 September 2003 paragraph 23.

53 Paragraph 26.

54 Paragraph 41.

55 Deuteronomy (21:6-7).

56 Kahan Commission comment: War Crimes, Crimes against Humanity, and Command Responsibility.

57 Article 17(1)(b).

58 For a detailed description of the legal structure of apartheid, see "Apartheid as a root cause of human rights violations," chapter 8 in a book I wrote titled *No More: The Battle against Human Rights Violations* (Toronto: Dundurn Press, 1994).

59 "Chantier sur la lutte contre le racisms et l'antisemitisme." Report presented October 19, 2004.

60 The original text is in French. The translation is my own.

61 Paragraph 98.

62 Paragraph 423.

63 Lucy Davidowicz, *The War against the Jews 1933–1945* (New York: Bantam, 1976), 122.

64 Article 4B.

65 Citizenship Act section 8(1)(b).

66 Article 116

67 See, for instance, section 15(2) of the Canadian Charter of Rights and Freedoms.

68 Article 4B.

69 Article 4A(a).

70 Leviticus 24:22.

71 Letter of April 2, 2002, to Honourable Bill Graham, Minister of Foreign Affairs.

72 This quote is posted on the Anglican Church website at www.anglican.ca as part of a message to Canadian Anglicans titled *Israel and Palestine*, dated April 5, 2002.

73 "Majority of Palestinians believe that Israel should be eliminated, poll says," *National Post*, June 12, 2002.

74 Preface, *The Covenant of the Islamic Resistance Movement*, August 18, 1988, found at the website for The Avalon Project at the Yale Law School.

75 Esther Webman, *Anti-Semitic Motifs in the Ideology of Hizballah and Hamas* (Tel-Aviv University, 1994).

76 Nicholas D. Kristof, "Arafat and the myth of Camp David," *New York Herald Tribune*, May 18–19, 2002.

77 Graeme Hamilton, "Concordia blocks Barak from speaking," *National Post*, October 5, 2004.

78 Robert Fulford, "Terrorism is Arafat's Medium," *National Post*, June 1, 2002 (quoted from Ellen Gordon in the *Jerusalem Post*).

79 Rami Amichai, "Rocket attack kills two Israeli children," the *Globe and Mail,* September 30, 2004.

80 See United Nations Declaration on the Granting of Independence to Colonial Countries and Peoples, General Assembly resolution of 1514(XV), December 14, 1960.

81 Letters to the Editor, *Commentary,* January 1990.

82 For the phrase "occupied State" see articles 56 and 70.

83 Paragraph 101.

84 Article 1(4).

85 The Protocol was adopted June 8, 1977, and entered into force on December 7, 1979.

86 "Occupied, undeniably," *Jerusalem Report,* August 8, 1991: 45.

87 "Annan's Careless Language," the *New York Times,* March 21, 2002.

88 Letter to Joseph Wilder, National Chair, Canada Israel Committee, April 3, 2002, from Kieran Predergast, Under-Secretary-General for Political Affairs, United Nations.

89 "Taking aim at justice," the *Globe and Mail,* April 12, 2002.

90 United States Department of State, "Patterns of Global Terrorism 2001," May 21, 2002, http://www.state.gov/s/ct/rls/pgtrpt/2001/html/10247.htm.

91 "Occupied Territories to "Disputed Territories," Viewpoints number 470, January 16, 2002.

92 Paragraph 10.

93 Paragraph 9.

94 Hebron, Status Report, August 2003.

95 *Re Drummond Wren,* [1945] O.R. 778. But see *Re Noble and Wolf* [1948] O.R. 579, affirmed [1949] O.R. 503.

96 Conveyancing and Law of Property Act, 1990 Revised Statutes of Ontario, chapter 34, section 22.

97 Article 49.

98 Commentary II, page 283.

99 Protocol Relating to the Protection of Victims of International Armed Conflict, Article 85(4)(a).

100 Article 85(1) and Article 146 of the Geneva Convention for the Protection of Civilian Persons in Time of War.

101 David Matas, "Freedom of Movement: The International Legal Framework," *Still Moving: Recent Jewish Migration in Comparative Perspective,* ed. Daniel J. Elazar and Morton Weinfeld (Transaction Publishers, 2000), 413.

102 World Factbook <www.cia.gov>.

103 "Surviving under Siege: The impact of movement restriction on the right to work," AI Index: MDE 15/064/2003.

104 1990, 39-39 Elizabeth II, Statutes of Canada, Chapter 14.

105 Section 3.
106 United Nations Document A/CONF.183/2/Add.1, April 14, 1998, Article 5 "War Crimes," paragraph B. (f) option 3 (i).
107 Article 22(2).
108 Elyakim Rubinstein, then Israeli Attorney General, "Yediot Ahronot," July 21, 1998.
109 Article 9(1).
110 Document PCNICC/1999/WGEC/INF/3, August 12, 1999.
111 Paragraph 120.
112 Paragraph 9.
113 Paragraphs 24 and 25.
114 Paragraph 121.
115 See Vienna Convention on the Law of Treaties, article 30.
116 Paragraph 97.
117 Article 142.
118 Article 32(6).
119 Article 13, Statute of the Court.
120 Article 8 "War Crimes " 2. (b)(viii).
121 Rubinstein, "Yediot Ahronot," July 21, 1998,
122 Article 12.
123 Marx Brothers, *Duck Soup*, 1933.
124 Molly Moore, "Israeli Supreme Court Orders Changes in Barrier," *Washington Post*, July 1, 2004.
125 David Makovsky and Ben Thein, "Unilaterally Constructed Barriers in Contested Areas " *Peacewatch*, number 465, July 8, 2004, www.washingtoninstitute.org.
126 Paragraph 139.
127 Israel Ministry of Foreign Affairs, "Saving Lives: Israel's Anti-Terrorist Fence — Answers to Questions," January 1, 2004, www.mfa.gov.il.
128 Article 96, paragraph 1.
129 Article 65
130 Paragraph 25.
131 Paragraph 21.
132 Order of January 30, 2004.
133 Article 10.
134 Article 11
135 Article 13
136 Charter of the United Nations Chapter VII.
137 Article 11(2)
138 Under Article 11(2) of the United Nations Charter
139 Resolution 1515(2003) of November 19, 2003.

140 Resolution 377 A (V).

141 Paragraph 31 of the judgment.

142 Article 65

143 Paragraph 40.

144 See Ruth Lapidoth, "The Right of Return in International Law with Special Reference to the Palestinian Refugees," *16 Israeli Yearbook of Human Rights* 103 (1986); and *The Oslo Accords: International Law and the Israel-Palestinian Peace Agreements* (Oxford University Press, 2000), 281–286.

145 See United Nations Human Rights Committee *Lovelace v. Canada*, Case 24/1977, July 30, 1981, paragraphs 15 and 16.

146 November 2, 1999, Article 12 CCPR/C/21/Rev.1/Add.9, CCPR General comment 27.

147 Resolution 181.

148 Article 22

149 Article 23.

150 Article 18.

151 Article 1.

152 For Human Rights Watch, see http://www.hrw.org/campaigns/israel/return. For Amnesty International, see AI Index: MDE 156/013/2001.

153 Judgment of April 6, 1955.

154 Paragraph 11.

155 See, for instance, UNGA resolution 3089 D (XXVIII) December 7, 1973; resolution 3235 (XXIX), November 22, 1974; resolution 35/169 A, December 15, 1980.

156 Article 53.

157 Article 15(1).

158 Resolution 55/153, December 12, 2000.

159 Article 1.

160 Section 3(a)(3)

161 Article 1(1) International Covenant on Civil and Political Rights.

162 David Aaronovitch, "Message to the Left: There is no all powerful Jewish lobby," the *Guardian*, May 27, 2003.

163 The letter has been posted on the website of Rights and Democracy at www.ichrdd.ca. However, this statement was not presented for our approval before it was made. I was on the board of directors of this organization at the time. I wrote to the Minister of Foreign Affairs expressing my personal disagreement.

164 "Without Distinction: Attacks on Civilians by Palestinian Armed Groups," AI Index MDE 02/004/2002.

165 "Shielded from scrutiny: IDF violations in Jenin and Nablus," AI Index MDE 15/149/2002.

166 March 25, 2002.

167 See, for instance, paragraph 3 of the concluding declaration of the Conference of High Contracting Parties to the Fourth Geneva Convention, Geneva, December 5, 2001.

168 "Baker Speaks at Concordia," the *Jewish Tribune*, February 7, 2002.

169 "Parents protest risk to children," the *Globe and Mail*, December 11, 2000.

170 Marina Jimenez, "61% of Muslims say Arabs not behind Sept. 11: poll," *National Post*, February 25, 2002.

171 Robert Fife, "Israel's security wall illegal, Layton says, clarifying position," *National Post*, October 1, 2004.

172 David Matas, "What is Hate Propaganda?," in *Bloody Words: Hate and Free Speech* (Winnipeg: Bain & Cox, 2000), 44–57.

173 Judgement of April 6, 1955.

174 See Chapter 7.

175 A more complete analysis of the legal assertions in the Rights and Democracy letter of April 2, 2002, can be found in a dissenting letter I wrote to Canadian Foreign Minister Bill Graham in June 2002.

176 David Matas, "What is Hate Propaganda?," in *Bloody Words: Hate and Free Speech* (Winnipeg: Bain & Cox, 2000), 44–57.

177 Resolution 2002/1.

178 David Rohde, "Rights Group Doubts Mass Death in Jenin, but Sees Signs of War Crimes," the *New York Times*, May 3, 2002.

179 AI Index MDE 15/04/2002.

180 Article 20(1) for war propaganda, article 20(2) for hate propaganda.

181 John Podhoretz, "Amnesty's Calumny," *New York Post*, April 23, 2002.

182 The website www.nog-monitor.org provides a wealth of examples of NGO anti-Zionist bias.

183 Sheema Khan, "The Prophet would be appalled," the *Globe and Mail*, March 29, 2002.

184 Nikla Gibson, "Chirac appeals to Muslim leaders," *National Post*, April 10, 2002.

185 For an example from Buddhism, see Paul Knox, "Drawing Conclusions: political Buddhism as a spent force," the *Globe and Mail*, February 1, 2002.

186 Gordon Allport, *The Nature of Prejudice* (Cambridge, Massachusetts: Addison-Wesley, 1954). Elisabeth Odio Benito, United Nations Centre for Human Rights, "Elimination of all forms of intolerance and discrimination based on religion or belief," Study series 2, 1989, page 40, paragraph 163.

187 See Asbjorn Eide, Protection of Minorities Working Paper, United Nations Document E/CN.4/Sub.2/1994/36, July 6, 1994, paragraph 15. Asbjorn Eide, Report Addendum 4, United Nations Document E/CN.4/Sub.2/1993/34, Add. 4, 11 August 1993, paragraph 5.

188 Rick Kardonne, "Calls for Hate on Palestinian TV," the *Jewish Tribune*, January 24, 2002.

189 MBD, Canadian Jewish News, February 21, 2002.

190 The *Globe and Mail*, February 16, 2002.

191 Anne Bayefsky, "The UN and the Jews," *Commentary Magazine*, February 2004; Anne Bayefsky, "Ending Bias in the Human Rights System," the *New York Times*, May 22, 2002.

192 See Malcolm Harper, "Comparison of United Nations Member States' Language in Relation to Israel and Palestine as Evidence by Resolutions in the UN Security Council and UN General Assembly," United Nations Association of the United Kingdom, August 2004.

193 Resolution 1.

194 Steven Edwards, "UN tainted by 'solidarity of the abusers'," *National Post*, April 23, 2002.

195 See Anne Bayefsky, "Ending Bias in the Human Rights System," the *New York Times*, May 22, 2002.

196 For 2002, see resolution 8. For 2003, see resolution 6.

197 United Nations Document E/CN.4/1997/71

198 Commission resolution 1997/125.

199 See Jonathan Fowler "UN investigator says West Bank settlements constitute war crime," Associated Press, June 14, 2002.

200 The Wednesday Watch, October 20, 2004, UN Watch.

201 Hillel C. Neuer, "The UN's Food Politics," *National Post*, September 6, 2004.

202 Quoted by Anne Bayefsky, "One Small Step," the *Wall Street Journal*, June 21, 2004.

203 United Nations document E/CN.4/2005/5, 5 July 2004, Report of the eleventh meeting of special rapporteurs/ representatives, independent experts and chairpersons of working groups of the special procedures of the Commission on Human Rights and of the advisory services programme (Geneva, 21-25 JUNE 2004) Annex.

204 "Actually, the world is wrong," *National Post*, April 11, 20002.

205 Article 10.

206 Ron Csillag, "Israel's UN isolation comes to an end," *Canadian Jewish News*, June 8, 2000

207 For 1999, see resolution A/RES/ES-10/6, February 24, 1999.

208 Ron Csillag, "Canada seeks to postpone territories conference," *Jewish Post and News*, July 28, 1999.

209 Paragraph 13.

210 Paragraph 12.

211 Michael Wines, "Killing of UN Aide by Israel Bares Right with Relief Agency," the *New York Times*, January 4, 2003.

212 Anne Bayefsky, "The UN and the Jews," *Commentary Magazine*, February 2004.

213 Sean Gordon, "Members of Hamas on UN payroll," *National Post*, October 4, 2004.

214 Stewart Bell, "Aid officials fear money going to terrorists," *National Post*, January 29, 2003.

215 "Palestinians embrace 'romance with death,'" *National Post*, April 12, 2002.

216 "The unseen hand behind suicide bombers," *National Post*, May 20, 2002.

217 Letter of Warren Allmand, President, to Honourable Bill Graham, Minister of Foreign Affairs, April 2, 2002, at www.ichrdd.ca.

218 Ami Eden, "Study: Palestinians Target Civilians," *Forward*, June 14, 2002 (www.forward.org).

219 Robert Fulford, "Murderous, barbaric — and utterly futile," *National Post*, June 22, 2002.

220 James Bennet, "Rash of New Suicide Bombers Showing No Pattern or Ties," the *New York Times*, June 21, 2002.

221 Associated press, "Iraq hikes payments to families of suicide bombers," *Winnipeg Free Press*, April 4, 2002.

222 Paul Lungen, "Hate crimes soar in 2001, Toronto Police reports," *Canadian Jewish News*, March 7, 2002.

223 Warren Silver, Karen Mihorean, and Andrea Taylor-Butts, "Hate Crime in Canada," *Juristat*, Canadian Centre for Justice Statistics, Statistics Canada, Volume 24, number 4, June 2004.

224 Reuters, "France Deploys Extra Police After Synagogues Burn," the *New York Times*, April 1, 2002.

225 See www.antisem.com.

226 Andrew Diamond, "French Jews fed up with antisemitism," *Canadian Jewish News*, January 31, 2002.

227 Claire Levy, "Report: British Jewry faces worrying antisemitic trend," *Jewish Post and News*, March 6, 2002.

228 "Cleric arrested," *Canadian Jewish News*, February 28, 2002.

229 See Stephen Scheinberg, "The New Antisemitism: The Transformation of Hate," *League for Human Rights*, B'nai Brith Canada, Audit of Antisemitic Incidents, 2001.

230 Steven Edward, "UN Study faults Arabs for Arab woes," *National Post*, July 3, 2002.

231 Rights and Democracy, "Democratic Development in the Middle East and North Africa," May 2002.

232 Saad Eddine Ibrahim, "Management and Mismanagement of Diversity: The case of ethnic conflict and state building in the Arab world," http://www.hf.uib.no.

233 See, for example, John Ibbitson, "A shift in policy on Mideast?" the *Globe and Mail*, October 15, 2004.

234 United Nations Charter, Article 1(1).

235 John Ibbitson, "Bush is making it simple for the Palestinians," the *Globe and Mail*, June 27, 2002.

236 Suzanne Goldenberg, "Public death for collaborators," the *Guardian*, January 15, 2001.

237 "Iran not cooperation with UN, IAEA head says," the *Globe and Mail* June 15, 2004.

238 Mark Landler, "Iran Threatens to Restart Nuclear Weapons," the *New York Times*, June 17. 2004

239 "Iran crosses another line," *National Post*, July 28, 2004.

240 "Iranians reported to be seeking nuclear-weapons booster," *National Post*, June 29, 2004

241 "Teheran demands membership in 'nuclear club,'" *Winnipeg Free Press*, June 13, 2004.

242 Peter Goodspeed, "Iran balks at nuclear restrictions," *National Post*, June 17, 2004.

243 Middle East Media & Research Institute, MEMRI Latest News, January 7, 2002, Special Dispatch No. 325.

244 Gerald M. Steinberg "When will the West confront Iran?," *National Post*, July 14, 2004.

245 Paul Hughes, "Iran claims successful field test of missile," *National Post*, August 12, 2004.

246 "Iran warns of pre-emptive strike to prevent attack on nuclear sites," AFP, August 18, 2004.

247 Ali Akbar Dareini, "Iran threatens nuclear revenge," *Winnipeg Free Press*, August 18, 2004.

248 "Iran's uranium vote," the *Globe and Mail*, November 3, 2004: A22.

249 Tom Lantos, "The Durban Debacle," *2002 Fletcher Forum of World Affairs*, Volume 26.

250 Christie Blatchford, "An Israeli weeps for a foe never fought," the *Globe and Mail*, August 16, 2004.

251 "Safeguarding the rule of law," *Canadian Jewish News*, July 13, 2000.

252 Michael Jordan, "Three Iranian Jews Released from Prison," *Canadian Jewish News*, October 31, 2002.

253 Veronique Mistiaen, "Memories of a slaughter in Iran," the *Toronto Star*, September 5, 2004.

254 Anti-Defamation League, "Investigation finds Iranian, Hezbollah and Syrian involvement in 1994 bombing of Argentine Jewish Community Centre," October 2003, www.adl.org.

255 *Peterson v. Iran*, D.C. District Court Civil Action No. 01-2094 (RCL).

256 Sheldon Kirshner, "Iran's goals in the Mideast threaten Israel," *Canadian Jewish News*, February 28, 2002.

257 Maurice Roumani, "Jewish Population in Arab Countries 1948–2001"; "The Jews from Arab Countries: A Neglected Issue," WOJAC, 1983; and *American Jewish Yearbook*: 1958, 1969, 1970, 1978, 1988, 2001 (Philadelphia: The Jewish Publication Society of America).

258 United Nations, "Official Records of the Second Session of the General Assembly Ad Hoc Committee on the Palestinian Question," Summary Records of Meetings, Lake Success, NY, September 25, 1947.

259 UN General Assembly, Second Session, Official Records, Ad Hoc Committee on the Palestinian Question, Summary Records of Meetings, Lake Success, NY, November 14, 1947: 185.

260 UN General Assembly, Second Session, Official Records, Verbatim Record of the Plenary Meeting, November 18, 1947: 1391.

261 Mallory Browne, "Jews in Grave Danger in All Moslem Lands, Nine hundred thousand in Africa and Asia face wrath of their foes," the *New York Times*, May 16, 1948.

262 Al-Kifah, March 28, 1949.

263 Article 10(4) of the Code. See Maurice de Wee, "La Nationalité Egyptienne, Commentaire de la loi du mai 1926," 35. See also law 26 of 1952.

264 H.J. Cohen, *The Jews of the Middle East, 1860 – 1972* (Tel-Aviv: Ha-Kibbutz ha-Me'uhad, 1973).

265   Egyptian Official Gazette, No. 88, November 1, 1957; confidential memorandum provided to the UN High Commissioner for Refugees, Auguste Lindt, on February 21, 1957.

266 Directive No. 189 issued under the authority of Military Proclamation No. 4; confidential memorandum provided to the UN High Commissioner for Refugees, Auguste Lindt, on February 21, 1957.

267 AP, November 26 and 29, 1956; *New York World Telegram*

268 Law No. 391 of 1956, section 1(a). See *Revue egyptienne de Droit International*, Vol. 12, 1956: 80.

269 Article 18.

270 See Carole Basri, "The Jewish Refugees from Arab Countries: An Examination of Legal Rights — A Case Study of the Human Rights Violations of Iraqi Jews," *2003 Fordham International Law Journal* , Volume 26: 656.

271 Law No. 51 of 1938, *Official Gazette*, July 24, 1938: 475 (English edition); Law No.11 of 1948 amending Law No. 51 of 1938, *Official Gazette*, November 14, 1948: 591 (English edition).

272 The *New York Times*, May 16, 1948

273 Law No. 5 of 1951 entitled "A law for the Supervision and Administration of the Property of Jews who have Forfeited Iraqi Nationality," *Official Gazette*, March 10, 1951: 17 (English edition), section 2(a). See also law No. 12 of 1951, supplementary to Law No. 5 as above, *Official Gazette*, January 27, 1952: 32 (English edition), Law No. 64 of 1967 (relating to ownership of shares in commercial companies), and Law No. 10 of 1968 (relating to banking restrictions).

274 Judith Miller and Laurie Mylroie, *Saddam Hussein and the Crisis in the Gulf* (New York: Random House, 1990), 34.

275 The *New York Times*, February 18, 1973.

276 Norman Stillman, *The Jews of Arab Lands in Modern Times* (Jewish Publication Society of America, 1991).

277 Article 1 of Law No.62 of March 1957; confidential memorandum to Prince Sadruddin Aga Khan, UN High Commissioner for Refugees, dated May 8, 1970.

278 Under the Law of December 31, 1958, a decree to this effect was issued by the President of the Executive Council of Tripolitania.

279 Law of May 24, 1961.

280 Royal Decree August 8, 1962.

281 Law No. 14 of February 7, 1970.

282 Note to File, UNHCR Archives, dated August 24, 1970.

283 Law of July 21, 1970.

284 Article 8(e).

285 Article 6B.

286 UN High Commissioner for Refugees, Report of the UNREF Executive Committee, Fourth Session — Geneva, January 29 to February 4, 1957.

287 United Nations High Commissioner for Refugees Document No. 7/2/3/Libya.

288 Stanley A. Urman (Director, Justice for Jews from Arab Countries), "The United Nations High Commissioner for Refugees (UNHCR) and Former Jewish Refugees from Arab Countries."

289 Office of the United Nations High Commissioner for Refugees, *Handbook on Procedures and Criteria for Determining Refugee Status*, paragraph 51.

290 Article 7(b).

291 UNHCR/IOM/8/68, UNHCR/BOM/10/68, paragraph 2.

292 Article 1D.

293 Note on the applicability of Article 1 D of the 1951 Convention Relating to the Status of Refugees to Palestinian refugees.

294 "Despite rhetoric, Arabs have not helped refugees," *Canadian Jewish News*, April 16, 2003.

295 See Alan Dershowitz, *The Case for Israel* (John Wiley & Sons, Inc., 2003), 78.

296 Stan Urman and David Matas, *Justice for Jews from Arab Countries* (New Jersey: Center for Peace in the Middle East, 2003).

297 Robert Fife, "Policy chaos as PM stumbles again," *National Post,* April 13, 2000.

298 Mike Trickey "Angry at a reported offer of a home, Palestinians burn Manley in effigy," the *Ottawa Citizen,* January 19, 2001.

299 "Canadians might understand now," *Canadian Jewish News,* February 22, 2001.

300 Resolution 242.

301 October 27, 1977.

302 Kara Stein, "The Madrid Peace Conference and the Refugee Working Group," an unpublished paper.

303 Findings, page 7.

304 Security Council Resolution 827.

305 Security Council Resolution 955.

306 David Matas with Ilana Simon, *Closing the Doors: The Failure of Refugee Protection* (Toronto: Summerhill Press, 1989).

307 Irving Abella and Harold Troper, *None Is Too Many: Canada and the Jews of Europe, 1933–1948* (Toronto: Lester & Orpen Dennys, 1982).

308 Howard Margolian, *Unauthorized Entry: The Truth about War Criminals in Canada, 1946-1956* (Toronto: University of Toronto Press, 2000).

309 David Matas with Susan Charendoff, *Justice Delayed: Nazi War Criminals in Canada* (Toronto: Summerhill Press, 1987), 77–78.

310 See Daniel Goldhagen, *Hitler's Willing Executioners: Ordinary Germans and the Holocaust* (New York: Alfred A. Knopf, 1996).

311 Lucy Davidowicz, *The War against the Jews 1933–1945* (New York: Bantam Edition, 1976), 543.

312 Daniel Goldhagen, "The Evolution of Eliminationist Antisemitism in Modern Germany" in *Hitler's Willing Executioners: Ordinary Germans and the Holocaust* (New York: Alfred A. Knopf, 1996), 49–79.

313 Articles 7 and 14.

314 Article 20(2).

315 Article 4(c).

316 David Matas, *Bloody Words: Hate and Free Speech* (Winnipeg: Bain & Cox, 2000), 93–94.

317 See Lucy Davidowicz, *The War against the Jews 1933–1945* (New York: Bantam Edition, 1976), 122.

318 See Steven T. Katz, "The Uniqueness of the Holocaust: The Historical Dimension" in *Is the Holocaust Unique?,* ed. Alan S. Rosenbaum (Westview Press, 1998).

319 David Matas, *No More: The Battle against Human Rights Violations* (Toronto: Dundurn Press, 1994), 212.

320 Jonathan Schell, *The Fate of the Earth* (New York: Avon Books, 1982), 146.

321 E. Thomas Wood and Stanislaw M. Jankowski, *Karski: How One Man Tried to Stop the Holocaust* (John Wiley & Sons, Inc., 1994).

322 David Matas, *Bloody Words: Hate and Free Speech* (Winnipeg: Bain & Cox, 2000), 58–59.

323 Irving Abella, "The Dark Years: 1930–1945" in *A Coat of Many Colours: Two Centuries of Jewish Life in Canada* (Toronto: Key Porter Books, 1990), 179–208.

324 See David Matas with Susan Charendoff, *Justice Delayed: Nazi War Criminals in Canada* (Toronto: Summerhill Press, 1987), 58–66.

325 See the Saskatoon Statement on Self Determination, March 6, 1993, adopted at the Martin Ennals Memorial Symposium.

326 Common article 1(1)

327 The International Covenant on Civil and Political Rights, preambular paragraph three; International Covenant on Economic, Social and Cultural Rights, preambular paragraph three.

328 Vienna Convention on the Law of Treaties, Article 31(1)

329 Universal Declaration of Human Rights, preambular paragraph 1; International Covenant on Civil and Political Rights, preambular paragraphs 1 and 2; International Covenant on Economic, Social and Cultural Rights, preambular paragraphs 1 and 2.

330 *Ward v. AG of Canada*, Supreme Court of Canada case number 21937, June 30, 1993, at pages 16, 37, and 38.

331 Universal Declaration of Human Rights, Article 14(1).

332 *Ward v. AG of Canada*, Supreme Court of Canada case number 21937, June 30, 1993, at page 36; *Zalzali v. M.E.I.* (1991) 3 F.C. 605 (F.C.A.); *M.E.I. v. Villafranca*, A-69-90, December 18, 1992, Federal Court of Appeal.

333 *Ward v. AG of Canada*, Supreme Court of Canada case number 21937, June 30, 1993, at pages 16, 37 and 38; *M.E.I. v. Satiacum* (1989) 99 N.R. 1717 (F.C.A.) at 176.

334 Universal Declaration of Human Rights, preambular paragraph 1; International Covenant on Civil and Political Rights, preambular paragraph 1; International Covenant on Economic, Social and Cultural Rights, preambular paragraph 1.

335 Article 55.

336 See Lucy Dawidowicz, "The War against the Jews 1933-1945 " Bantam edition, 1976.

337 Irving Abella and Harold Troper, *None is Too Many: Canada and the Jews of Europe, 1933–1948* (Toronto: Lester & Orpen Dennys, 1982).

338 Universal Declaration of Human Rights preambular paragraph 2.

339 *Re Kindler and Minister of Justice* (1991) 67 C.C.C.(3d) 1 at 11. (S.C.C.).

340 1951 Convention Relating to the Status of Refugees, Article 1C(5); Immigration Act, Continuing Consolidation of the Statutes of Canada, Chapter I-2, section 2(3); United Nations High Commissioner for Refugees Handbook on Procedures and Criteria for Determining Refugee Status, paragraph 136.

341 *M.E.I. v. Obstoj* (1992) 2 F.C. 739 (F.C.A.); *Hassan and Hassan v. M.E.I.*, A-653-92, May 4, 1994 (F.C.T.D.)

342 Universal Declaration of Human Rights preambular paragraph 2.

343 Universal Declaration of Human Rights preambular paragraph 3.

344 Articles 1(2), 55; David Matas "Can Quebec separate?," *1975 McGill Law Journal*, 387 at 399

345 Universal Declaration of Human Rights preambular paragraph 5; United Nations Charter article 55(a)

346 Universal Declaration of Human Rights preambular paragraph 7

347 Universal Declaration of Human Rights Article 14.

348 Universal Declaration of Human Rights Article 7, International Covenant on Civil and Political Rights Article 20(2), Convention on the Elimination of All Forms of Racial Discrimination Article 4(c).

349 United Nations Principles on International Cooperation in the Detection, Arrest, Extradition and Punishment of Persons Guilty of War Crimes and Crimes against Humanity, General Assembly Resolution 3074 (XXVIII) December 3, 1973.

350 See the Saskatoon Statement on Self Determination, March 6, 1993, adopted at the Martin Ennals Memorial Symposium.

351 International Covenant on Civil and Political Rights article 2 (1), International Covenant on Economic Social and Cultural Rights article 2(2).

352 Paragraphs 46 and 79 of the NGO Forum Declaration.

353 Paragraph 61.

354 Paragraph 53.

355 Article 12(4).

356 David Matas, *Bloody Words: Hate and Free Speech* (Winnipeg: Bain & Cox, 2000).

357 David Matas, "Armed Opposition Groups," *1997 Manitoba Law Journal*, 621.

358 This point is elaborated in David Matas, "Individual and Collective Rights," in *Bloody Words: Hate and Free Speech* (Winnipeg: Bain & Cox, 2000), 36–43.

359 "Fire and Broken Glass: The Rise of Antisemitism in Europe," May 2002.

360 See "Antisemitism, Xenophobia and Religious Persecution in Russia's Regions, 1999–2000." February 8, 2001, at www.fsumonitor.com.

361 See David Matas, "Armed Opposition Groups," *1997 Manitoba Law Journal*, 621.

362 Will Offley, "David Icke and the Politics of Madness." PublicEye.Org, February 29, 2000, www.publicete.org.

363 Speech to the Jacob Blaustein Institute, seminar on Human Rights and Antisemitism, Vienna, June 18, 2003.

364 See David Matas, "Non-governmental Organizations at the United Nations," *No More: The Battle against Human Rights Violations* (Toronto: Dundurn Press, 1996,) 174–184.

365 Resolution 1373 (2001), September 28, 2001.

366 Volume 135, Issue number 8, *Canada Gazette* Part II, December 18, 2001

367 *In the Path of Hizbullah* (Syracuse University Press, 2004).

368 July 29, 2002.

369 November 4, 2002.

370 Federal Court file number T-1977-02

371 P.C. 2002-2154 and P.C. 2002-2155, December 10, 2002.

372 Article XXII. The agreement was signed in Washington, D.C., on September 28, 1995.

373 See Anne Bayefsky, "One Small Step," the *Wall Street Journal,* June 21, 2004.

374 "Palestinian bomber, 14, thwarted before attack," *International Herald Tribune*, March 25, 2004.

375 Article 3(1).

376 Article 19.

377 Article 29.

378 Articles 60/59/139/155 of the four Conventions.

379 Article 32.

380 Article 39.

381 Article 7.

382 Article 20.

383 Article 4.

384 "Don't Judge Judaism by the Numbers," the *New York Times*, November 20, 2002.

385 "The Holocaust and the State of Israel: Their Relation," in *A Holocaust Reader*, ed. Michael Morgan (Oxford University Press, 2001), 131–133.

386 "Arguing Israel and the Holocaust," *2001 First Things*, 109 (January 2001): 11–14.

387 Exodus, chapter 1, verses 8 to 11.

388 Stewart Bell, *Cold Terror: How Canada Nurtures and Exports Terrorism to the World* (Toronto: John Wiley & Sons, Inc., 2004), 106.

389 This quote has many different versions naming different groups in different orders. Niemoller himself used different versions. See Harold Marcuse, "Martin Niemoller's famous quotation," www.history.ucsb.edu/faculty/marcuse/niem.htm.